Led by Language

Modern and Contemporary Poetics

Led by Language

The Poetry and Poetics of Susan Howe

Rachel Tzvia Back

The University of Alabama Press

Tuscaloosa and London

Typefaces: Legacy Sans, Legacy Serif

New Directions Publishing Corp. has generously granted its permission for the use
of extended quotations from the following copyrighted materials: *Frame Structures*
by Susan Howe, copyright © 1974, 1975, 1978, 1979, 1996 by Susan Howe, and *The
Nonconformist's Memorial* by Susan Howe, copyright © 1993 by Susan Howe.

Sun & Moon Press has generously granted permission for the use of extended
quotations from *The Europe of Trusts* by Susan Howe, 1990.

The paper on which this book is printed meets the minimum requirements of
American National Standard for Information Science–Permanence of Paper for
Printed Library Materials, ANSI Z39.48–1984.

Library of Congress Cataloging-in-Publication Data

Back, Rachel Tzvia, 1960-
Led by language : the poetry and poetics of Susan Howe /
Rachel Tzvia Back.
p. cm.
Includes bibliographical references and index.
ISBN 0-8173-1126-2 (cloth : alk. paper) —
ISBN 0-8173-1132-7 (pbk. : alk. paper)
1. Howe, Susan, 1949—Criticism and interpretation.   2. Women and
literature—United States—History—20th century.   3. Autobiography in
literature.   4. Self in literature.   I. Title.
PS3558.O8935 Z58 2002
811'.54—dc21
2001004607

British Library Cataloguing-in-Publication Data available

Contents

Illustrations

Acknowledgments

One of the many pleasures of seeing a book to publication is the opportunity to thank those whose presence is strongly felt in the work, though not necessarily fully articulated. Given this opportunity, I would like to thank Shimon Sandbank for his advice, comments, and guidance through the years of my researching and writing this book. I am deeply grateful to Marjorie Perloff for her wonderful revision suggestions, her kind encouragement, her great generosity of spirit, and for the example she has set for me—through her indispensable and remarkable books—of literary criticism that enriches and illuminates the worlds of poetry. I am beholden to Lynn Keller for her careful reading of this work, for her valuable critique of it, and, most of all, for her own important scholarship on Howe, which made my own work possible. To Hank Lazer I owe special gratitude for reading this manuscript with such great care and attention, for generously sharing with me his own significant insights into Howe's work, for leading me to Howe criticism that I had overlooked, and for gently pushing me to hone my ideas and make this book that much clearer and stronger. To all the scholars and poets whose work I have relied on, and reveled in, during the process of writing this book, I am grateful. As Howe says in *The Birth-mark,* "It is the grace of scholarship. I am indebted to everyone."

I am deeply grateful to Dan Waterman, Curtis Clark, and Jon Berry, my editors at The University of Alabama Press, for their enthusiastic support of this book, for their patience and good humor, and for guiding the manuscript through the production process with professional grace and talent. To all three, my thanks for being so delightful to work with and for transforming these last months into a period of such positive collaborative energy and real pleasure. To Monica Phillips many thanks for her careful and exacting copyediting of the manuscript.

To my parents, Nathan and Toby Ticktin Back, I am grateful for a love of learning originating in their home, and for always supporting my academic and creative endeavors. To my father I owe special thanks for the quick and careful research he did for me in the Buffalo Rare Books library, and for the example he has always set, through his four decades of professional life, of integrity and unfailing commitment to research. Many thanks to my parents-in-law, Joe and Jose Grossman, for their loving and attentive support and assistance, for helping with child care at crucial moments, and for always accepting this work and its importance to me.

Deep thanks to my sister Sara for providing invaluable—often long-distance—computer assistance, and to my sister Adina, who read all my chapters and whose comments on the work were both generous and useful. To both my sisters, and to my brothers, Ephraim and Aaron, I am grateful for their emotional support and their love. I thank my sons, Daniel and Ariel, for allowing me to monopolize the computer, for enduring and understanding my absences from family outings, and, most of all, for their exquisite love that sustains me. To my daughter, Talya—in utero during the final stages of writing—I am grateful for accompanying me in the creating process and providing me with perspective and, finally, great joy. I thank also my partner, Yoni, for his endless patience with this project and with me, and for his steady and loving spirit that imbues the nurturing environment in which our family creates and thinks.

Finally, I thank Nita Schechet, whose careful, tireless, and devoted editing of this work improved it immeasurably, whose unfailing enthusiasm for my research and for Howe's poetry have bolstered and strengthened me in numerous ways, whose own scholarship and passion for literature have served as a steady model for me, and whose presence in my life—as dear friend and sister-lover of literature—has made the writing of this work possible. It is to Nita that I dedicate this book, with love and boundless thanks.

1

Introduction

The Poetry and Poetics of Susan Howe

mark   mar   ha   forest   1   boundary   manic   a   land   a
tract   indicate   position   2   record   bunting   interval
—Susan Howe, *Secret History* (1978)

Take Mark—. . . The mark of an enclosure. The border between. That which mars the undifferentiated, soils the soil, establishes identity, fixes territory, announces sovereignty. For what's been marked is claimed, possessed—the sign of a stake (state). At the same time, a mark is a token, that which stands for something else, the visible trace of a sign, metaphor for a word, substitute for a signature and so standing for a name.—An artist makes her mark . . ."
—Charles Bernstein, "'Passed by Examination': Paragraphs for Susan Howe" (1986)

Mark: a singular word of multiple denotations and connotations; a four-letter signifier of complex and variable etymological roots ("ME, from OE *mearc;* akin to OHG *marha* boundary, boundary land, ON *mork* boundary land, forest, wilderness, Goth marka boundary . . . L *margo* edge, border, boundary, OIr *mruig* boundary . . .");[1] a noun and verb both; a proper name with historical and Christian, literary and legendary resonances. Mark: a symbol signaling an absence through its presence; a visible impression which serves as identifying trait. A birthmark—mole, spot, blemish, stutter, literary trope—as distinguishing trait; the mark on a landscape (boundary stake, fence, homestead enclosure) made by surveyors and settlers, invaders and immigrants, the mark of first wars and recurrent violence; the textual mark, printer's mark, watermark, the mark in the text's margin. What is the *mark* of Susan Howe's experimental poetry? An opening consideration of this word as it reoccurs through Howe's poetry illuminates the poetics of this challenging poet and provides an entryway into her dense, often enigmatic work.

I start with the personal: Mark is the first name of Howe's father (Mark DeWolfe Howe), the name of her son, the name of her patriarchal grandfather and great grandfather, too; it is a name handed down through generations of Howe men, marking a lineage of New England writers, devoted biographers and documenters of local history.[2] Already in the intense historical investigations[3] under way in her early poem "Secret History of the Dividing Line"[4]—which opens with the word *mark* and its seeming disintegration (see epigraph and chap. 2, p. 17)—Howe informs her reader of the autobiographical significance of the word/name *mark* by dedicating the poem to "Mark, my father, and Mark my son" (*Frame Structures* 91).[5] Thus, the reader is alerted at the outset to the fact that the historical terrain Howe's poetry traverses is at all times informed and propelled by the personal; as Hank Lazer aptly frames it, "Howe's historically oriented poetry" is always "also a story of 'home' and 'family'" (1996: 62). This biographical component of Howe's work is foregrounded by the poet herself, who disperses biographical information throughout her prose and poetry; indeed, in order to sketch Howe's family tree or identify the significant figures, locales, and dates in her biography, one need do no more investigative work than closely read her oeuvre.[6] In my own reading of Howe, I have followed the abundant cues, and clues, she herself provides (that is, dedications, cover photos and sketches, organizing textual motifs, recurrent biographically significant geographic locales) in assigning and developing an understanding of the personal dimensions of a particular work.

From the mark (and Marks) of Howe's stubbornly individualistic historical project, I turn to the mark on a landscape and the role of place in Howe's poetics. The unraveling mark opening *Secret History* signals a connection between the word *mark* and issues of territory ("a land," "a/tract"), the establishing of borders ("boundary"), and possible resulting conflicts ("indicate position"). Howe is preoccupied both with the marks marring the once wild landscapes she inhabits and with the arrogance, possessiveness, and greed of those making their marks on the land. In contrast to the Indian perception of land as "communal rather than proprietary" (Pazicky 1998: 38), the Puritans—Howe's American ancestors and the protagonists of much of her American poetry—saw land as "the currency of culture" (Pazicky 1998: 36), something to be acquired and used (and used up) as they saw fit. "[W]hat is left when spirits have fled from holy places?" asks Howe in the prose preface to her poem "Thorow." As all places, to a certain degree, are holy—for poetry emanates from them—Howe's absorption in history's imprint on the land—marks made by trappers, traders, surveyors, speculators, soldiers, settlers, and missionaries—is a tracking of first crimes committed against the sacred. This tracking of colonialism and imperialism's cumulative marks on an entire continent also constitutes the poet's attempt to remember that which is outside the realm of memory and, through imaginative recall, to access the generative power embedded in first landscapes: "I stood on the shores of a history of the world," writes Howe, "where forms of wildness brought up by memory become desire and multiply" (*Singularities* 41).

Howe's "poetic investigations" of temporal and spatial marks "take place as and in language" (Naylor 1999: 9)—which is to say that Howe's poetic texts are themselves marked icons, whose textual marks are self-reflexively foregrounded. This distinction between *marked* text and *unmarked* text is eloquently drawn by Johanna Drucker, who explains that the unmarked text is the text "in which the words on the page 'appear to speak themselves' without the invisible intervention of author or printer. Such a text appears to possess an authority which transcends the mere material presence of words on a page" (1994: 95). In contrast, the marked text flouts poetic conventions and the norm of "the single grey block of undisturbed text" by utilizing a wide variety of typographic deviations, emphasizing the malleable materiality of the text and the very specific presence—and impact—of author, and printer, in each text's creation and dissemination. The marked text is defiantly nontranscendent and resists singular and authoritarian interpretations. Indeed, the marked text means to "unsettl[e] the grid of the page" (Dworkin 1996: 391)—a grid which evokes enclosure and delineated meaning[7]—and through this unsettling of the grid to liberate the reader from the limitations of normative reading procedures and to subvert the possibility of a passive reception of the work. The wide range of typographic marks on Howe's texts include different letter fonts and sizes, words crossed out or disrupted and unraveling, lines set at odd angles, upside down, or typed over each other, text pushed to the page's margins or arranged on the page to represent a plastic image. A close reading of these textual marks is central to our understanding of Howe's poetry and poetics,[8] for "the visual surface of [Howe's] pages illustrates at a literal, physical, spatial level the much more complicated lessons of the texts' thematic, semantic and conceptual planes" (Dworkin 1996: 396). Howe's visual experimentation may be considered one of the pivotal "distinguishing mark(s)" of her distinctive and difficult work, that which Perloff has termed the poet's "signature" (1999: 413).

I offer this initial tracking of Howe's use of the word *mark* in order to foreground my own methodology in reading Howe's poetry (I follow her words), and to mark certain motifs central to Howe's oeuvre and hence to my discussion of her work. In the next section of the introductory chapter, I will expand upon the three tropes introduced through the word *mark*—which I believe are central to Howe's poetics: (a) the function and impact of the radical visual and language experimentations fundamental to Howe's dense and challenging highly marked texts; (b) the role of place in Howe's work; (c) Howe's autobiographically propelled historical project. Finally, I will briefly consider Howe's place among her contemporaries.

On the "Difficulty" of Howe's Poetry

> Ignoring the difficulty of their work is a disservice to [these] poets and their poetry . . . these contemporary writers do continue the modernist assault on the ossification of language, which results in an assault on conventional forms of poetry, which results, in turn, in a "difficult" text.
> —Paul Naylor, *Poetic Investigations* (1999)

> She was intolerable to them because she called attention to the failure of language to work according to their expectation.
> —Patricia Caldwell, "The Antinomian Language Controversy" (1976)

The difficulty of the poetry of avant-garde American poet Susan Howe and the demands it makes of its readers has led more than one critic to question the purpose of these language intricacies/conundrums, and of the (seemingly willful) concealment of meaning behind radical linguistic and visual experimentation, labeling her techniques "arch" or "elitist." Asked her opinion regarding the objection to experimental writing such as hers on the grounds that it reaches only "a very narrow, highly educated" audience composed of readers who have to have "tremendous intellectual confidence even to grapple with these texts," Howe names this objection a manifestation of "a really frightening anti-intellectualism in our culture." She continues: "Why should things please a large audience? And isn't claiming that the work is too intellectually demanding also saying a majority of people are stupid? Different poets will have different audiences." Howe ends this exchange by emphasizing that what has been termed the difficulty of her work is not a *chosen* attribute but rather where she is led by language, where the process of poetry-writing takes her (Keller 1995: 23–24). In an earlier interview, Howe's response to the charge that her poetry is "inaccessible" is that "it's accessible to whoever really wants access to it" (Falon 1989: 41), rerouting attention from the difficulty of her work to the reader and his or her efforts and desires vis-à-vis her work. Through my reading of her work in this study, I argue that the great complexity, density, and, sometimes, opacity of Howe's poetry is not the product of coy and self-serving strategies external to and imposed on the work, but is rather intrinsic to her writing process as well as being an outcome of the thematic and formal foci of her poetry. That is to say, the enigmatic nature of Howe's poetry invites a rejection of the supremacy of monolithic meaning and an understanding of her literary works—like the historical tales she is so often embroiled in—as containing within them multiple, variable, unexpected, and often half-buried significances. To read Howe's work becomes, in James McCorkle's terms, "a series of retrievals," a recognition and embrace of the numerous "Possibilities" embedded in poetic language (1999: para. 8).[9] It is crucial to stress that Howe's rejection of an authoritative reading is a rejection also of authoritative patriarchy, and Howe's radical language experiments constitute a feminist commitment to dismantling "the grammar of control and the syntax of command" (Bernstein 1992: 202). "In prose and poetry she explored the implications of breaking the law just short of breaking off communication with the reader," writes Howe of Emily Dickinson (*My Emily Dickinson* 11),[10] describing writing strategies that apply equally to Howe herself.

The insistence on multiple possibilities intrinsic to Howe's work does not translate into a poetic field open to random and wholly individual associations on the part of the reader. In terms borrowed from psychoanalytic literary criticism, Howe's work, "like the analytic patient, *provides the terms of its interpretation,* and the reader has to learn to wrestle with this idiom rather than replace it with prepacked theories";[11] indeed, the reader must cultivate "the art of listening [in place of] the seizure of meaning" (Ellmann 1994: 10–11; my italics).[12] The linguistic and visual choices that Howe makes are not arbitrary, just as their meaning(s) is not open-ended: her poetry is propelled by an inner logic that is determined, first and foremost, by sound-associations, and then by the visual form of the unfolding text, its emotional dynamic and thematic concerns. The sometimes elusive and elliptical nature of Howe's work may also be read as resulting from its poetic and political commitment to sustaining and incorporating "rival possibilities" (Perloff

1981: 137), from its attention to and emphasis on language as itself dynamic, volatile, and protean, and from the very real difficulty—experienced in the texts by writer and reader both—of tracking (forgotten voices, lost footsteps) through overgrown and obliterating literary and historical landscapes.

The difficulty of Howe's poetry is also intricately connected to her vision of the role of the reader in the writer-reader complex. "Reader I do not wish to hide / in you to hide from you," states Howe in *The Nonconformist's Memorial* (30), and in her most recent collection *Pierce-Arrow* she writes: "Please indifferent reader you / into whose hands this book / may fall" (119), leaving the appeal open-ended. These addresses to the reader[13] foreground the centrality of the reader in the making of meaning—a centrality of which Howe is not only aware but also wholly embraces. Rather than a poetry of elitism, as some have maintained, I read Howe's work as a type of democratization of poetry, with the reader a full citizen of the textual terrain, with equal rights and obligations in the making of meaning.[14] In fact, rather than intending to block entry and leave the reader without, Howe's work is at all times engaged in bringing the reader more deeply *into* the text, toward effectuating greater participation on the part of the reader in the process of making meaning from a poetic text. "I wouldn't want the reader to be just a passive consumer," states Howe in the Keller interview. "I would want my readers to play, to enter the mystery of language, and to follow words where they lead, to let language lead them" (1995: 31). Howe's imagery here suggests that the reader's role is a paradoxical one that involves both active engagement ("To follow words where they lead") and a type of surrender ("to let language lead them"); what unifies these two positions is their close and intimate relationship with the text. I believe that what is defined as elliptical and obscure in Howe's poetry actually serves to pull the reader into this intimate relationship with the text, not allowing her distance and implicating her in the text that is made, in part, by her. Parallel to this paradoxical intimacy, the enigmatic text in general and Howe's in particular establishes a complex, equally paradoxical, network of power-dynamics between reader and text; the reader is at once powerless before "the aggressively restive, almost alien language" about which she "must struggle to say anything at all" (Dworkin 1996: 396), and also cast in the powerful role of "lift[ing] voices"—together with Howe, *through* Howe—"from the dark side of history" (*Europe of Trusts* 14), from the brink of erasure. Utilizing a terminology central in my later consideration of the pivotal role of the captivity narrative in Howe's work (chap. 2, pp. 37–45), I see the reader of Howe's work as *taken captive* by her language—as forced to "give up on refuge in the familiar or the same" (Heidegger, qtd. in McCorkle 1999: para. 4). Through this experience of captivity, through surrender to the unfamiliar and the unknown, which is also a surrender to the Other (within and without), the reader finds a voice—new and forceful—with which to speak.[15]

Howe's radical linguistic and visual strategies invite the reader to employ a "reading" process that is multifaceted and more varied than what is conventionally thought of as reading functions. The reader, first of all, *listens* to words and their musical patterns, which may, in fact, have no ready translation or interpretation. The reader then *looks* at the page's design, as one would look at a painting, foregoing—momentarily—entanglement in the semantic level of a word in order to consider its visual features, its placement, and its function on the white canvas. Thirdly, the reader sometimes becomes *tactually* engaged with the physicality of the book—turning it upside-down and around—as the conventions of top-to-bottom or left-margin to right-margin line arrangements are abandoned, replaced by the sense of the page as a three-dimensional entity whose depth has yet to be understood and of words as semiphysical (mythical) creatures liberated from the stagnancy and strictures of standard poetic usage. Finally, the reader engages the semantics and the narrative(s) (often in nonnarrative form) of the work, though always with the recognition that interpretive opportunities are multiple and that this particular reading offers "a complete and satisfying version of the work, but at the same time makes it incomplete for us, because it cannot simultaneously give us the other artistic solutions which the work may admit" (Eco 1989: 15).[16]

For the reader willing to place herself *in the midst*[17] of strange words and language relationships, tolerating a degree of unknowing[18] and forfeiting mastery over the text—engagement with a Howe text promises a reading experience that is challenging, ongoing, active, and rich with possibilities. Within this mode of engagement, which is, like the writing process itself, resistant to hegemonic interpretations and insistent on its own multiple nature, rests the promise of making something new in the reading process. The text—in part because of its mysterious and complex nature—remains a well of the as-yet untold and undiscovered: thus, "[e]very performance [or reading] *explains* the composition but does not *exhaust* it" (Eco 1989: 15). In this mode of engagement, the something new that is made may in fact be the reader herself, for "poetry is not only self-knowledge but self-creation," and the reader of avant-garde, experimental poetry in particular—by surrendering self to a realm of the dynamic and the unknown—"repeats the poet's experience of self-creation, and poetry becomes incarnate in history" (Paz 1974: 60).

On the Role of Place

> The tale and the place are tied in a mysterious and profound way . . . Trust the place to form the voice.
> —Susan Howe, *The Talisman Interviews* (1990)

> But now we are all, in all places, strangers and pilgrims upon earth. Our dwelling is but a wandering . . .
> —Robert Cushman, *Reasons and Considerations Touching the Lawfulness of Removing out of England into the Parts of America* (1622)[19]

Howe's relationship to place is complex and contradictory. She is intensely and intimately connected to specific landscapes and sensibilities of certain peoples and lands, naming herself the direct product of both her patriarchal New England lineage and upbringing and the matriarchal Irish identity that reverberates throughout her work. Place is, for Howe, a site of specific voices that need to be listened to—voices of literal territories (that is, New York State's Lake George, Dublin's the Liberties) that she traverses, inhabits, examines, and that at all times infiltrate and influence the form and content of her work. Place is also a reflection of the work's integrity, as expressed in her poetry's exclusive preoccupation with landscapes to which she feels she in some way belongs, is connected to, and created by: poetry is, for Howe, an act of self-involvement and self-revelation—hence she does not trespass in places where she can be only an observer. However, this identification and expression of self through the literary nooks and historical crannies of specific places (for example, "I can't get away from New England . . . It's in my heart and practice" [1989: 21]) is coupled with an equally intense sense of herself as a foreigner wherever she is, an outsider and an exile,[20] crossing borders in order to cross more borders, never fully reaching home. I read her as foreigner both biographically and as an outcome of her engagement with and understanding of language and its structures. In the lengthy and autobiographical prose introduction to the works collected in *Frame Structures: Early Poems, 1974–1979,* where Howe chronicles the intricate life tales of her patriarchal and matriarchal ancestors, what stands out most clearly is the abundance of displacements, disappearances, and long absences characterizing the family history and marking those left behind. "When [my mother] was a child," she writes, "her father [a doctor in the ranks of the British Empire's Colonial Service] was almost always living in another country and his father before him" (11). Due to familial circumstances, war, and promises hoped for elsewhere, the men in her mother's family were always "[l]eaving leaving arriving arriving" (12). Similarly engaged in various modes of wandering, her father's forefathers were sea-captains, privateers, and slave traders: trading, exploring, conquering, and colonizing, they were travelers all. Howe's mother continued her father's tradition of peregrination by crossing the Atlantic Ocean and making her life in the foreign soil of North America, though her identity remained both fiercely Irish and nomadic.[21] I would argue that Howe's heritage of displacements has made her more attentive to the centrality of place in one's emotional makeup and more suspect, perhaps, of ever completely belonging. "Exile begets exile," writes Edward Said in his essay "The Mind of Winter: Reflections on Life in Exile" (1984: 51), and the exile of Mary Manning from her Irish homeland—while an exile of choice—as well as the exiles of her father and grandfather before her, are manifest in the poet-daughter's exilic identity and modes of expression.

In the aforementioned essay, Said characterizes the state of exile as one of being "led outside the habitual order. It is nomadic, decentered, contrapuntal" (55). Howe's language usage may be described in similar terms, and I believe that her sense of her own foreignness, in the midst of such deep identification with particular places, landscapes, and even nationalities, is due in great part to her attitude toward and understanding of language. "Linguistic nature is always foreign," declares Howe in *"The Difficulties* Interview" (Beckett 1989: 26), and it is just this otherness of language—its restlessness and refusal to settle in one place, its pull toward the margins and the unexpected, its musical ability to contain both itself and its counterpoint—that Howe uncovers, cultivates, and foregrounds in her work. Language, like exile, "is never the state of being satisfied, placid or secure" (Said 1984: 55). It is a place, for Howe, typified by constant movement, by an awareness of what is not being said, by the risk of disturbing consensus and being censured, silenced, or banished and,[22] finally, by a deep and compelling desire for the other, the absent and the always faraway. "The mouth that utters the place, that can tell the right story of the place," writes Zali Gurevitch, "must be of the place. Only the native is the right story-teller" (1995: 207). Due to her own history and attitude toward language, Howe's location in the storyteller's relationship to place is more complex than Gurevitch's formulation: both native and immigrant/foreigner, she is deeply intimate with the American and Irish landscapes she writes from, even as she speaks (also) in the cadences of the exiled. This doubleness of identity is cultivated and embraced through work that always insists on the mystery of language, the multiplicity of voices, and the certainty that there is, finally, no "*right* story of the place" (my italics).

A final prefatory word on the function and expression of place in Howe's work: most of the figures whose tales she unfolds in her wanderings through and across history were themselves engaged, in one form or another, in issues of belonging to a landscape and in the realities of exile. Those banished (Anne Hutchinson, Cordelia, Mary Magdalene), lost in the wilderness (Mary Rowlandson, Hope Atherton), uprooted expatriates (Swift's Stella),[23] and those with lifelong divided allegiances (Swift), all people her poetry and, for most, home is that which one will always long for, an unreachable place. These figures—together with the early immigrant Puritans of her North American lineage who could never decide if they had reached the Promised Land or a "howling wilderness" whose strangeness they could not penetrate, together with the multitudes of Irish emigrants/exiled whose absences marked an emerging national identity—are embodied in and shape the paradoxical and complex attitude toward place that unfolds in Howe's work.

Howe's Historical Project

It is when one has been able to reach the moment of opening oneself completely to the other that the scene of the other, which is more specifically the scene of History, will be able to take place in a very vast way.
          —Helene Cixous, "From the Scene of the Unconscious
          to the Scene of History" (1989)

My poems always seem to be concerned with history. No matter what I thought my original intentions were that's where they go. The past is present when I write.
          —Susan Howe, "*The Difficulties* Interview" (1989)

Historical imagination gathers in the missing.
          —Susan Howe, "Frame Structures" (1995)

Howe's poetics are intricately informed by the desire to "gather in the missing" from history's annals, to document the "'undocumented' people" (Said 1984: 50), mark their absence and exclusion, and, perhaps, thereby lend them presence, substance, and even voice in her work. Her ear is attuned to silences as her eye is trained on the gaps in traditional historical renderings. One may trace Howe's pull toward history back to her childhood when the subject "was my favorite . . . in school. I devoured historical novels" (*Talisman* 1994: 50), and when her law professor father was himself intensely engaged in narrativizing the past, devoting his time to writing the biography of Justice Oliver Wendell Holmes. However, this pull toward history may be traced not only to these early sites of exposure to the discipline but also to a primary understanding of her exclusion *from* history—from the making of history and the telling of it both: "There was a sense, I suppose from my father," states Howe, "that because I was feminine, anything would do *except* law or history. Those disciplines were for men" (Falon 1989: 29). Howe's historical/ poetic project involves a commitment to infiltrating this arena traditionally—patriarchally—inscribed as off-limits to her and, through this infiltration, asserting not only herself (into the future through the past)[24] but also those marginalized and forgotten individuals—most often women—silenced and slighted, if not altogether obliterated, in the standard chronicles. Indeed, her historical poetry is driven by a poetic ethos that "[o]ne must protect the living and the dead. For it is possible to kill the dead, too, one can bury them, erase them into infinity" (Cixous 1989: 6).

Howe's poetic recuperation "from the dark side of history . . . [of] voices that are anonymous, slighted—inarticulate" (*Europe of Trusts* 14) differs from that of many other mainstream contemporary poets committed to giving voice to the silenced. A formal distinction of great import is that in Howe's poetry—like that of other avant-garde writers—the investigation into history's erased figures and the resulting critique of contemporary culture "takes places as and in language," through "various transgressions of form" (Naylor 1999: 9, 11). Avant-garde writer Nathaniel Mackey's incisive critique of other marginalized writers who place "far too much emphasis on accessibility" is relevant here (qtd. in Naylor 1999: 13). Like Mackey, Howe refuses to simplify the complex issues involved in history's silencing tactics or to obliterate or undervalue the great effort of retrieving lost voices. Thus, Howe's poetry—dense, difficult, resistant to easy penetration—formally enacts the arduous process of tracking back through thick and overgrown landscapes in search of history's missing. In addition, the radical language experiments of Howe's work present "a formal as well as thematic challenge to the structure of authority under which history has been written" (Naylor 1999: 14).

A second factor that sets Howe's revisionist historiography apart—this time from other avant-garde writers engaged in historical retellings—is a central component of her work, already mentioned in my opening examination of the word *mark:* the highly autobiographical nature of her work. The charting of her own childhood and ancestral geographies, the uncovering of the points of convergence between biography and history, and the frank foregrounding of the intensely personal are foundational to Howe's poetry and poetics. The uncovering of each historical tale is propelled *also* by the wholly individual and idiosyncratic historical details of the poet's own life. Thus Howe's expansions and rewritings of Puritan history may be read as "a communing with her father [himself a serious student of Puritan history] as well as a skeptical investigation of the history that his generation of Harvard scholars [that is, Perry Miller, F. O. Matthiessen] produced" (Lazer 1996: 62). And yet, Howe's poetry is fundamentally different from the personally charged work of mainstream contemporary poets whose lyric "I" dominates the poems' focus, obliterating all else. The speaking voice in Howe's work—particular, personal, self-revealing—is not authoritative or unified: as Perloff frames it, the perspective "is always shifting and . . . the subject, far from being at the center of the discourse . . . is located at its interstices" (1999: 432).

Howe closes her own chronicle of her family's history in "Frame Structures" with the following qualifier: "I may have mixed up some of the sordidly spectacular relatives but this is the general genealogical picture, a postmodern version. It could be called a record of mistakes" (*Frame Structures* 23). Every historical narrative—even a personal one composed of an individual's reflections, recollections, and redactions on available family information—is, for Howe, intrinsically fallible, conjectural, and unstable. Howe foregrounds the presence of history's tellers and the crucial impact of their particular vantage points, interests, and intentions on historical renderings that, contrary to common belief, are always variable, always versions of a tale that scrutiny and contemplation open to debate and further interpretation. She herself has no intention or desire to offer an alternative *authoritative* history in her poetry's account of the past. Her objective, rather, is to lead "the reader to assume consciousness of the erasures and choices that are inherent in any attempt to narrativize history" (Williams 1997: 131), while giving voice to the unvoiced.

History is, for Howe, the site of the other, though it is always and only through one's own involvement and identification with the sought-after other that the other is accessed. In quoting from Herman Melville's description (as recorded in his Holy Land *Journal*) of his encounter with a nameless woman prostrating herself over a fresh grave, calling "'to the dead . . .' Why don't you speak to me? 'My God—it is I!'" what strikes Howe most forcefully in the scene is that through his documentation of the woman's words, through his silent witnessing of and later reflection on her anguish, Melville[25] carries some of that anguish and he too "is saying 'My God—it is I!' He is the woman. There is everything in that to me. She's calling to the dead. Who has been buried? Is it her husband, a parent, a child? Melville doesn't know her . . . She is herself, and he sees himself in her. I think that detail holds everything" (*Talisman* 1994: 66).

Similarly, in her quest after the lost voices and shadowy figures of Stella, Hutchinson, Hope Atherton, Mary Magdalene, and others, Howe sees herself in them; the movement toward the lost other is also a movement toward the self, which is, for Howe, the self defined and marked *by* loss. The biographic absences, disappearances, and displacements that frame her understanding of place also underlie her absorption in the absent, the disappeared, and the displaced of history's archives and records, in a "writing backward . . . [in] pursuit of origins" (Williams 1997: 114). Writing is a "passageway" toward, though never all the way to, "the other that I am and am not" (Cixous 1987: 85). "You must go on as if I was an open door," writes Howe, addressing herself and reader both, "[g]o right on through me I can't answer all your questions" (*Frame Structures* 25).

Finally, history as Howe reads and renders it is often characterized by scenes of violence, portrayed through visual and aural violence on the page: battles, beheadings, scalpings, banishment, abandonment to starvation, cold, and madness, crucifixions, and conquering forces are all abundantly present in her poetry. The violence, of course, is perpetrated in the justifying name of a god, a ruling ideology, or a religious framework, and Howe's poetry is committed not only to uncovering lost voices and tales but also, through those lost voices and tales, to investigating the roots of that violence in her society. Behind the most decorous and civil facades, she argues, lies "an instinct for murder, erasure and authoritarianism" (*Talisman* 1994: 64). Howe's poetics of historical revision is propelled by a desire and a need to know "Why are we such a violent nation? Why do we have such contempt for powerlessness? I feel compelled in my work to go back, not to the Hittites, but to the invasion or settling . . . of this place. I am trying to understand what went wrong" (*Talisman* 1994: 55).

Howe and Her Contemporaries

The violence that permeates Howe's work may be read as a consequence of her specific historical consciousness formed, in part, by her being born *into* the destruction and chaos of World War II and coming into first cognition with pictures of the Holocaust and the war's devastation imprinting violence on her mind and in her heart.[26] Similarly, her father's sudden disappearance in 1941 into that war and his five-year absence (in addition to her mother's consequent going off to work at that time [Falon 1989: 31]) certainly established radical instability, the insecurity of structures, and the ever-present threat of loss as constitutive elements in Howe's emotional and, hence, poetic identity. I begin this brief consideration of Howe's position among her contemporaries in experimental American writing with this biographic information as it is, in part, Howe's year of birth and her resulting preoccupation with issues of history and violence that set her apart from many of the language-centered poets with whom she has traditionally been grouped.[27] Howe herself names chronology as one reason why she is not "really" a Language poet, stating that "for one thing I'm older than most of the people I consider to be Language poets" (Keller 1995: 19). As most of the poets identified with Language writing were born between 1940 and 1950 (Hartley 1989: xi) and Howe was born in 1937, the difference in their ages may seem insignificant. However, because of the centrality of the Second World War to her formative years—her childhood experiences unfolding *in the midst* of that war's chaos when complete destruction felt like a real possibility (rather than on the tail ends of it or shortly after, as is the case for the others)—this distinction is significant and is, I believe, expressed in both the *immediacy* and in the *fiercely personal* nature of her work's historical focus. This is not to say that other contemporary writing is not significantly informed by the events of the Second World War; indeed, Charles Bernstein convincingly argues that "much of the innovative poetry these soon-to-be fifty years following the war register the twined events of extermination in the West and Holocaust in the east" (1992: 197).[28] However, these "twined events" are registered by contemporary writers born after the war "as an historical event, something past and gone" (Bernstein 1992: 194); for Howe, the historical event is present and reverberating.[29]

Howe establishes an additional set of criteria that, in her mind, sets her apart from the Language poets. She identifies the group—or groups[30]—of Language writers as originating within the framework of the universities in the sixties, as being theoretically based (Keller 1995: 20), and as writing according to what Perelman names a set of "goals, procedures, habits and verbal textures" bonding these poets together, though without a fully articulated "uniform literary program" (1996: 12–13). In contrast, Howe asserts both her zealous Puritan individualism and her passionate belief in language, art, and life's intrinsic unpredictability and chance nature by stating that "I seem to have been led into writing by accident [and] . . . I have never followed an agenda or program" (Keller 1995: 20). These disclaimers aside, Howe has, in fact, "moved in the orbit of Language writing" (McGann 1993: 104), has always expressed appreciation of the work being done by Language writers and, most importantly, does share some significant conceptions and strategies with language-centered writing. Like Language writing, Howe's poetry always insists on "language as the center of whatever activity poems might be" (Silliman in *Alcheringa* 1.2 (1975): 118, qtd. in Hartley 1989: xii), rejecting poetry that advances and cultivates the supposed transparency of language. A corollary of the above is Howe's interest, like that of her Language-writing contemporaries, in "breaking the automatism of the poetic 'I' and its naturalized voice" together with "foregrounding textuality and formal devices" (Perelman 1996: 13). Finally, as discussed earlier in this introduction, Howe's poetry shares with the writings of the Language-centered poets a commitment to transforming the reader into an active participant in the process of the poem—one who recognizes "his or her part in the social process of production" (Hartley 1989: xiii)—resisting thus the supremacy of the authoritative master-narrative and the move toward textual closure that characterize, in her view, dominant poetic discourse.

Despite these similarities between Howe and the Language poets, I believe that Howe's work has the unique characteristic of emanating from opposing forces and tendencies. Thus, her intense preoccupation with her culture's history, her fierce interest in obscure archival materials, forgotten manuscripts, and lost documents, her abundant use and apparent favoring of "the [impersonal] voice of the chronicler" is matched by an equally intense and fierce preoccupation with understanding and investigating the personal, the autobiographical, and the highly intimate. The combining of similarly conflicting forces is apparent in the lyricism of Howe's radical prosody. An "absolutist of the word" (McGann 1993: 104) and of the *music* inherent in words, Howe is an avant-garde writer located firmly within an age-old tradition of lyrical poetry, even as she subverts many of the premises of that tradition. I believe she would agree wholeheartedly with Carlyle's declaration that "Poetry, therefore, we call musical thought. The Poet is he who thinks in that manner.... See deeply enough, and you see musically" (qtd. in Duncan 1966-73: 219). Howe is a version of Walter Benjamin's winged figure, evoked in the cover picture of her book *The Liberties*, propelled by her radical poetics into a future of the new even as her form is fully facing, and pulling from, the past (see chap. 3, pp. 102–106). The mysteries and materialities of language are, for Howe, as inseparable as are the past and future that inhabit her present. It is this distinctive meeting of opposites as enacted

in Howe's work that has led me to devote an entire book to her oeuvre; it is
this distinctiveness that lies behind the choice to analyze her work not by
comparing and contrasting it to that of her contemporaries but by examin-
ing her poetry and poetics within their own historical and poetic framework.
I believe that this approach will render a greater understanding of this icono-
clastic image-maker,[31] this exuberantly spiritual skeptic,[32] this postmodern
Puritan.

Thus, in chapter 2 of this study I analyze Howe's "American" works—*Se-
cret History of the Dividing Line, Articulation of Sound Forms in Time* and *Thorow*. I
am interested in understanding what is specifically American in the content
and, even more importantly, in the form of these works, and how they reflect
not only the early Puritan context of the New World but also express Puritan
sensibility in their approach to language and frequent slippage into stutter.
In this chapter I also trace the presence of two early American women whom
Howe identifies as foremothers and whose voices resonate in her work—
antinomian Ann Hutchinson and encaptured Mary Rowlandson.

In chapter 3 I shift my focus to the more European—specifically Irish—
context and content of Howe's *The Liberties* and the classically framed
Pythagorean Silence. My analysis of these texts, which are engaged in a project
of historical revision, is informed by Walter Benjamin's ideas on history, as
outlined in his essay "Theses on the Philosophy of History." Howe's efforts
to retrieve a range of female figures and voices lost on "the dark side of his-
tory" in *The Liberties* narrow to the individual child and her individual losses
in *Pythagorean Silence*, and in my reading of that more autobiographic poetry
I find Lacan's ideas of identity formation a useful and enlightening gloss on
the work. Finally, chapter 4 offers an analysis of what may be Howe's most
challenging work—*A Bibliography of the King's Book or, Eikon Basilike*—and of a
more recent text, *The Nonconformist's Memorial*. In my readings of these works,
I explore Howe's attitudes toward the materialities of the printed text as ex-
pressed in her work, investigating the avid anticanonical stance of these po-
etic texts that revolve around original works of uncertain authorship and
her insistence on "opening up" the literary text. In addition, I develop the
notion of Howe as a late-twentieth-century antinomian and iconoclast, work-
ing in the extended tradition of her Puritan ancestors. I hope through these
close readings and investigations both to explore the poetry and poetics of
this important contemporary poet and to provide possible bridges for those
readers willing to cross them in an engagement with her work.

2

From the American Wilderness

A Reading of *Secret History of the Dividing Line,*
Articulation of Sound Forms in Time, and *Thorow*

Though our Handsome Sailor had as much of masculine beauty as one can
expect anywhere to see; nevertheless, like the beautiful woman in one of
Hawthorne's minor tales, there was just one thing amiss in him. No visible
blemish indeed, as with the lady; no, but an occasional liability to vocal defect.
Though in the hour of elemental uproar or peril he was everything that a sailor
should be, yet under sudden provocation of strong heart-feeling his voice, oth-
erwise singularly musical, as if expressive of the harmony within, was apt to
develop an organic hesitancy, in fact more or less of a stutter.
  —Herman Melville, *Billy Budd, Sailor* (1892)

It's the stutter in American literature that interests me. I hear the stutter as the
sounding of uncertainty. What is silenced or not quite silenced. All the broken
dreams. . . .We are the wilderness. We have come on to the stage stammering.
  —Susan Howe, *Talisman Interviews* (1994)

"*D*efenestration *[of Prague]* is Irish," explains Susan Howe in a 1989 interview.
"*Secret History* is American. Most people don't think of their writing in such
a weird way, but it's what I do" (Falon 1989: 40). Certainly, the works col-
lected in her 1990 volume entitled *Singularities,* including the longer poems
Articulation of Sound Forms in Time and *Thorow,* must be categorized as Ameri-
can also, but what exactly does that appellation mean, how does it foreground
certain ideological concerns, how does it help explain radical language us-
ages, and in what way should it inform our readings of those texts? Indeed,
Secret History of the Dividing Line (1978), *Articulation of Sound Forms in Time*
(1987), and *Thorow* (1990) draw much of their thematic material from

American history and situate themselves in American—specifically New England—landscapes;[1] in addition, Howe's American work seems to adopt and extend literary forms first popularized and, in the case of the captivity narrative, initiated in the New World. However, the Americanness of this material seems to me more deeply rooted than thematics or literary form, emerging as it does from two liminal moments in American history: Columbus's discovery and conquest of America in 1492 and the Puritans' immigration to and settling of the American wilderness in the early 1600s. In *The Conquest of America: The Question of the Other*—an investigation into "the discovery self makes of the other" as expressed in early American history— Tzvetan Todorov marks the year that Columbus crossed the Atlantic as the beginning of the modern age, the moment "that heralds and establishes our present identity" (1984: 5). "The entire history of the discovery of America," he explains, "the first episode of the conquest is marked by this ambiguity: human alterity is at once revealed and rejected" (49–50). The interaction with the external other who cannot be assimilated and, hence, must be enslaved if not annihilated emerges as a central constitutive factor in American identity. Howe's American work is at all times concerned with this interaction, extending definitions of "otherness" to include the internal other, frustrating categorization by foregrounding the other/outsider status of the conquering/questing figures themselves, and avoiding a self-righteous stance by placing herself within the complexities of the tale. "You are of me & I of you, I cannot tell / Where you leave off and I begin," she states in *Thorow*, addressing as much her own conquering ancestors as the Indians who were conquered (*Singularities* 58).

The seventeenth-century Puritan voice and approach to life—"a fabric woven almost entirely out of paradoxes"—are the second origin of these works' particular and "peculiar" Americanness (Erikson 1966: 50). Commonly considered a rigidly steady and self-righteous community, the Puritans were in fact an extremely uncertain and, hence, psychologically fragile people.[2] Their doctrine of predestination, whereby God's will alone determines if one will be saved or condemned to eternal damnation, relegated the Puritan to a position of powerlessness, a life spent in desperate search of signs of one's election. The entire faith system revolved around intense uncertainty and the human limits of knowing. Even in one's public assertion of saving grace— the conversion narrative recounting the moment one "knew" god, which each Puritan was expected to deliver in church as a condition of church membership—one had to accommodate uncertainty, for "the surest mark distinguishing true assurance from false was its continuing imperfection . . . : in order to be sure one must be unsure" (Morgan 1963: 70). The American Puritans in particular were bound, at times paralyzed, by their powerlessness in the most central tenets of their faith, heightened as that powerlessness was by their isolation in the New World, their distance from the familiar and safe in Europe, and all the unknowns—real and imagined—of their new landscapes (Cohen 1986; Middlekauf 1971). In her seminal text *The Puritan Conversion Narrative,* Patricia Caldwell identifies these earliest examples of American self-expression as more open-ended than their English counterparts and more clearly propelled by a "sense of strain, the meagreness of genuine, fulfilling relief" and the "nervous, repeated invocation of doubt" (1983: 121). I believe that many of Howe's language strategies and avant-garde doubling and dismemberings of words hark back to this Puritan doubt[3]—a literary landscape of language wrestling with what it cannot say and can never entirely know, a literary landscape delineated in no small degree by the psychological, physical, and linguistic violence within and without its boundaries. As Howe says in her 1989 interview with Janet Ruth Falon (comparing herself to Wallace Stevens), "I am unable to speak with as *sure* a voice. I can't be direct . . . My own work is doomed to be hesitant" (28). In this chapter I intend to articulate the American—specifically Puritan—nature of *Secret History of the Dividing Line, Articulation of Sound Forms in Time,* and *Thorow,* first by examining the historical and literary works interwoven through these texts and secondly by tracing their soundings of earlier and ongoing struggles with self and Other in the New World.

Secret History of the Dividing Line (1978)

Two primary texts central to our understanding of *Secret History of the Dividing Line* (henceforth to be called *Secret History*) are William Byrd of Virginia's "History of the Dividing Line" (1728) and *Touched with Fire: Civil War Letters and Diary of Oliver Wendell Holmes, Jr. (1861–1864).* The first serves as a frame[4]—textual and ideological—for the disparate materials and forms of *Secret History,* while the second serves as a sourcebook—scripturelike—for the work's recurrent images and tropes. William Byrd, son of a wealthy Virginia planter, merchant and Indian trader, educated in England where he continued to live for a good portion of his life, was a member of a surveying commission established in 1728 to determine the much-disputed borderline between the states of Virginia and North Carolina. The account that Byrd wrote of the four-month, six-hundred-mile surveying expedition, entitled in full "The History of the Dividing Line Betwixt Virginia and North Carolina Run in the Year of our Lord 1728," though not published until 1841, was at once circulated among London readers, providing them with an entertaining and highly informative report of the natural details and Indian lore of the New World. The problematics of establishing the boundary between Virginia and North Carolina foreground both the "lexical drift" (*FS* 22) of time and place and the arrogance and ignorance of the colonizers.[5] All agreed that the boundary was "[t]o run from the north end of Currituck Inlet, due west to Weyanoke Creek, lying within or about the degree of thirty-six and thirty minutes of northern latitude, and from thence west, in a direct line, as far as the South Sea" (Wright 1958: 534). The problem was that the Weyanoke Creek had, in fact, *lost its name,* resulting in a controversy as to where exactly it lay. The Virginians insisted that the Weyanoke was the creek now known as the Wicocon, while the North Carolina authorities insisted it was the Nottoway River. Fifteen miles separated the Wicocon from the Nottoway—hence, a significant amount of land was in dispute.

With the addition of the word *secret* (to be discussed at greater length later), Howe adopts Byrd's title as her own, thus naming the issue of territorial markings as fundamental to her work. *Secret History,* a tale of wanderings "westward and still westward" (95), marked by violence and loss, seeks to trace these first journeys and the ensuing claims on place and power—all efforts to delineate oneself in this world's canvas. The framing function of Byrd's text about boundaries is foregrounded by the first and last pages of Howe's poem—rectangles of seemingly arbitrary words and word parts connected only by the insistent return to the words *boundary, land* and *mark.* The first reading of *Secret History*'s first page tosses one into a space of disparate voices and language movements:

```
mark   mar   ha   forest   1   a   boundary   manic   a   land   a
tract   indicate   position   2   record   bunting   interval
free   also   event   starting   the   slightly   position   of
O   about   both   or   don't   something   INDICATION   Americ

made   or   also   symbol   sachem   maimed   as   on   her   for
ar   in   teacher   duct   excellent   figure   MARK   lead   be
knife   knows   his   hogs   dogs   a   boundary   model   nucle
hearted   land   land   land   district   boundary   times   un
                                                    (FS 89)
```

Language seems to disintegrate from the first word on the page, where the first syllable of "mark" is repeated in "mar" which then becomes nothing more than the open breath sound of "ha"—as though the speaker is trapped in a stutter that finally eliminates the possibility of future speech. The Arabic numeral "1" intervenes at this point, introducing an alternative mode of communication—a discourse based on the rational, the quantifiable and definable: "1 a boundary manic a land a / tract." However, by the next two words of the poem's second line—"indicate position"—an additional voice infiltrates: that of the authoritarian commander instructing the soldier or spy to name his placement. The opening surface uncertainty of the stutterer, diverted for a moment by the rational, returns as the subterranean and unspoken anxiety of the isolated listener receiving the directive "indicate position." However, this voice fades, too, as words pile up on the page in an attempt to tell a tale that resists telling: "O about both or don't something INDICATION Americ." While the tale remains nebulous, its American nature is signaled through the aborted naming of place ("Americ"—what has interfered?), the Indian associated "sachem" of the second stanza and the popular American trope of birth-mark in "maimed as on her for." The sense of speech interrupted leads one to fill in the missing and complete the final word of this line as "forehead"—thus fleshing out the picture of the marked woman.

The two shifts into words in uppercase letters indicate, perhaps, a louder or more insistent voice intruding; more importantly, though, the capital letters foreground the word as word, physical entity, "black riders" on the blank page (McGann 1993).[6] Indeed, the wordness of the uppercase words signals the source of this opening text: the first and, in part, last pages of *Secret History* are in fact extracts from a dictionary entry at the word *MARK*.[7] Howe has lifted the left-margin words and word-pieces from this entry, skipping lines at will, then doubling back to the right margin in order to create her text (see fig. 2.1). Howe's text places that which is literally on the margins of language's most authoritative book—the dictionary—into the center, negotiating all the while the dictionary's arbitrary separation of words to fit into columns with her own careful attentiveness to the look and meaning of every group of letters. The authority of a dictionary entry is subverted by Howe's alternative reading strategy *down* the page instead of across, resulting in an alertness to the subjectivity of cultural marks and markings. Finally, the evolution of the word *mark* from words indicating boundary (the Old High German *marha*), land, forest, wilderness (the Old Norse *mork*), edges and borders (the Gothic *marka*) sets the reader—and the text to follow—firmly in the unsettled and unsettling American expanse that William Byrd and party contended with, attempting—and ultimately failing—to tame.[8]

A final direct reference to Byrd's text appears on the sixth page of *Secret History* and introduces another central motif in the poem. On this page, the title of the poem written in bold letters across the middle of the page is mirrored by itself upside down and inverted, beneath a dividing line

¹**mark** \'märk, 'måk\ *n* -s [ME, fr. OE *mearc;* akin to OHG *marha* boundary, boundary land, ON *mörk* boundary land, forest, wilderness, Goth *marka* boundary, boundary land, L *margo* edge, border, boundary, OIr *mruig* boundary land, district, W *bro* region, Per *marz* boundary land, district] **1 a** (1) : ²MARCH 1 (2) [G, fr. OHG *marha* boundary, boundary land] : a tract of land held in common by a Germanic village community in primitive or medieval times ⟨a share in the common ∼ . . . made up of the uncultivated land —Alfons Dopsch⟩; *also* : the community holding such a tract **b** : something placed or set up to serve as a guide or to indicate position: as (1) : a conspicuous object of known position serving as a guide for travelers ⟨a ∼ for pilots⟩ (2) : something (as a line, notch, or fixed object) designed to record position (3) : one of the bits of leather or colored bunting placed on a sounding line at irregular but frequent intervals — compare DEEP (4) : PLIMSOLL MARK **c** (1) : something toward which a missile is directed : a thing aimed at : TARGET ⟨hit the ∼ squarely in the center⟩ ⟨the officers, being on horseback, were . . . picked out as ∼s —Benjamin Franklin⟩ (2) : the jack in the game of bowls; *also* : a proper bowling distance or position allowed for the jack (3) : the pit of the stomach in boxing (4) : a spot (as that marked by the heel of a player in making a fair catch) at which a free kick or a penalty kick is allowed in rugby football; *also* : a fair catch in rugby (5) : the starting line in a track event ⟨got off the ∼ very quickly⟩ (6) : a position on the starting line assigned to a contestant in a track event; *also* : the relaxed position taken by a runner or swimmer at or slightly behind the starting line immediately prior to the position or attitude of readiness which precedes the firing of the starting gun — usu. used in pl. (7) — used as a skeet shooter's command for the release of the low-house target **d** (1) : an end in view : GOAL, OBJECT ⟨120 mph is not a hard ∼ to achieve —*Ford Times*⟩ ⟨developed enough musicianship to fix his own ∼s at which to aim —Marcia Davenport⟩ (2) : an object of attack, ridicule, or abuse : BUTT ⟨would have to explain and deny and make a general ∼ of himself —Theodore Dreiser⟩ ⟨would have to go about, a ∼ for the talkers —George Meredith⟩; *specif* : a prospective or actual victim of a confidence game or other swindle ⟨lead the ∼ to her apartment —W.H.Murray⟩ ⟨the ∼s don't know no different —W.L.Gresham⟩ (3) : the point desired to be made : the question under discussion — often used in the phrase *beside the mark* ⟨both seem curiously beside the ∼ —*Times Lit. Supp.*⟩ ⟨it is beside the ∼ to argue that a culture consists of something more than plastic compounds —Waldemar Kaempffert⟩ (4) : the actual facts or true state of affairs : condition of being correct or accurate ⟨was perhaps near the ∼ —*Times Lit. Supp.*⟩ ⟨even the initial diagnosis was widely off the ∼ —Martin Gardner⟩ (5) : a standard or acceptable level of performance, quality, or condition : NORM — usu. used in the phrase *up to the mark* ⟨weren't feeling up to the ∼ lately —Michael McLaverty⟩ ⟨that's the great thing about persecution: it keeps you up to the ∼ —Bruce Marshall⟩ ⟨both of these performances were very far from being up to the ∼ —Claud Cockburn⟩; *also* : the limit of what is reasonable or acceptable ⟨wanted fifteen hundred pounds for it and I don't think that was beyond the ∼ —H.J.Laski⟩ **2 a** (1) : something that gives evidence of something else : SIGN, INDICATION, TOKEN ⟨as a ∼ of their change of sentiment —T.B.Costain⟩ ⟨his writings . . . bear ∼s of haste —*Encyc. Americana*⟩ ⟨a sure ∼ of the families' social position —Bernard Smith⟩ (2) : a narrow deep hollow on the surface of the crown of a horse's incisor tooth that gradually becomes obliterated by the wearing away of the crown and therefore is indicative of the animal's age and usu. disappears from the lower central incisors about the sixth year while traces may remain in the upper until the eleventh (3) : an impression or trace (as a scar or stain) made on something (4) : CHARACTERISTIC ⟨the ∼ of every Christian —*Commonweal*⟩ (5) : a distinguishing characteristic or essential attribute in logic : DIFFERENTIA **b** (1) : a character usu. in the form of a cross made as a substitute for a signature by a person who cannot or is unwilling to write and often witnessed by another; *also* : a personal cipher used in place of a signature ⟨the symbols above the lion represent the ∼ of . . . the chief sachem —Allan Forbes & R.M.Eastman⟩ (2) : a visible sign (as a badge or sign of honor, rank, office, or stigma) assumed by or put upon a person ⟨the vermilion ∼ of marriage remained on her forehead —Nilima Devi⟩ ⟨other distinguishing ∼s may be worn by navy men . . . who have won certain distinctions —*All Hands*⟩; *specif* : a small plate of gold or silver worn by a master Mason (3) : a character, device, label, brand, seal, or other sign put on an article esp. to show the maker or owner, to certify quality, or for identification : TRADEMARK ⟨the owner of a ∼ can secure relief only where the infringer uses it on goods . . . closely resembling the owner's —*Harvard Law Rev.*⟩ (4) : a small heraldic bearing used or added as a distinctive sign — compare CADENCY MARK (5) : a written or printed symbol ⟨punctuation ∼s⟩ (6) : an identifying mark (as an ear notch) cut on livestock with a knife — distinguished from *brand* ⟨every mountaineer knows his hogs by his ∼ —*Amer. Guide Series: Tenn.*⟩ (7) : a brand on a log indicating ownership (8) : POSTMARK (9) *usu cap* [G *marke* mark, label, brand, fr. OHG *marha* boundary] — used with a numeral to designate a particular model of a weapon, machine, or article of equipment ⟨this nuclear power plant, known as *Mark I* —*Birmingham (Ala.) News*⟩ — abbr. Mk **c** : a number or other character used in registering or evaluating: as (1) : a symbol used by a teacher to represent his estimate of a student's work or conduct ⟨had several late ∼s against him⟩; *esp* : GRADE ⟨gets excellent ∼s at school⟩ ⟨the highest ∼ in the class⟩ (2) : a figure registering a point or level reached or achieved ⟨within six months the population . . . topped the 500 ∼ —J.D. Hillaby⟩ ⟨more than 125 have passed the half-century ∼ —*Amer. Guide Series: Minn.*⟩ ⟨the 1954 figure is expected to be around that ∼ —Wayne Hughes⟩; *specif* : RECORD ⟨the ∼, almost twenty miles faster than the previous record, wasn't allowed —*Collier's Yr. Bk.*⟩ **3 a** : ATTENTION, NOTICE ⟨nothing worthy of ∼ occurred in your absence⟩ **b** : IMPORTANCE, DISTINCTION ⟨might easily become a figure of ∼ —H.J.Laski⟩ ⟨stands out as a man of ∼ —John Bright †1889⟩ — often used in the phrase *make one's mark* ⟨has made his ∼ in many ways —Milton MacKaye⟩ **c** : a lasting or strong impression : an enduring effect — usu. used in the phrase *make one's mark* ⟨had made their ∼ in evolutionary history —W.E.Swinton⟩ ⟨made a ∼ in western history —R.W. Southern⟩; *esp* : a strong favorable impression ⟨anxious to make a ∼ with my first major book —Charles Breasted⟩ ⟨works that have made their ∼ with the general public —William Murray⟩ ⟨as office boy I made such a ∼ that they gave me the post of a junior clerk —W.S.Gilbert⟩ **d** : an assessment of merits : RATING ⟨would have had ∼ against him —F.M.Ford⟩ ⟨could get higher ∼s . . . for telling warmhearted, democratic lies about the people —*New Republic*⟩

(see fig. 2.2). Similarly, Byrd's "History of the Dividing Line" was mirrored by a second text he wrote about the expedition, entitled "The Secret History of the Line." This second account, indeed secret and not intended for publication, is radically different from the first.[9] Half as long as the official report, "The Secret History of the Line" focuses almost exclusively on the squabbles between the members of the expedition, parodying the main characters and attaching to them humorous pseudonyms. The juxtaposition of these two texts speaks of the gap between public and private utterances—a fundamental paradox in the Puritan world, where the most private religious concerns were shared in the public arena, resulting in what Patricia Caldwell terms a "New Englandly" discourse, a mode of communication characterized by linguistic struggle and formal open-endedness (1983: 41). Furthermore, by directing her reader's attention to this public/private gap, Howe foregrounds the possibility of multiple private versions to every public and seemingly authoritative tale told. As Howe insists, for the anonymous, the marginalized, and the silenced, "the gaps and silences are where you find yourself" (Foster 1994:50).

The second foundational text of *Secret History* is *Touched by Fire: Civil War Letters and Diary of Oliver Wendell Holmes, Jr. (1861–1864)*, edited by Mark DeWolfe Howe, Susan Howe's father—with Holmes's "Memorial Day Address" of 1884 serving as an additional central beam in the structure of the poem. Without explicitly naming in her poem the source texts she is using,[10] Howe lifts entire passages from Holmes's war letters home,[11] diary and memorial address, inserting them directly into her poem. The first such insertion appears already on the second page of *Secret History*, with the phrase "[w]hen next I looked he was gone"—a reference by Holmes to the sudden death of a fellow officer whom he had just saluted before battle.[12] In Howe's poem the entire passage reads as follows:

> When next I looked he was gone
>   Frame of our Universe
>   Our intellectual wilderness
>   no longer boundless
>   west
>   when next I looked he was gone.
>   (*FS* 90)

This loss of a comrade-in-arms is adopted and rewritten by Howe as the sudden and monumental loss of God, "Frame of our Universe"; the fragility and fleeting nature of life as experienced on the battlefield exposes the excruciating fragility of faith. *Secret History* thus announces itself as the descendant of

SECRET HISTORY OF THE DIVIDING LINE
SECRET HISTORY OF THE DIVIDING LINE

Fig. 2.2. The Sixth page of *Secret History of the Dividing Line* (*Frame Structures* 94).

the Puritan Conversion Narrative wherein, ironically, doubt resounds. Caldwell convincingly argues that it was the shift to and experience of America that caused this great unsteadiness, as though "the experience of America is felt as a numbing blow from which the narrator [of the conversion narrative] never quite revives" (1983: 125). The journey westward to the New World had promised redemption; the arrival in the New World halts the journey at the edges of what is perceived as a "howling wilderness," and a psychological boundary now stands in the way of the imagined and longed-for "promised land"—"[o]ur intellectual universe / no longer boundless / west"—and the promise of redemption remains unfulfilled.

In addition to specific phrases and passages, Howe adopts Holmes's epistolary form, foregrounding thus the figure of the solitary soldier immersed in thoughts of home and family. However, the reworkings of Holmes's letters through grammar slightly unsettled and the juxtaposition of incongruent clauses subtly signals distress beneath the seemingly calm accounts the soldier pens. For example, on the third page of *Secret History*, Howe writes:

Dear Parents
I am writing by candlelight
All right so far

after a long series of collisions
had a good night's rest.

Belief in the right of our cause
Tomorrow we move

from hence
from hence
from hence
(*FS* 91)

The absence of a referent in the sixth line of this passage (whose belief?), as though the soldier dares not express himself fully, makes one suspect the surface steadiness of the voice. What is not being said? Similarly, the repetition of the phrase "from hence" closing this passage undermines the preceding calm, the words echoing hollowly as though they alone inhabit the war-ravaged and now unpeopled landscape. Indeed, the text referred to—Holmes's December 20, 1862, letter to his father—is quite different in tone when completed:

I never I believe have shown, as you seemed to hint, any wavering in my *belief in the right of our cause*—it is my disbelief in our success by arms in wh. I differ from you . . . I think in that matter I have better chances of judging than you—and I believe I represent the conviction of the army . . . I think you are hopeful be- cause (excuse me) you are ignorant. But if it is true that we [the northern states] represent civilization wh. is in its nature, as well as slavery, diffusive & aggres- sive, and if civ & progress are the better things why they will conquer in the long run, we may be sure, and will stand a better chance in their proper prov- ince—peace—than in war, the brother of slavery . . . At any rate dear Father don't, because I say these things imply or think that I am the meaner for say- ing them—I am, to be sure, heartily tired and half worn out of body and mind by this life. (79–80; my italics)

Almost two years into a war that would continue for another two years, the twenty-one-year-old Holmes is daring to say the unsayable: that the war has been comprised mostly of "infamous butchery" due to strategies "forced by popular clamor" (79–80). The hedging quality of the repeated qualifiers "I think" and "I believe"—indicative of the strain involved in speaking these words—is countered in full by the sheer audacity of calling his father "igno- rant." Finally, what emerges most forcefully from Holmes's letter and what resonates in Howe's text is the vulnerability of the individual before the vio- lence and destruction that so often characterize "the march of progress." Indeed, all that young Holmes can be absolutely sure of is that he is "heartily tired and half worn out of body and mind." *Secret History* highlights the par- ticular absurdity of war's habit of "sacrificing" the youth by inserting lower down on this same page the boldface line, "AND THIS IS THE FRUIT OF YOUR LABOR" and providing a reference, again in boldface, to the first child born in the New World. I read this "labor" as referring firstly to childbirthing, the struggle and reward of procreation superseding the word's other deno- tations, and the boldface voice—directive, even accusatory—forces us to look back, and look differently, at the soldier/boy abandoned in a Civil War trench, demands that we read again, and read differently, his words. The suspect nature of first readings and surface meanings is exposed; we are drawn into language's "wild interiority" (1989: 26)—what is spoken in the silences.

The letter presented three pages into the text is mirrored by a letter ap- pearing three pages from *Secret History*'s end—an additional internal frame to the text:

Dear Parents

A thousand lovely thoughts this sunny morning.
At all events I have tried and decided

nothing especial

except a new line of earthworks
in the rear of the old ones.
(*FS* 120)

The expectation of some significant decision having been made established
with the phrase "I have tried and decided" is heightened by the stanza break
following it; the "nothing especial" rejoinder is incongruent and, conse-
quently, suspect. The speaker seems to have censored himself in midsentence,
and the reader must read as much meaning into the space between the lines
and between the stanzas as in the lines and stanzas themselves. A voice that
is subterranean[13]—or "sub-paginal"—has entered the text, directing the
reader's attention once again to the presence of the unspoken in every utter-
ance and to the deceptive nature of surfaces.

The silence between the lines may also direct the reader back to the source-
text and what has been lost in the "translation"—the "carrying across" from
one text to another. Holmes's letters and diary entries relevant to this sec-
tion of *Secret History* stretch out over five pages and continue as follows:

June 5. . . . . ., 1864
Dear Parents
    [. . .] *A thousand loving thoughts this Sunday morng*—The earlier part of wh. has
been spent on the front line of works drawing them & dodging bullets—(140)

June 7/64
Dear Mother
    [. . .] These days of comparative rest though constant loss allow my thoughts
to turn longingly & lovingly homeward again—which they couldn't—as I told
you—in the wear and tear of alternate march and fight.
    The campaign has been most terrible yet believe me I was not demoralized
when I announced my intention to leave the service next winter if I lived so
long—[. . .]
    I hope this will meet your approbation—you are so sure to be right—*at all
events I have tried* to decide conscientiously *& I have decided*—[to waive promo-
tion and leave the service] (141–143)
[Diary]
June 8–9, 10, 11
    In camp—*nothing especial except running a new line of earthworks in rear of the old
ones* by wh. to fall back—(144; my italics)

The slight though significant shifts from "loving" into "lovely" and "Sunday" into "sunny"—together with the omission of bullets dodged and the wear and tear of the campaign—push what is originally a battlefield scene closer to the pastoral and enact the ear's tendency to hear what it wants to so that the mind's eye may see what it would rather see. The monumental decision to leave the army is similarly deleted, so that a text of debate and struggle is converted into a report of the routine holding of the line. Howe's "poetics of intervening absence" (*Birth-mark* 27) results in this letter/poem that is a patchwork of omissions—holes stitched together.[14]

Howe's choice of *Touched by Fire* as a foundational text for *Secret History* is obviously connected to her father's role as editor of the volume. Mark DeWolfe Howe, Howe's Harvard-law-professor father, spent the better portion of his professional life editing Holmes's papers and writing a biography of the famous judge. In *The Difficulties* interview with Janet Ruth Falon, Howe conveys the sense of her father having sacrificed his life for the work: "I don't think that my two sisters and I will ever get used to the shock of our father's sudden death [twenty years ago] . . . He tired himself out. His biography of Justice Holmes hung over us all like lead. We didn't pay enough attention to the work he did but we knew he was working terribly hard over something— a Life of someone none of us particularly like. We should have paid more attention because he was working himself quietly to death" ("Speaking with Susan Howe" 1989: 39). Thus Holmes's letters to his father function as an opening for Howe to enter into a dialogue with her own father as she belatedly pays attention to his life's work. Certainly, *Secret History* may be read without knowledge of the prominent role played by Holmes's text in shaping and informing the poem. However, *Secret History* may *not* be read without acknowledgment of its individual and highly personal dimension. Often perceived as work that is "impersonal" due to its shifting or absent "I" and relentless focus on language, Howe's poetry is, in fact, "everywhere charged with her presence" (Perloff 1990: 310). Indeed, in a striking departure from literary conventions, Howe's dedication of *Secret History* to her father and her son is inserted into the body of the text, appearing at the bottom of the poem's third page: *"for Mark my father, and Mark my son"* (91). Due to this dedication, the recurrent usage of the word *mark* in its multiple denotations and connotations doubles as a mantra-like calling of father and son—and a naming of oneself and one's losses in that calling. In this poetic retelling of history—propelled by its belief "in the necessity of 'seeking the truth' and in the obligation of making it known" (Todorov 1984: 247)—the poet's positioning of self within the telling and within the tale is an ethical stand. Already in her choice of Jean Dean Dubreuil's etching entitled "The Practice of

SECRET HISTORY
OF THE DIVIDING LINE

Fig. 2.3. Jean Dean Dubreuil's etching from *The Practice of Perspective*.
Used as cover illustration for *Secret History of the Dividing Line*.

Perspective" as the cover picture of *Secret History,* Howe is announcing the subjectivity of perception due to the individuality of viewpoint as a central theme: the forest looks different depending on where one is standing (see fig. 2.3).

The issue of self-positioning is foregrounded in additional ways already in the opening pages of *Secret History.* On the second page of the text, Howe writes:

> We sailed north
> it was March
> White sands
> and fragrant woods
> the permanence
> of endless distance.

Howe is quoting here from William Carlos Williams's *In the American Grain,* his "source book of highly individual and radical discoveries" in the guise of a collection of narratives on American history (1956: xii). The relevant passage in Williams's original text is describing the search of Ponce de Leon—brutal Spanish conqueror of Puerto Rico—for the fabled fountain of youth and reads as follows: "They sailed North. It was March. In the wind, what? Beauty the eternal. White sands and fragrant woods, fruits, riches, truth! The sea, the home of permanence, drew them on into its endless distances. Again the new! Do you feel it? The murderer, the enslaver, the terror striker, the destroyer of beauty, drawn on by beauty across the glancing tropical seas- . . . They even put in at Guanahani for water—Columbus' first landfall; then populous, inviting; now desolate, defeated, murdered—unpeopled" (1933: 43).

By shifting Williams's use of the third-person-plural pronoun ("[t]hey sailed") to first-person plural ("[w]e sailed") at the passage's opening, Howe collapses the time spectrum and places herself among the conquering forces, enjoying none of the distance or self-righteousness of Williams's narrator; as Howe integrates outside sources into her poem, this twentieth-century poet integrates herself into the earliest tales of conquest and violence on the American continent. Any attempt at naming herself as distinct and separate—such as the disclaimer "I am another generation" appearing toward the bottom of this second page—is quietly and quickly undone, in this case by the urgency and insistence of the now italicized *"when next I looked he was gone."* Repeated here for the third time (paralleling the tripled "from hence" on the opposite page), the phrase functions as a relentless reminder of loss as the speaker looks toward a horizon suddenly emptied and marked by the absence.

Secret History is in all ways "the old old / myth // march // month of victims and saviors // girl on the dirt track" (93)—the age-old tale that is, nonetheless, as singular in each retelling as the solitary girl on a dirt track. The poem's movement through "a vast geography both physical and spiritual" (Caldwell 1983: 30) seems to be always leading *back* to literary, historical, and psychological origins. The mark that enters the text as the colonizers' attempts at delineating a border becomes the individual heritage and family mark each person carries, and the backdrop of the Civil War recalls the first mark in the Bible, the consequence of brother killing brother. In Genesis 4, in the first tale of murder, it is written:

> 8: And Cain talked with Abel his brother: and it came to pass, when they were in the field, that Cain rose up against Abel his brother, and slew him.
> 10: And [the Lord] said What hast thou done? the voice of thy brother's blood crieth unto me from the ground.
> 11: And now art thou cursed from the earth, which hath opened her mouth to receive thy brother's blood from thy hand;
> 12: . . . a fugitive and a vagabond shalt thou be in the earth.
> 15: . . . And the Lord set a mark upon Cain, lest any finding him should kill him.

Cain's mark, protecting and separating him, reflects the anthromorphized mark of Abel's blood crying out from the land. In a reversal of roles, the earth-as-mother drinks from her son's body. That blood-mark of first violence is the birth-mark and the border-mark of the New World landscapes in Howe's early poetry.

Following the first four pages of *Secret History*—and with the exception of the mirrorings on pages 94 and 113 and the quotation from *A Midsummer's Night Dream* on page 114—the remainder of the thirty-four-page text is visually more "normative" in nature, comprised of poems of mostly couplets aligned along the left margin of the page. The crowding of words, the irregular use of page space, and the unexpected shifts into boldface or italics characterizing the *Secret History*'s opening pages recede, together with the urgency they conveyed: the scene has been set, major themes introduced, and the wandering now takes on a more habitual, routine nature. Ancient figures and scenes dominate the text, all marked by their absence of innocence and their aggression. In landscapes of first creation Adam is already covering his nakedness, a "cadaverous throng"—Babel-like—communicate through "pose and gesture" alone, and the animals, still possessing the power of speech, are "impaled again / in a netting of fences" (96). First explorers and settlers are represented by the exiled Erik the Red—Norwegian navigator of the tenth century—whose connection to America is through his son Leif Erikson, said to be the first European to have discovered the coast of North America. It is, however, Erik the Red's brutally ambitious daughter Freydis whose voice is most clearly heard (110):

up from my cabin
my sea-gown scarfed around me in the dark

belly that will bear a child forward into battle

the hieratic night is violent and visible.

This portrait of Freydis, based on one sketched by Williams in the opening essay of "Red Eric" in *The American Grain* (1956: 4–5), foregrounds the paradoxical Figure of Fertility bearing also murderous intentions and names the first culprits as male and female both. Indeed, Howe may be suggesting that the attempt of the individual to make space for himself in the world, which is a world of "Others," marks even his prenatal self and maps the direction of his future. As Todorov frames it, "human life is confined between these two extremes, one where the *I* invades the world, and one where the world ultimately absorbs the *I* in the form of a corpse or of ashes" (1982: 247). The pregnant belly, vulnerable and invading at one and the same time, pushes forward in space and time: a prefiguration of the exploring and conquering North American progenitors, a prophecy of violence—regenerative in part—to follow.

"I take SPACE to be the central fact to man born in America, from Folsom cave to now," writes Charles Olson in *Call Me Ishmael,* a critical/creative representation of Melville. "I spell it large," he continues, "because it comes Large, and without mercy" (1967: 15). The movement toward and through this space—the North American *space* which Howe names as constitutive of North American identity through its impact on "memory, war, and history"— serves as a central thematic of *Secret History* (1995: 5). The constant movement westward in Howe's poem seems to be an adoption of the traditional notions of *translatio imperii* or *translatio religionis* whereby world history is characterized by the transfer of power, wisdom, and religious thought from East

MORNING
SHEET OF WATER AT THE EDGE OF WOODS

Fig. 2.4. The twenty-fifth page of *Secret History of the Dividing Line* (*Frame Structures* 113).

to West.[15] However, Howe presents these notions in order to subvert them: the movement westward in *Secret History* is typified by frenetic energy and a deeply rooted ambivalence—"body backward / in a tremendous forward direction" (112). Indeed, the movement most dominant in the text—reactive rather than directional—is the involuntary and pointless physical flurry of the freezing figures that wander through Howe's always cold landscapes. From the "technique of traveling over sea ice / silent // before great landscapes and glittering processions" to "pacing the floes nervously" of first journeys westward (95)—from the "snow hanging in her hair" (106) and falling "on open pages" (104) to all the "frosty darkness" (107), "icy tremors" (109), "[t]rembling fathers" (110), and "sleep under frost and stars" (120) of the history to follow—this vast landscape is an ice-field[16] where the stuttering of its figures is as much due to the cold chattering of teeth as to uncertainty or congenital defect. The image of "troops of marble messengers [that] move before our eyes" (111) collapses the history of the continent into a single ice-icon—a palimpsest of marble tombstones marking the place of the many dead over the freezing soldiers occupying "a cold, bleak hill" (120) over the ghosts of all the first settlers who "howl 'wilderness'" through the first winter (110) over the icebergs, finally, of an unpeopled place.

The notion of *translatio imperii* is in the end subverted altogether by the absence of motion in the frozen-lake images marking the text. The mirrored word image on page 94 (see fig. 2.2) anticipates the more explicit verbal picture on page 113 (fig. 2.4): "It is winter / the lake is frozen over," explains the text a few pages earlier (98), and the reader now understands that Howe is sketching with words the image of the lake frozen over, in the tradition of Apollinaire and other writers of "concrete" or "visual" poetry.[17] Visual poetry, explains William Bohn in *The Aesthetics of Visual Poetry*, "seeks to alter our concept of reading as well as writing." In their dual role as both visual and verbal signs, the words on the page ask the reader to *look* at the text in addition to reading it—"that is, to acknowledge its physical authority" (1986: 67). As much as directing the reader's attention to whatever currents and creatures may move beneath the ice, Howe's frozen lake image/picture expresses an interest in the surface itself—the startling solidity of waters and words, the material mystery that often resists penetration. One may also read the rigid line drawn across the page, dividing the words into two camps—like foot soldiers on two fronts—as commentary on the artificial and arbitrary nature of borders. Indeed, this land/ice border will be undone once the thaw sets in.

The frozen lake image/picture also foregrounds the motif of reflections prominent in Howe's American works. The "mirroring impulse" in her poetry seems to have evolved from her beginnings as a visual artist in general and her interests in Marcel Duchamp's work in particular (Keller 1995: 9). Duchamp's most famous work, *The Bride Stripped Bare by Her Bachelors, Even*—also known as the *Large Glass*—created in the years 1915 through 1923, when it was abandoned and declared by Duchamp definitively "incompleted," is directly referred to in *Secret History*:

> "What's in a lake?"
> "Glass and sky."
>
> Calling the glass
> partners in this marriage
>
> glass bride
> and her metal frame
>
> inside
>
> thread, thread
> ambiguous conclusion
> (98)

The bride and her bachelors are separated from one another by their distinct frames, and though the bachelors may undress her with their gaze and mechanical maneuverings, the image is one of desire suspended—or desire, literally, in suspension.[18] "Words are only frames," writes Howe in *The Birthmark*, there are "[n]o comfortable conclusions" (1993: 141). The very indeterminacy of Howe's text and Duchamp's sculpture suspend the possibility of traditional "consummation" in the form of an authoritative or final meaning applied to either artwork—both artists present work that refuses "to 'mean' in conventional ways" (Perloff 1981: 34). Thus, the reader/viewer—proposing various interpretations that reflect as much her own context and concerns as the artist's—is part of and party to the work's suspended nature. In his discussion of Duchamp's erotic masterpiece, John Golding argues that Duchamp's choice of material may have emanated from his unconscious attraction to the idea "that when studying a work of art executed on glass the viewer would see himself and his surroundings to a certain extent mirrored in the object of his contemplation, thus involving a further degree of participation on his part" (1973: 68-69). Similarly, the reader gazing at the mirror images of *Secret History* cannot depend on conventional reading strategies and through her necessarily individual approach implicates her self—and thus is reflected—in the text. The individual's first encounter with her own reflection is, in part, an encounter with the "Other"—a pivotal moment of loss and gain identified by psychoanalytic theorists as a central stage in identity formation.[19] The "Other" in the wild American landscapes of *Secret History* is always, in part, oneself.

"If the 'dream' of New England fails to provide a proper conclusion, where does the speaker—where does the *story*—go from there?" asks Caldwell in her discussion of the open-endedness of the American Puritan conversion narratives (1983: 34). The speaker and the story of the similarly open-ended *Secret History of the Dividing Line* go back to primary literary forms, as though partial comfort, if not conclusion, can be found in the rhythms of legend and fairy tale:

> Ancient of days
> shadow of your wing
> hint of what light
> the open sky
> my refuge
>
> Came there all naked
> thorns were there
> many fair shields
> and Beauty lost
> was the Beast found
> descended from harmony
> enduring in unity
> far back in some story
> heard long ago
>
> (121)

The transcendent light is only hinted at, and the protective wing is no more than a shadow. And yet Howe identifies that "open sky"—the place where "[h]istorical imagination gathers in the missing" (*Frame Structures* 3)—as her "refuge." The "missing" portions of this tale are often represented by the lost child who has wandered through violent territory, hiding "under a bush crying bitterly // or nearly perishing with cold" (100). Toward the poem's end, a voice intent upon soothing that child intervenes:

```
poppy   sh  snow  flee  falcon  fathom  sh
flame   orison  sh  children  lost  fleece
sh  jagged  woof  subdued  foliage  sh
spinet  stain  clair  sh  chara  sh  mirac
                    (116)
```

The description seems to be of a deep interior, each separate word carrying the full weight of loss, in the enduring dialectic and dark fairy-tale reversal of "Beauty lost" and the "Beast found." The repeated "sh" sound weaves its way through this landscape, calling the child home, textual crumbs marking a possible path to safety. In the final page of the poem—another rectangle of separate words paralleling the word-rectangles of the poem's opening page, another frame to the text as a whole—the "sh" sound is again repeated, around and between words lifted from the dictionary entry at "mark" (see fig. 2.1):

```
sh  dispel  iris  sh  snow  sward  wide  ha
forest  1  a  boundary  manic  a  land  sh
whit  thing  :  target  cadence  marked  on
O  about  both  or  don't  INDICATION  Americ
sh  woof  subdued  toward  foliage  free  sh
                    (122)
```

The word-rectangle becomes territory—a snow-covered field or a forest of dense foliage perhaps—where the public and private voices, the authoritative and the alternative, the past and the present contend with each other for space and primacy. While the dividing line is, ultimately, never set, the poem's final line—framed as it is with the soothing "sh"—seems to end this poetic surveying trip with a cool hand to the forehead and the possibility of rest.

Articulation of Sound Forms in Time and *Thorow* (1990)

Howe's 1990 collection entitled *Singularities*, which includes both *Articulation of Sound Forms in Time* and *Thorow*, opens with the following two epigraphs:

> She was looking for the fragments of the dead Osiris, dead and scattered asunder, dead, torn apart, and thrown in fragments over the wide world.
> —D. H. Lawrence

under her drift of veils,
and she carried a book.
—H.D.[20]

It is evident with Howe's choice to inscribe her book first with the quotation from Lawrence that the poems to follow will wander through the landscapes of fratricide and gratuitous violence already encountered in *Secret History*. Indeed, the Lawrence quotation repeats the word *dead* three times in as many lines, twice mentions Osiris's fragments of flesh, and twice more refers to Seth's brutal ripping asunder of his brother's body. The singular female pronoun[21] opening the passage—the female presence of Isis, who will search to reclaim and bury every piece of her dead husband/brother's body—is overpowered, even obliterated, by the savagery and destruction of what follows. And yet, the soundings of hitherto silenced female voices from these literary and historical landscapes appears to be Howe's particular concern in these later American poems. The passage from H.D.—announcing its own fragmented nature through incomplete syntax and interrupted story—directs attention back to "she" who has entered the scene, book in her hands.[22] "How do I, choosing messages from the code of others in order to participate in the universal theme of Language," asks Howe in her earlier critical work *My Emily Dickinson*, "pull SHE from all the myriad symbols and sightings of HE" (1985: 16–17). *Articulation of Sound Forms in Time* and *Thorow* not only "pull SHE" to the forefront, but they do so by wrestling with and finally debunking Howe's own earlier formulation of Language as a "universal theme."

The figures and voices of the Puritan women Mary Rowlandson and Anne Hutchinson are crucial to our understanding of *Articulation of Sound Forms in Time* (henceforth to be called *Articulation*), as their stories seem to generate the content and influence the poetic praxis of the work. "I think Mary Rowlandson is the mother of us all. American writers I mean," writes Howe in *The Birth-mark* (167). "Already in 1681," she continues, "the first narrative written by a white Anglo-American woman is alive with rage and contradiction." Howe credits Rowlandson with this progenitor literary role due to her captivity narrative of 1682, "the first and by far the most widely distributed book devoted to a single captivity" (Slotkin 1973: 95). Mary Rowlandson's *Narrative of the Captivity and Restoration of Mrs. Mary Rowlandson*[23] chronicles the tale of her abduction by the Narragansett Indians from her home in Lancaster, Massachusetts, in the winter of 1676 and the eleven weeks she spent as their captive. During her time of captivity, Rowlandson—separated from her older children at the outset and uncertain of their fate throughout—has her wounded six-year-old daughter, Sarah, die in her arms; witnesses multiple killings by clubbing, shooting, and burning; and herself suffers from starvation, cold, and extreme fatigue. As Slotkin argues, the New England Indian captivity narrative, with Rowlandson's text as the prototype, "functioned as a myth [from the moment of its literary genesis], reducing the Puritan state of mind and world view, along with the events of colonization and settlement, into archetypal drama" (1973: 94). An isolated individual on the American frontier, most often a woman,[24] is subjugated by and forced to interact with the Indian, the one perceived as the devilish Other—"those black creatures in the night" whose "roaring, and singing, and dancing, and yelling . . . made the place a lively resemblance of hell!" (qtd. in Andrews 1992: 29). This interaction with the Other, strangely characterized by the intimacies of sharing food and blanket, was then interpreted as God's testing of his faithful; one's ultimate redemption from the Other was proof of God's divine providence and boundless grace. Polemical use aside, it seems evident that the great popularity of these narratives in their day in America and abroad[25] attests to the overwhelming fascination that the white settlers and their families in England had with the unknown Other, the "barbarous" Indians just beyond the boundaries of their villages. The captive provided an insider's view, enacting a forbidden intimacy; the captive gendered female foregrounded the settlers' particular fear of the Other's physicality and sexuality.[26]

It was on the heels of writing her article on Mary Rowlandson ("The Captivity and Restoration of Mary Rowlandson," in *Temblor* 2 [1985]; now collected in *Birth-mark* 89-130) and while continuing her research into Native American raids of that period that Howe first encountered the story of Hope Atherton: "I was up in the stacks of Sterling Library . . . [which] houses books that aren't used often, so it has an aura of death [. . .] I was turning the pages of a history of [the New England town of] Hadley, and Hope's name just caught me. It was the emblematical name. Here was this person. A man with a woman's name. He had this border-line, half-wilderness, half-Indian, insanity-sanity experience. He was a minister accompanying an army. The enemy thought he might have been God" (Foster 57). Having challenged traditional readings of the now canonized Rowlandson narrative in her creative/ critical article, Howe uncovers an uncanonized voice of American captivity literature—a voice and figure composed entirely of paradoxes, a voice and figure uncategorizable and hence threatening to the established readings of this New World literary genre. What most interests Howe in Hope's story— what is present though has most often been ignored in Rowlandson's—is the fashion in which the encounter with the Other changes Hope to such a degree that he becomes a "stranger to his community" (*Singularities* 4). *Articulation of Sound Forms in Time* is, in a phrase Howe borrows from Emmanuel Levinas and adopts as a statement of poetics, a work concerned with the "*movement of the Same towards the Other which never returns to the Same*" (*Birthmark* 37). Paralleling Hope's "movement . . . towards the Other" is Howe's movement toward Hope, effected by her "assum[ing] Hope Atherton's excursion": putting it upon herself, as one would a piece of clothing—performing his transformative journey through her transformations of language (4).

The three-page prose opening of *Articulation* dryly catalogs the savagery of the white settlers toward the Indians and of the Indians toward the white settlers: bodies are indiscriminately shot, drowned, dashed against rocks, and burned with dry thatch. Both sides seem intent upon eradicating the other, children and women included; neither side seems aware of the other as human. Accompanying the army until he is unhorsed and left behind, Hope Atherton, "minister of the gospel, at Hatfield, a gentleman of publick spirit" (3), wanders through this bloody arena—a strange "little man with a black coat and without any hat" (5), whose straying too far into forbidden territory places him outside the bounds of his community. Hope's tale deviates from the norms of the captivity narrative in that the Indians reject him, and he ends up wandering lost through the wilds. I am suggesting that he is, in fact, captured, and captivated, by the wilderness: the captivity that marks the entire American literary tradition. Upon returning to his own community, Atherton is labeled as "beside himself" (5), deviant, and the account he gives of his experiences with the Indians is thus easily and wholly discredited.[27] The sixteen poems of section 2, entitled "Hope Atherton's Wanderings," constitute Atherton's discredited account and, with their complete abandonment of normative language functions, ask to be read both as the wild rantings of a madman and as language being remade to reflect the particularities of place and experience.

The first two poems of section 2 of *Articulation* read as follows:

Prest try to set after grandmother
revived by and laid down left ly
little distant each other and fro
Saw digression hobbling driftwood
forage two rotted beans & etc.
Redy to faint slaughter story so
Gone and signal through deep water
Mr. Atherton's story Hope Atherton

Clog nutmeg abt noon
scraping cano muzzell
foot path sand and so
gravel rubbish vandal
horse flesh ryal tabl
sand enemys flood sun
Danielle Warnare Servt
Turner Falls Fight us
Next wearer April One

(6)[28]

From the outset, with the subject of this tangled narrative absented—who is "[p]rest try to set," who "[s]aw digression hobbling," and who is "[r]edy to faint"?—and the ordering effect of syntax abandoned, the role of language seems to have little to do with the relaying of experience and everything to do with its reenactment.[29] The poetic landscape is a clutter of verbs and nouns that the reader, together with the speaker, crashes into—unbuffered by the gradual evolution of a normative sentence. Similarly, through the abridgment of words ("ly," "cano," "abt") and the discarding of all time adverbs, time is condensed from a spectrum into a spot, as though each moment in this wilderness is both the only moment and every moment. The poems rush forth with the urgency and breathlessness of a person in flight. However, the flight is within a territory bounded on all sides, and while the semantic "[b]onds [are] loosd" in the telling of this "[r]ash catastrophe" (9), the poems themselves remain severely delineated by the left and right margins of the page. The combination of unruliness within and restriction without—like a madman in a locked room—seems to represent a central strain in American literature, the legacy of Puritan parents seeking—and imposing—the semblance of stability at all costs, despite the uncertainty at their core and the extreme wildness on all their borders.

The third-person reference to self ("Mr. Atherton's story Hope Atherton") in the poem's opening conveys both the sense of madness of an individual literally "beside himself" and introduces the small child's voice who has not yet recognized the first-person pronoun as herself. With the repetition of "Hope Atherton," the child's voice lingers—insistent, petulant, wanting to be understood. *Articulation* is, in many ways, "a myth of beginning" (12), a journey back to origins, to first places—linguistic, geographic, historical, and psychological. Indeed, the repeated references throughout section 2 to "deep water" and "falls" evoke not only the actual battle site where Hope, and hope, too, were first lost, but also the womb environment of insulation and isolation. From this prelanguage "conch," Howe/Hope "signal[s]" instead of speaks, offering up "sound forms" in the place of words: "drumm amonoosuck y" (10). From this prelanguage "catacomb" (the word crossed out in the text, pushed deeper into the page), Hope emerges at section's end and declares as though in valediction:

> We march from our camp a little
> and come home
> Lost the beaten track and so
> River section dark all this time
> We must not worry
> how few we are and fall from each other
> More than language can express
> Hope for the artist in America & etc
> This is my birthday
> These are the old home trees
>
> (16)

Howe seems to be suggesting that just as Hope Atherton is transformed by his wanderings in the American wilderness, away from his own known identity and away from the "beaten track"—so too will the "American artist" be transformed and reborn by her willingness to stray from the wide community of conventional language usage, to wander with a few others into the unknown territory of "More than language can express," where, paradoxically, she will find herself among "the old home trees."

The notion of "signaling" prominent in section 2 of *Articulation* enacts also the only mode of communication possible from behind enemy lines: the sending of encoded messages. Through the encoded message, language admits that which otherwise remains only implicit: words are anything but transparent, they "mean" in multiple ways, and they participate in varying forms of deception and subterfuge. On pages 13–15 in particular, each word— separate, seemingly unconnected to what precedes and what follows, plotted in straight lines across the page to form "blocks" of text—demands attention, carrying the weight of meaning embedded within:

Posit gaze level diminish lamp and asleep(selv)cannot see

is notion most open apparition past Halo view border redden

possess remote so abstract life are lost spatio-temporal hum

Maoris empirical Kantian a little lesson concatenation up

tree fifty shower see step shot Immanence force to Mohegan

blue glare(essence)cow bed leg extinct draw scribe   upside
even blue(A)ash-tree fleece comfort(B)draw scribe   sideup

(14)

Though the text above is enigmatic and resistant to interpretation, it seems evident to me that the words of the text are anything but haphazard and have, in fact, been chosen and placed on the page with great deliberateness. The changing amount of space between words and between lines, the occasional use of parentheses and hyphens, the repetition of certain words and the highlighting of others through italics or capital letters all signal the presence of a *language system*, which signals the presence of meaning. The first and final words of the text—"[p]osit gaze" and "sideup"—may be read as instructions for the decoding procedure: look at the text and then turn it. Indeed, the facing page is an upside down and inverted mirror image of the middle four lines of the text, with all spaces extracted and capitals added:

MoheganToForceImmanenceShotStepSeeShowerFiftyTree

UpConcatenationLessonLittleAKantianEmpiricalMaoris

HumTemporal-spatioLostAreLifeAbstractSoRemotePossess

ReddenBorderViewHaloPastApparitionOpenMostNotion *is*

(15)

The opening line seems to provide the message we have been awaiting: the attack of Mohegan Indians is imminent (conveyed through the sound similarity to "Immanence"), shots have been heard in an area of fifty trees. However, our desire for one authoritative reading is quickly frustrated by language's own links—the "[c]oncatenation" of sounds and shapes in a particular moment in time. Thus, "Mohegan" leads to "Maoris"—another indigenous people conquered and colonized—through the alliterative connection, and establishes the humming *m*—internal, reverberative, and continuous—as the text's dominant sound ("Immanence," "Empirical," "Hum," "Temporal," Remote," and "Most"). Similarly, the repeated alliteration of *l* in "LessonLittle" and "LostAreLife"—in addition to their central placement in the middle of the middle two lines of the text—highlight those word groups as though they alone carry the passage's core and hidden meaning: the insignificance of the "lesson" learned from this tale in the face of the loss of life experienced. The italicized *"is"* at the passage's end, the only word standing separate and not capitalized, supports this reading: the sanctity of that which lives, that which *"is,"* supersedes all. However, this reading too is challenged by the words preceding it: empirical understandings of the world are partial at best, the halo and the apparition—all that is mysterious and at the borders of understanding—have a genuine power over and purpose in our lives. Howe's text, which can never fully be decoded, embraces the enigmatic as an engagement with a multiple and generative landscape.

The reader's inability to "make meaning" out of the text also reflects Howe's poetic praxis of what Bob Perelman names "composition in the field of other users of language" (1996: 111).[30] Howe's work emerges from and enacts a rejection of linguistic hegemony—an ideological position that informs all of her poetry. In these American works in particular, Howe's unconventional language usages may be read as her answer to the first conqueror's rejection of language diversity in the New World. As Todorov argues,

> Columbus's failure to recognize the diversity of languages permits him, when he confronts a foreign language, only two possible, and complementary, forms of behavior: to acknowledge it as a language but to refuse to believe it is different; or to acknowledge its difference but to refuse to admit it is a language ... This latter reaction is provoked by the Indians he encounters at the very beginning, on October 12, 1492; seeing them, he promises himself: "If it please Our Lord, at the moment of my departure I shall take from this place six of them to Your Highnesses, so that they may learn to speak." (1982: 30)

Columbus's perception of Indian languages does shift from this extreme position over time; however, as cataloged in Todorov's readings of original documents, including diary entries and letters, a profound disinterest in and disdain for the Other's modes of communication continues to characterize all his encounters with the Indians. *Articulation* and *Thorow* may be read as Howe's response to the conquerors' and settlers' early language practices, which continue to haunt the American literary tradition. In the place of an imperialistic assumption that the Other—which includes the reader—speaks the same language, or *should* speak the same language, the failure-to-understand and the not-being-understood become, as Perloff states, Howe's "point of departure" (1990: 303).[31]

Anne Hutchinson, the second Puritan female figure wandering through *Articulation,* needs to be considered at this point. Hutchinson was at the forefront of the 1636–38 Antinomian Controversy in New England, a controversy that has been considered "the most momentous event in the first decade of settlement," though also a tremendously "confusing affair, even to its most active participants" (Erikson 1966: 74). Cotton Mather recorded in his *Magnalia Christi Americana* that "multitudes of people, who took in with both parties [of the Antinomian debate], did never to their dying hour understand what their difference was" (1853: I, 508). Many of the texts devoted to discussions regarding the Antinomian Controversy speak in generalities and fail, finally, to elucidate the exact nature of the conflict. The core of the conflict returns us to the issue of uncertainty in the Puritan worldview: Hutchinson was claiming that the perfect Christian was "the one who, emptied of self and conflict in Christ, waits *passively* for the moment when his dependence is rewarded with *sure* knowledge of salvation" (Lang 1987: 20; italics added for emphasis). Hutchinson was challenging the doctrine as it had evolved in New England usage whereby "good works" may secure one's salvation, though one would remain in doubt to the end. As a purist, she applied a literal reading to the Covenant of Grace, accusing the religious figures of her day of preaching still the long-broken Covenant of Works.[32] The church fathers refuted this accusation, claiming that Hutchinson had brashly overstepped the perimeters of her female role and that they "do not mean to discourse with those of [her] sex" (Hutchinson 1768: 484). Hutchinson and her accusers agreed on little, seemed to understand each other even less, and the records from her civil trial of November 1637 and her church trial of March 1638 exhibit the two parties employing radically different language systems, resulting in a complete breakdown in communication. In her brilliant article "The Antinomian Language Controversy," Patricia Caldwell develops this reading of the controversy, explaining the confusion characterizing the trial documents and the later accounts of this history as the result of a profound linguistic division between the parties involved. "[W]hatever else it may have been," argues Caldwell, "the Antinomian Controversy was a monumental crisis of language. The trial documents suggest that Mrs. Hutchinson . . . was speaking what amounts to a different language—different from that of her adversaries . . . and that other people may have been speaking and hearing as she was, and that what happened to them all had serious literary consequences in America" (1976: 346–347).

Hutchinson's location "outside the linguistic fold" (1976: 351) of her community resulted from her various "aberrant" doctrinal beliefs and language practices.[33] Firstly, while Scripture remained for her the absolute authority in all matters of faith, interpretations *applied to* Scripture could never be more than partial, reflective of the interpreting individual, open to doubt and debate. As Caldwell states, Hutchinson's "final answer is always, Scripture, yes; agreement on interpretation, no. God, yes; man, no" (1976: 351). The fallibility of human understanding and the limitations of human articulation were intrinsic to her worldview—an oddly postmodern sensibility coupled with the completely seventeenth-century embracing of God's perfection in all matters. Hutchinson's own language is "infinitely open," characterized by an abundance of questions and her tendency to contradict herself, every articulation containing itself and its opposite. Language is unsettled, wandering in search of what it might say, in search of what is sayable. The profusion of passive forms in her speech pushes the language user even further into the background. "Distancing herself from her own words and from her hearers," writes Caldwell, "she conveys a sense that verbal expressions are independent objects which may be acted upon and which are not inevitably 'connected' to the will although they may be aligned with it. Words are part of what one has, not part of what one is. They can be set askew, can change or disintegrate, because fundamentally they *are* things" (1976: 356). It seems to me that "Taking the Forest"—the third section of *Articulation*—and the poem as a whole return the reader to this "primordial struggle of North American literary expression" (*Birth-mark* 4): the question of what words *are*, what their degree of reliability is, and how one is to proceed in a world where the language landscape is, finally and willfully, unstable.

The twenty-five sections of "Taking the Forest" are visually normative in nature: arranged in couplets and single lines with aligned left margins and standard, unfragmented English words, the poems utilize no obvious avant-garde or experimental language strategies. And yet, one has only to read a section or two to realize that the words of this text are propelled by an alternative set of language rules or, perhaps, by the absence of a set of language rules. The experience of reading these texts is a frustrating one: what seems accessible is, in fact, not, and words, disconnected from subject or object, pile up on the page, like stones forming a wall. I will quote at length from this section's third poem in order to convey a sense of the text's density:

> Double penetrable foreign sequel
> By face to know helm
> Prey to destroy in dark theme
> Emblem of fictitious narrative
>
> Step and system

Collision and impulsion

Asides and reminders to myself

Lives to be seen pressing and alien

Fix fleeting communication

Carried away before a pursuer
Demonstration in a string of definitions

To walk a little
Night's kingdom lamentation dimming

Snatched idea
Recollection fallen away from ruin

Slide into elect unalterable

slipping from known to utmost bound

Paper plague odd ends reap

Faint legend is day

(*Singularities* 19)

Referents are all but absent: whose face will know what helm, is the prey
subject or object, who will walk and who slide? In a line like "[p]aper plague
odd ends reap," the syntactical role of each word is uncertain; hence, the
relationship between words and the meanings these relationships might make
are multiple, open to debate, questions, and queries. This dark and dense
language-forest is, first and foremost, a "[s]phere of sound," a "[b]ody of ar-
ticulation chattering," which the reader may enter into though not conquer
(26). The title of this section has to be read as ironic, for reader and speaker
are not, in fact, "[t]aking the forest"—the forest "takes" them, takes over,
with the sturdiness of its "[g]reen tree girdled against splitting" and its "[g]irl
with forest shoulder" (31). The life force of the forest resides in the rejection
of singularity, the suspension of "cold intellect" (34), the surrender to a place
of "soft origin" where words make their own connections: "vat" leads to "co-
vert" (32), "mad" to "made" and "collision" to "collusion" (33). "Dear Un-
conscious scatter syntax / scythe mower surrender hereafter," writes Howe
(36), linking the liberation of language from syntax with a type of immortal-
ity, a triumph over death as it appears in the guise of the scythe mower. This
refusal to curb one's original vision, this celebration of life and language's
chaotic and contradictory nature, recalls Hutchinson at her trial defiantly

speaking in paradox, insisting that now, "having seen him which is invisible," she is unafraid of what "man can do unto me" (Hutchinson 1768: 509).

The language of "Taking the Forest" is further characterized by the sparse use of articles, possessives, and prepositions: each word is its own weighty entity, unmediated and unqualified. In addition, and resonant again of Hutchinson's language usages, the passive voice predominates in the text, coupled with an all but absent speaking subject. In the single poem quoted above, something is "[c]arried away," "[l]ives to be seen" are pressing and alien, and "[r]ecollection [has] fallen away from ruin." Even the adjective of "[s]natched idea" resonates of the passive form through the evoking of verb and absented agent. The language spoken here calls attention to that which it has liberated itself from: the authoritative "I," the singular interpretation, and the "captive compulsion" (17) of the Puritan forefather "to hold meaning steady" (Caldwell 1976: 360).

I read Hutchinson as the single constant figure in "Taking the Forest." I see the text's language strategies as emanating from this American foremother and her desire and struggle to define for herself and her accusers "the meaning of knowing" (25). It is, finally, her own boldness and directness of speech that results in her banishment: during her civil trial, Hutchinson makes the heretical claim that she has had a direct revelation of God, unmediated by Church ministering (Hutchinson 1768: 508–514). Having provided her judges with adequate reason, she is "banished from out of our jurisdiction as being a woman unfit for our society." When Hutchinson, strangely unaware of the utter stalemate in communication, persists and demands to know "wherefore am I banished," Governor Winthrop silences her once and for all with the following: "Say no more, the court knows wherefore and is satisfied" (520). It is an Anne Hutchinson, with the advantage of retrospect and the understanding of the danger in words, who speaks in Howe's text: "Destiny of calamitous silence / Mouth condemning me to absence" (25). The absence and silence are both figurative and gruesomely literal: in the late summer of 1643, in the wilds and isolation of the Long Island Sound where she settled upon banishment from her community, Hutchinson and five of her children were slaughtered by Indians (Battis 1962: 248).

In the five months between her civil and church trials, Anne Hutchinson delivered a stillborn baby. The fetus was reported to be deformed and "monstrous"—proof to her male accusers that their judgment of her was correct, for "as she had vented misshapen opinions, so she must bring forth deformed monsters" (Theodore Weld's preface to Winthrop's *Short Story*, qtd. in Kibbey 1986: 112).[34] Winthrop himself so fused the "material shape and figurative image" that when he "heard of Hutchinson's stillborn, malformed child, he dug up the buried corpse to see for himself the material, visible *figura* of the 'misshapen opinions'" (Kibbey 1986: 113). It is, finally, *as* maternal figure, mother of the malformed, that Hutchinson is cast out completely; it is as mother that Howe reintroduces her into our literary landscape. "Taking the Forest" repeatedly refers to mother figures—the ones who "from their windows look" (18), Sarah and Rachel (20), Eve and the Norse Eve figure of Embla (32), "[s]traw mother" (20), "[m]other and maiden" (24). "Mother my name" (23), proclaims the speaker, the rare first-person possessive pronoun foregrounding the weight of the statement and of the role, with the inverted syntax highlighting a sense of strain and difficulty. Indeed, this mother cannot protect her children in the volatile landscape they inhabit, their cries opening "to the words inside them / Cries hurled through the Woods" (23). By poem's end, Hutchinson is far off, "dim outline // Little figure of mother" (37), lost with her children to the forest.[35]

The personal "I" that has been avoided throughout the text and intervenes in the text's final poem is, to recast Reinfeld's formulation regarding language, an "I" "broken and made strange by the history it seeks to articulate" (1992: 127). As something "broken" and "made strange," this "I" speaks in a voice that has been opened to its own multiplicity, its places of origin, and its losses. The tale of the final poem of *Articulation* is an age-old one, made new by the twenty-four meditations preceding it:

> To kin I call in the Iron-Woods
> Turn I to dark Fells last alway
>
> Theirs was an archheathen theme
> Soon seen stumbled in lag Clock
>
> Still we call bitterly bitterly
> Stern norse terse ethical pathos
>
> Archaic presentiment of rupture
> Voicing desire no more from here
>
> Far flung North Atlantic littorals
>   (38)

These final images of isolation and abandonment—the "I" calling to kin who will not answer, the "we" calling bitterly from "[f]ar flung North Atlantic" shores, the Rowlandsons, Athertons, and Hutchinsons lost to the literal and figurative forests of the New World—are the focus of Howe's poetic project and praxis. Between "the crumbled masonry" marking failed human efforts and the "windswept hickory" (38) that will endure, within the "[o]ccult ferocity" (30) of all first settlers, with their myths of sacred violence, within the "[o]ccult ferocity" of the "howling wilderness" itself, she locates the birthplace of American literature. What was originally seen as the "[e]nd of the world" is, for Howe, the place of "trial or possible / trail" (27).

"Our nationality which answers to the name of American . . . is a language," writes Horace Gregory in his introduction to *In the American Grain*, "and it requires a particularly alive and discerning imagination to keep pace with it and to speak it truly" (Williams 1956: xii). From the dark ending of *Articulation* to the multiple openings of *Thorow*, from a work located in the troubled end of the seventeenth century to a work associated with a transcendentalist of the mid-1800s, Howe's poetry seems to be "keeping pace" with shifts in sensibility and self-awareness that characterize American history. While *Articulation* and *Thorow* are independent works, they are nonetheless linked by their juxtaposition in *Singularities*, and one senses that the landscapes of *Thorow* that open up into desire and rejuvenation do so as a direct result of the chaos and violence unearthed and enacted in the previous work. This is not an embracing of Williams's notion of "rich regenerative violence," but rather an insistence on the richness and regeneration involved in *admitting to* the violence, the original savagery—the regeneration of "[r]evealing traces" (46). In the "Narrative in Non-Narrative" introduction to *Thorow*, on the shores of Lake George, New York—a site marked, as all Howe's American landscapes are, by violence perpetrated by foreign invaders on native and nature alike,[36] Howe writes: "In the seventeenth century European adventurer-traders burst through the forest to discover this particular clear body of fresh water. They brought our story to it. Pathfinding believers in God and grammar spelled the lake into *place* . . . In paternal colonial systems a positivist efficiency appropriates primal indeterminacy" (*Singularities* 41). Howe is *part of* the "European adventurer-traders" story—"our story," she writes (see Perelman 1996: 132)—even as she is apart from their attempts "to spell" the lake into place. Having wandered through the "paternal colonial systems" of her forefathers and having uncovered its affects in *Secret History* and *Articulation*, Howe intends in *Thorow* to reinstate the "primal indeterminacy" long denied.

Already from the text's title, Howe announces the multiple and indeterminate as intrinsic to that which is commonly perceived as individual and singular: the proper name. This alternative spelling of Henry David Thoreau's name originates in the letters of Hawthorne, where he writes: "Mr. Thorow dined with us yesterday. He is a singular character—a young man with much of wild original nature still remaining in him" (Baym 1994: 1388). Why Hawthorne spells Thoreau's name thus is not known, though it may have been an indication of the original pronunciation of the name.[37] Regardless, this name "thrown open" (Reinfeld 1989: 97) becomes the text's point of departure, an entryway into "the instantaneous apprehension of [the] multiplicity" in names (*Singularities* 44) and an invitation to call the very act of naming into question. "The first gesture Columbus makes upon contact with the newly discovered lands," writes Todorov, "is an act of extended nomination," which is an act of possessing (1982: 28). "'My desire,' writes Columbus during the first voyage, 'was to pass by no single island without taking possession of it' (15/10/1492)" (Todorov 1982: 45). In *Thorow,* names "on both sides of the European/Indian divide" (Perelman 1996: 133) are misspelled and "made more crooked," in a rejection of ownership,[38] an "outstripp[ing]" of possession, the "[f]ence blown down in a winter storm" (*Singularities* 44). From the surveyor's markings and boundary-making in *Secret History,* through the claustrophobic forms and delineating forest of *Articulation,* Howe has reached in *Thorow* an American landscape that opens up into "a possible field of work //. . . expanse of unconcealment" (55).

The title of *Thorow* may also be read as the archaic spelling of "through," advancing the notion of this text as a movement toward, an opening up, a passage through—in seeming affirmation of Sir Humfrey Gilbert's assertion that "there is no thorow passage navigable," as quoted by Howe in *Thorow*'s "Narrative in Non-Narrative" preface (42). Certainly through this use of such archaic spellings, Howe is not only in dialogue with the "Pathfinding believers in God and grammar" who "spelled" America into place; she also means to "lend authenticity and historicity to her poem"—articulating thus the ongoing, often obscured, "complicity between the past and the present (Naylor 1999: 53, 52).[39] However, I believe that Howe's central objective in employing archaic word forms—which appear as misspellings to the contemporary reader—is to "unspell" America. The following extracts provide a few examples of this "unspelling" technique, with almost every third or fourth word deviating from rules of conventional orthography:

at Fort Stanwix the <u>Charroke</u>
<u>paice</u>
[. . . .]

[. . . .]
Irruptives

thorow out all
the Five Nations

To cut our wete

of the Jentlemen

Fort the same
Nuteral

Revealing traces
Regulating traces

---

(46)

[. . . .]
Let us gether and bury

limbs and leves

Is a great Loast

Cant say for us now

Stillest the storm world
Thought

The snow
is still hear

Wood and feld
all covered with ise

seem world anew
[. . . .]

(48; my underlinings)

To utilize in reverse Thoreau's own terminology quoted in the opening of
Thorow, the language here, like the names, is "made more crooked"—which
means it is "straightened out," more accurately representing the cultural di-
vide between settlers and Indians and the historical divide between the twen-

tieth-century reader and the seventeenth- or early-nineteenth-century sub-
ject. "The snow / is still hear" states the final poem of section 1, insisting
that we listen to this landscape in addition to visualizing it, for sight is lim-
ited and through the deviant and alternative soundings we may apprehend
that which otherwise evades detection.

The motif of listening closely is evoked in *Thorow* also through the stance
the speaker adopts: she is "acting the part of a scout" (51). The origins of the
word *scout* are from the Old French *escoute*, "listener," or *escouter*, "to listen."
The scout sets out alone, ahead of all others, to gather information, to ex-
plore and spy on, to stand watch and forewarn. The scout of *Thorow* is not
settler or settler's outcast, not Indian or Indian's victim; this scout has "snow
shoes and Indian shoes" both (43) and seems intent upon traveling between
the two sides, following her own "track of Desire" (45). "If men inherit souls,"
writes Williams *In the American Grain*, "this is the color of mine. We are, too,
the others" (1956: 41). Williams's Europeans inherit and are dominated by
the souls of the Indians they have massacred. Howe's scout, neither Euro-
pean nor Indian, seems to carry the souls of both sides in a merging of Self
and Other possible only after the tale with "traces of blood" in it has been
told. Howe herself carries a name appropriate for the scout: "Howe" is a vari-
ant of "Hugh," signifying one who dwells on a projecting ridge of land or a
promontory.[40] The promontory, ledge between water and land, is the perfect
topographical placement for the one who must stand watch and witness,
and also conjures up places of first encounters and first clashes between the
European and the India.

Both sections 1 and 2 of *Thorow* introduce imagery of thawing into the
text. "When ice breaks up / at the farthest North / of Adirondack peaks,"
states the third poem in section 1, "Go back for your body" (43). In section 2,
the "[t]haw has washed away snow / covering the old ice" (51). Indeed, *Thorow*
as a text of thawing, a moving through ("thorow") a transition from rigid
positions into a flowing, is suggested already in the final page of *Articulation*,
where the Norse god Balder—slain by the jealous Loki in a pseudo-fratri-
cide—is mentioned. Folk belief says that the thaw after a frost indicates that
"all things weep for Balder" (Davidson 1969: 187). With the final section of
Thorow, the frozen lake of *Secret History* melts. Using the same principles of
mirroring, Howe has the two pages invert and more or less reflect each other;
however, the mirrorings in *Thorow* abandon entirely the highly structured
format present in *Secret History* (*FS* 94) and *Articulation* (*Singularities* 14–15)
and display instead what Howe calls "the scattering effect" (Keller 1995: 9;
see figs. 2.5 and 2.6). On both sides of the book's seam, words drift apart,
turn, and crash into each other at odd angles, like pieces of ice breaking away

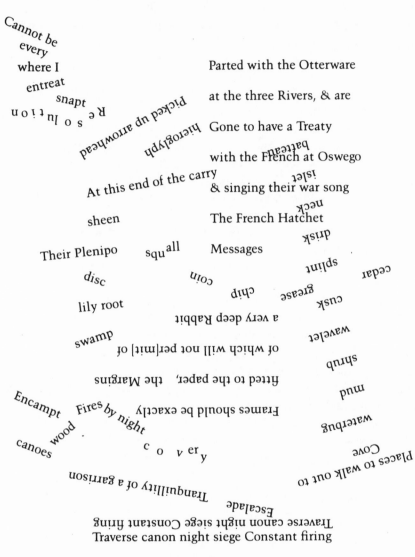

Fig. 2.5. Page 56 from *Thorow*.

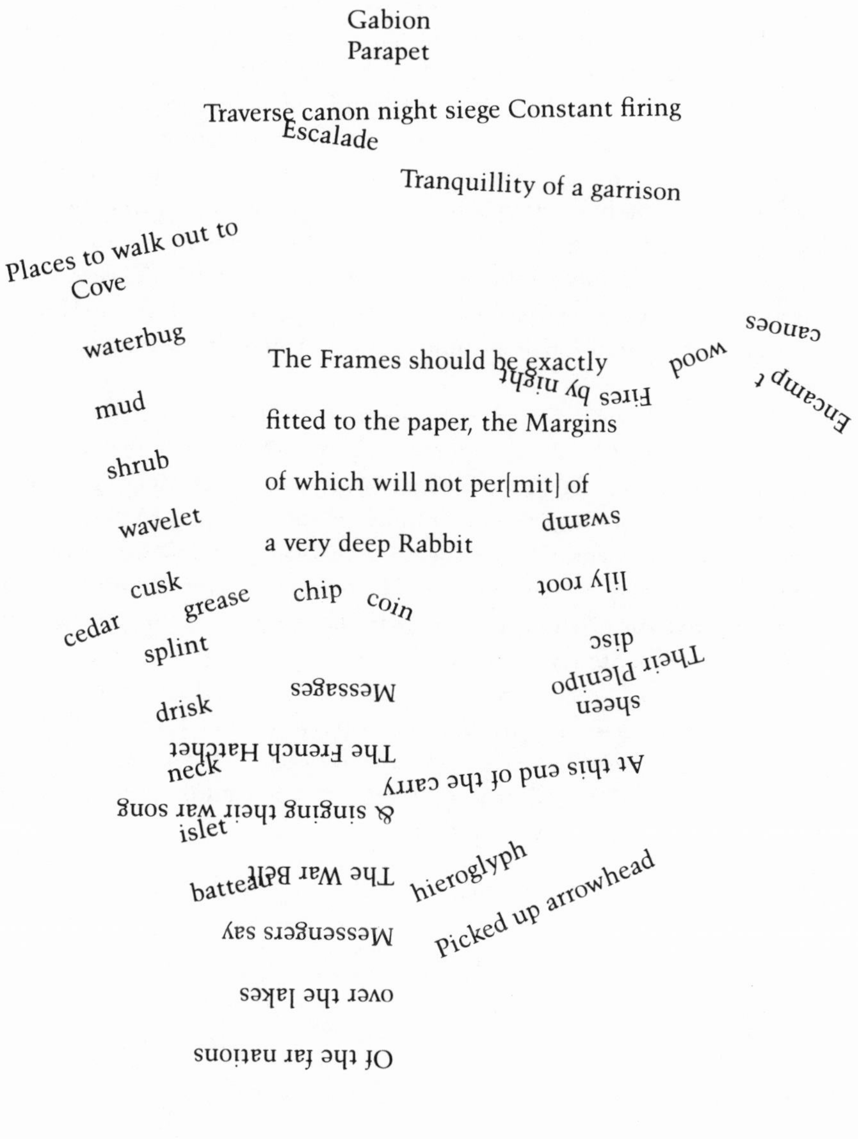

Gabion
Parapet

Traverse canon night siege Constant firing
Escalade

Tranquillity of a garrison

Places to walk out to
Cove

waterbug

canoes

mud

wood

Encamp't

The Frames should be exactly
Fires by night
fitted to the paper, the Margins
of which will not per[mit] of
a very deep Rabbit

shrub

swamp

wavelet

cusk
cedar grease chip coin
splint
drisk Messages

lily root
disc
Their plentipo
sheen

The French Hatchet
neck
At this end of the carry
& singing their war song
islet

battered The War Bell hieroglyph

Picked up arrowhead

Messengers say

over the lakes

Of the far nations

Fig. 2.6. Page 57 from *Thorow*.

from the whole, like floes flowing. If the captivity narrative is also, as Charles Bernstein argues, "the story of our own language held hostage" (1989: 86), these two pages of *Thorow* enact language's liberation, its release from the bonds of syntax, word units, and normative use of page space. The word landscape, like nature before the arrival of the first "spoilers and looters," is returning to its "[u]ninterrupted" and unordered origin (Beckett 1989: 20–21). Words indicating European military strength—"[g]abion," "[P]arapet," "garrison," "canon," and so on—collide with "canoe" and "arrowhead," intermingle with the half-water/ half-land landscapes taking over, the "swamp" and the "mud," the "islet" and the "cove." "The essential American soul," writes Lawrence in *Studies in Classic American Literature*, "is hard, isolate, stoic, and a killer. It has never yet melted." The "American soul" re-created in Howe's poetry escapes definition in its multiplicity, and, in her representation of it, it is melting.

"Dark here in the driftings / in the spaces of drifting," writes Howe in the final poem of section 2, "Complicity battling redemption." Howe's work seems always concerned with the possibility that in the attempt to give voice to the unvoiced of the early American landscapes, it may fail, voice only itself, and, thus, become an accomplice in the deceptions and erasures of literature and history.[41] Referring to the "disc" separated from "covery" toward the bottom of page 56 (not reflected on the opposite page), Perelman writes: "While Howe's writing works toward discovery of semi-erased traces . . . she seems aware that . . . she [may be] simply adding another layer over what it wants to reveal: 'discovery' may always be 'covery'" (1996: 136). These doubts, I believe, are intrinsic to her poetic praxis, for they lead to experimentation and invention. The final page of *Thorow* is a collection of strange and unidentifiable words, or word-pieces:

anthen	uplispth	enend
adamap	blue wov	thefthe
folled	floted	keen

Themis

thou sculling me
Thiefth

These sounds, half-stutter/half-lisp, themselves floating on the open page, represent this American poet's commitment to inventing original terms for the "crooked" history of her continent. "Poets are always beginning again," states Howe in the 1989 *Difficulties* interview. Both adopting and challenging a conqueror/quester's frame of reference in her choice of imagery, she continues: "They sail away to a place they hope they can name . . . Only a few strike home" (Beckett 1989: 26). Howe's American work ends with the sea-travel image of "thou sculling me"—where an Indian landscape of canoes and scalpings is embedded in, perhaps engulfed by, the admission of strange intimacy and complete interdependence between self and Other in this American wilderness.

3

Brushing History against the Grain

A Reading of *The Liberties* and *Pythagorean Silence*

According to traditional practice, the spoils [of history] are carried along in [a] procession. They are called cultural treasures, and a historical materialist views them with curious detachment. For without exception the cultural treasures have an origin which he cannot contemplate without horror. They owe their existence not only to the efforts of the great minds and talents who have created them, but also to the anonymous toil of their contemporaries. There is no document of civilization which is not at the same time a document of barbarism. And just as such a document is not free of barbarism, barbarism taints also the manner in which it is transmitted . . . A historical materialist therefore dissociates himself from it as far as possible. He regards it as his task to brush history against the grain.

—Walter Benjamin, "Theses on the Philosophy of History" (1940)[1]

In my poetry, time and again, questions of assigning *the cause* of history dictate the sound of what is thought . . . I write to break out into perfect primeval Consent. I wish I could tenderly lift from the dark side of history, voices that are anonymous, slighted—inarticulate.

—Susan Howe, *The Europe of Trusts* (1990)

In the spring of 1940, in the space of three months, the armies of Nazi Germany invaded and occupied Norway, Denmark, Holland, Belgium, Luxembourg, and France. The German-Jewish philosopher Walter Benjamin, then a refugee in Paris, was completing in this period what was to be his final work—"Theses on the Philosophy of History"—an essay on the misperceptions and deceptions of traditional historicism and the illuminations and (partial) human redemption possible through a historical materialist approach to the past and the present. The historical materialist, argues Benjamin, means to provide a past "citable in all its moments," without distinction between minor or major events, wresting from the "oppressors" their monopoly on the telling of the tale (Benjamin 1968: 254). The essay itself wanders around its theme(s), approaching it from different and seemingly random avenues like the figure of the aimless city stroller, the *flaneur* to whom Benjamin is so often compared. Indeed, "[t]he title of Benjamin's last work," argues Rolf Tiedemann, "promises a discussion of the *concept* of history." However, Tiedemann continues, "[l]ittle could be more characteristic of the author and less typical of the time . . . than the fact that there is no discursive expli-cation at the center of the text but an *image* instead. History itself seems to do away with philosophy's old conceptual games, and transform concepts into images which spoil the promises offered by logic: identity and the ab-sence of contradiction" (1989: 176). Not only is there no "discursive explica-tion" at the center of Benjamin's essay, but there seems to be no identifiable center to the text at all, as the essay is composed of twenty separate sections, each its own entity, proffering diverse images, quoting from different sources, and approaching the theme of history from changing vantage points. This is not to imply that Benjamin does not have a coherent and comprehensive idea as to how history must now be read, recorded, and transmitted, or that this idea is not, finally, conveyed through the "piling up" of the range of images, voices, and commentaries of the complete work. However, the style of this essay—juxtaposing separate units with seemingly disparate approaches to the theme (or themes) at hand—insists that just as history must be read as the jagged discontinuum it has always been, so must the individual's intel-lectual and artistic activities emanate from and reflect that discontinuum.

In this chapter I intend to offer an analysis of two of Howe's most significant European works: *The Liberties* (1980) and *Pythagorean Silence* (1982).[2] Why then open this analysis with the ideas and words of Walter Ben-jamin? The reasons are multiple and extend from questions of content, style, and particular motifs utilized by both Benjamin and Howe, to the two writ-ers' individual positionings in time and place—which produce, I believe, analo-gous "historical consciousness" (*Europe of Trusts* 13). The passionate interest in history, the insistence that the past must be read and written differently—must be "brush[ed] against the grain"—the understanding of one's world through its figurative and literal topography, and the refusal to conform to genre limits and genre norms are a few of the traits shared by Benjamin and Howe. In an interview with Lynn Keller, Howe maintains that some of Benjamin's essays should actually be called poems, naming also his "interest in very short essays, his interest in the fragment, the material object, and the entrance of the messianic into the material object" as significant to her own work (1995: 29). As a European forefather, one who is preoccupied with history and is also profoundly affected by World War II[3]—as Howe herself was—Benjamin serves as a useful entry point into the historical and literary rewritings of *The Liberties* and the historically contextualized self-explorations of *Pythagorean Silence*. These works' European identity, in contrast to the avid Americanness of *The Secret History of the Dividing Line, Articulation of Sound Forms in Time,* and *Thorow,* is foregrounded by Howe's return to first and primal places, as represented by her mother's Ireland, the early myths and fairy tales of her own disrupted childhood, and the enduring absence of a father pulled away by history.

The Liberties (1980)

If one asks, writes Benjamin in the seventh section of "Theses on the Philosophy of History," "whom the adherents of historicism actually empathize . . . [t]he answer is inevitable: with the victor. And all the rulers are the heirs of those who conquered before them" (256).[4] He continues: "Only that historian will have the gift of fanning the spark of hope in the past who is firmly convinced that *even the dead* will not be safe from the enemy if [the victor] wins" (255). Developing ideas first articulated by Marx and Engels in *The German Ideology,* Benjamin sees the victor as the dominant class whose interests are consistently served and upheld by society's economic structure. Because economic structure is the foundation of society, and because it is structured to secure the needs of the ruling class, the present and future are held hostage to the past as victor begets victor and change seems impossible. Utilizing a formulation strikingly similar to Benjamin's, Howe writes in her prose introduction to *The Europe of Trusts* that "[h]istory is the record of winners. Documents were written by the Masters" (11). For Howe, too, the question is who is forgotten in historical documentation; however, Howe's focus is more often—though not exclusively—on issues of gender rather than class. "Masters" signals here first the privileges of maleness and only then the privileges of a higher economic status. In *The Liberties,* Howe returns to tales of Jonathan Swift and Stella, tales she first heard in childhood from her Irish mother and which were for her "like another Grimm's fairy tale" (Foster 1994: 56),[5] to "lift from the dark side of history" (14) the figure of Stella which, she believes, has hitherto remained hidden. Her poetic project seems propelled by the belief that *especially the dead*—in this case Stella—are not "safe from the enemy," who can erase complete lives in their literary and historical presentations of the past. In the process of uncovering Stella, Howe reconsiders, recovers, and even creates other female figures ranging from Lear's Cordelia,

The Liberties—an outline

(Introduction)
- **"FRAGMENTS OF A LIQUIDATION"**: pp. 149–156

I. **"TRAVELS"**
   (i)
   - "her diary soared . . . " (one-page introduction to *"Book of Stella"*):
     p. 158
   - **"THEIR // Book of Stella"** : pp. 159–169

   (ii)
   - (nine-line quotation from *King Lear*—introduction to *"Book of Cordelia"*): p. 170
   - **"WHITE FOOLSCAP // Book of Cordelia"** : pp. 171–180

II.
   - **"God's Spies"** (a play): pp. 183–199

III.
   - word (stone)column beginning with "White Marble": p. 203
   - word-grids with "I," "S" or "C" heading: pp. 204–208
   - word-puzzle(s): p. 209
   - poetry more visually normative: pp. 210–213
   - **"HEAR"** (a play fragment): pp. 214–217

Fig. 3.1. An outline of *The Liberties*. (The parenthetical asides are my interpretation of the section's formal role and the bold-faced words and numerals are the poem's own titles/ headings.)

a mythological female Icarus, Howe's own mother, and some version of her own Irish self.

Due to the formal complexity of this seventy-one-page poem, I feel that an outline of *The Liberties'* subsections might help in providing an overview of the text and a visible scaffolding for the analysis to follow (see fig. 3.1). Preceding an epigraph extracted from Swift's *Journal to Stella* (to be discussed at greater length later), *The Liberties* opens with an eight-page prose intro- duction entitled "FRAGMENTS OF A LIQUIDATION." The prose of this section is periodically interrupted by poetry fragments from Swift, Sheridan, and Yeats. Section I of the poem, also preceded by an epigraph from Swift's *Journal to Stella,* follows and is entitled "TRAVELS" (with the title placed above the Roman numeral marking the section). The twenty-three pages of poetry in this section are divided into two major subsections: "THEIR // *Book of Stella*" and "WHITE FOOLSCAP // *Book of Cordelia.*"[6] Each of these subsec- tions is preceded by a one-page introduction, the first a poem apparently about Stella ("her diary soared above her house," 158) and the second the opening exchange between Lear and Cordelia from *King Lear* (170). Section II of *The Liberties* is a seventeen-page play entitled *"God's Spies"* and features the characters of Stella, Cordelia, and the Ghost of Jonathan Swift. The clos- ing and untitled section of the poem, section III, is fifteen pages long and includes pages of "word-grids" attributed to Stella, Cordelia, or Howe, a page of word puzzles, more standard poetry, and a closing play fragment. The entire text is framed by the opening picture of an old Irish stamp and the closing picture of what appears to be a fragment of a map of Ireland.

From the very title of *The Liberties* the reader is alerted to the thematic centrality of *place* in the text to follow. The Liberties refers to the southwest- ern end of Dublin, Ireland—an old section of the city traditionally inhabited by the poor working class. In earlier times this low-lying area was periodi- cally flooded by the Poddle, a subterranean tributary of the Liffey, causing considerable damage to the neighborhood and spreading disease amongst the poverty-stricken population (Weston 1977: 453–54; Fabricant 1982: 25– 30). On the lowest ground of the Liberties stands St. Patrick's Cathedral, where Jonathan Swift was installed as dean in 1713 and where both he and Stella are buried. It was while visiting her Irish mother, who was lying sick in a hospital located in the Liberties, that Howe first began composing this text (Foster 1994: 56). Thus, from the very opening of this difficult poem, the multiple concerns and themes to be considered in the text—Stella and her strange relationship with Swift, other individuals (often women) situated in figurative (and literal) "low-lying" areas whose stories are lost to history,

Howe's return to an ancestral homeland and her "charting [of] her own Irishness" (Butterick 1987: 317)—all converge in the overdetermined title. Perhaps the meanings of the title, which resonate most loudly and which take on new meaning within the context of the poem, are the dictionary's most common denotations of the singular form of *liberties*—the condition of being free of restriction or control, and the right to act in a manner of one's own choosing. *The Liberties* means to release Stella from her imprisonment in Swift's arena and to reinstate to her, to Cordelia, and to Howe herself the liberties of owning, and knowing, one's own tale.

Esther Johnson, renamed Stella by Swift, was born in March 1680 in Richmond, Surrey, met Swift when she was eight and he was twenty-two, was tutored by him in her childhood, and for twenty-eight years—from the age of nineteen until her death at the age of forty-seven—followed Swift to and around Ireland, serving as his most faithful shadow, transcribing his poems, presiding over his dinner parties, supervising his household, and nursing him when he fell ill. Throughout their life together, Swift continued to instruct Stella on how best to utilize her mind, how to conduct herself in matters of the heart, even how to improve her penmanship—so that it should most resemble his. "No one," states John Fischer in his book on Swift's poetry, "could have been more Swift's own creature than Stella was" (1978: 123). Yet despite this intertwining of lives, Stella never had an official role in Swift's world, was never alone with him in a room, never received a letter from him addressed only to her,[7] and finally was to die alone, buried at midnight in St. Patrick's Cathedral without Swift present. He was, apparently, too ill to attend.[8] These biographic details and others are provided in spare, straightforward prose in the eight-page introduction to *The Liberties*. However, as indicated by the introduction's title—"Fragments of a Liquidation"—this "biography" is composed only of fragments that together serve to eradicate rather than portray the figure of Stella. Indeed, the choice of the word "liquidation," with its relationship both to the worlds of business and physical violence, positions Stella at the outset as a liability to be settled or as an "unwanted person" to be "eliminated."[9] The latter denotation—in common usage since the 1920s—cloaks brutality in the benign and neutral language of science or commerce, thereby distancing the reader from the bloody reality of the deed. As C. S. Lewis states in *Abolition of Man*, "[o]nce we killed bad men: now we liquidate unsocial elements" (1943: iii, 37). The euphemism involved in the word *liquidation* establishes a chain reaction whereby the victims of this violence are dehumanized by their classification as "elements." From the very opening of *The Liberties*, Howe is alerting us to the ways in which language manipulates our perception of the world, and to the fact that language, in the service of androcentric readings of this particular literature and history, have hidden Stella from sight, have "liquidated" her. Swift's portrayal of Stella has been consistently taken as gospel. Thus, in his introduction to Swift's *Journal to Stella,* Harold Williams asserts that "there is every reason to believe" that Stella was content with the part she played in Swift's life and with the unfolding circumstances of her own life, naming his assumptions a "judicious characterization" as they are "borne out by all that Swift himself tells us" (1948: xxx, xxxvi).

"Fragments of a Liquidation" is preceded by an epigraph-like quotation taken from the *Journal to Stella—*the collection of letters sent by Swift to Stella between the years of 1710 and 1713. During this period Swift resided in London as an emissary of the Church of Ireland while Stella remained behind at his residence in Dublin.[10] The letters are in the form of diary entries wherein Swift recorded the minutia of his daily life in London and conducted an ongoing dialogue with Stella and her companion Rebecca Dingley. The extract Howe quotes here, from a March 1712 letter, is not immediately decipherable to the reader unacquainted with the "little language" Swift used in his communications with Stella and Dingley. The journal extract reads as follows: *"so adieu deelest MD MD MD FW FW Me Me / Fais I don't conceal a bitt. As hope sav'd"* (Swift 1948: 529; italics and lineation added by Howe). Indeed the extract is in code and, as codes *are* meant to hide meaning, thus belies Swift's assertion in the second line that he does not "conceal a bitt." Within the context of the entire letter, Swift's claim that he is not concealing a thing is a reference to his frankness regarding his recent illness and the course of his recuperation.[11] Furthermore, the coded language of the letters is more or less consistent throughout his correspondence, making the substitutions— once known—straightforward and the decoding an easy task.[12] Nonetheless, Howe's strategy—like Walter Benjamin's—is to tear "fragments out of their context and arrange them afresh in such a way that they illustrate . . . their *raison d'etre* in a free-floating state" (Arendt 1968: 47). In this free-floating state, the words take on a new and, in this case, ironic meaning, as Howe foregrounds a central theme of the poem to follow: how effectively and completely history as relayed by society's "victors" conceals more than "a bitt"— indeed, conceals entire worlds. In addition, Howe focuses the reader's attention at the very outset on two central traits of the journal: firstly, this communication between Swift and Stella is not, in David Nokes's words, "a dialogue of equals" due to "the paraphernalia of Swift's 'little language'" (the abbreviations, the letter substitutions, the repetitions, the fatherly endearments, and the scolding tone he often adopts with Stella, the "baby talk" he seems so fond of), which all serve to infantilize her (1985: 118). Secondly, no response from Stella is available; Swift destroyed all her letters to him, thus assuring that their relationship would be viewed from his perspective only.

Just as Swift's voice preempts the attempt to focus on Stella, so does his voice repeatedly intervene in the eight pages that follow. Howe interrupts her prose with fragments of Swift's letters and poetry, which provide a range of his observations and thoughts—including how, at the age of forty, Stella's face is "crack't" and how much she eats (152), his concern lest Stella die in the deanery and embarrass him (153), and, after her death, his preoccupations with his own failing health (155–56). Not a page is unmarked by Swift's words, and by the end of "Fragments of a Liquidation" it is evident that the retrieval of Stella, or some piece of her, will demand of the poet radically unconventional literary measures. "To articulate the past," writes Benjamin, "means to seize hold of a memory as it flashes up at a moment of danger" (1968: 255). Through her literary return to Ireland, which is also a return to her Irish mother, through myth, fantasy, and first landscapes, Howe means "to seize hold" of shared memories that may provide a glimpse of Stella, memories that are at every moment in danger of being lost.

"Fragments of a Liquidation" closes with the Latin epitaph that Swift wrote for himself and with the English revisionary rendering of the original by his compatriot Yeats. The two epitaphs read as follows:

Here lies the body of Jonathan Swift, S.T.D.
    Dean of this Cathedral
   Where savage Indignation
Can no longer lacerate His Heart.
     Go, Traveler,
   And emulate, if you can,
    The heroic exertions
of this Champion of Liberty.
       —Swift (trans. Kenney 1974: 47)

Swift has sailed into his rest;
Savage indignation there
Cannot lacerate his breast.
Imitate him if you dare,
World-besotted traveller; he
Served human liberty.
       —Yeats

If we are to take this epitaph as his final sense of his worldly accomplishments, it seems that Swift wanted to be remembered, or believed he would be remembered, not for his literary output but for the role he had in championing the liberties of the Irish people in the face of British oppression.[13] However, Howe's choice of inserting these two texts—which formally and syntactically build toward the word *liberty*—is not to provide an insight into Swift's sense of self but to follow the word *liberty* where it may lead. "If you follow [a] word to a certain extent," Howe tells Foster in his interview with her, "you may never come back . . . the word becomes an infinite chain leading us underground" (1994: 66). Howe's manner of accepting the challenge to "Go, traveler / and emulate" Swift is by tracking the word *liberty* to Ireland, underground toward where Stella is literally and figuratively buried, toward where she was first concealed, controlled, and restrained by Swift, the "Champion of Liberty."

Before the start of section I—entitled "TRAVELS," as though emphasizing that this poet *is* a late-twentieth-century version of the "traveller" Swift just addressed—an additional epigraph-like quotation from the *Journal to Stella* is provided. However, the source of this quotation, in contrast to the first, is not credited—the effect being that for the reader who has not read Swift's letters in full the passage seems mythical rather than literal. The extract from a March 1711 letter reads as follows: *"As for Patrick's bird, he brought him for his tameness, and now he is grown the wildest I ever saw. His wings have been quilled thrice, and are now up again: he will be able to fly after us to Ireland, if he be willing—Yes, Mrs. Stella . . ."* (Swift 1948: 209; italics added by Howe). Patrick is, in fact, Swift's manservant who bought "a poor linnet . . . as tame as a dor-mouse. I believe," continues Swift in a letter from six months earlier, "he does not know he is a bird: where you put him, there he stands, and seems to have neither hope nor fear" (1948: 156). However, this tame little bird eventually grows wild, even though the manservant tries to control it by "keep[ing] it in a closet" (1948: 188). The narrative of this bird as encapsulated in the single passage Howe uses in her text takes on a metaphoric level: Patrick, patron saint of Ireland, seems to stand for the beleaguered island and its inhabitants—a place and people that have been subjected to centuries of invasion and occupation. As "one of the longest-colonized countries in the world," Ireland is "like a man in prison," writes Robert Smith—without "the years of freedom needed to grow and develop," the imprisoned one barely knows what he is or what he can do (1979: 2). I read Howe's use of this passage as hopeful: she has appropriated Swift's own words to speak of the *possibility* of freedom—for Stella, for Ireland, for other female figures who wander through her text (Cordelia first among them), and for herself. The tame bird who has grown wild and whose wings have been quilled three times will, despite all odds, fly free.

Section I of *The Liberties*—the beginning of the work's poetry—is divided into two subsections: "THEIR / *Book of Stella*" and "WHITE FOOLSCAP / *Book of Cordelia*," with a one-page introduction preceding each subsection (see fig. 3.1). The very first image encountered in this section is "her diary soared above her house" (158). The bird imagery of a page earlier, the desire and attempt to be liberated, and the liberating effect of historical and literary documentation converge in this single image. The diary which we do not know if Stella kept, the diary which would have given us her history—unmediated and uncontrolled by Swift's words—takes flight, soaring above her house, above the heads of nameless people. What seems to me most telling in this image is its two-sidedness: what may be read as a metaphor of liberation has a darker, more literal side—the pages of the diary (if it existed), when burnt (by Swift, perhaps), became ash and cinders, took to the sky, and were lost forever. *The Liberties* is a text wherein double meanings abound and uncertainty is formally and thematically intrinsic to our understanding of the work. Howe is never clear what she can retrieve of Stella, if anything; neither does she know where a return to Ireland will lead her. She is tracking footsteps "there in me / them in me" (160), negotiating the uncertain terrain between mythology and history, between "fictional direction" and a real "region" (169). "*O cinders of Eve,*" the speaker exclaims a few pages into the *Book of Stella* (166), "*what is my quest?*" She knows she is searching; however, the mother figure/guide is as insubstantial and as fragmented as cinders, and the object of her search is multiple, often unnamable, changing in the very process of the search.

"Patrick's bird" and the soaring diary are only the first of many winged images in *The Liberties*. Birds abound in the text, from wild geese (158, 184, 196, 197) and a falcon (184)[14] to wrens, robins (179), and a dove (193). The wild geese, mentioned most frequently, certainly refer also to the generations of young Irish men who, exiled from their homeland, fought in European battles and were known by all as the Wild Geese.[15] It is estimated that between 1691 and 1791 half a million Irishmen fought abroad and more than 50,000 died on European battlefields (Welch 1996: 598). At all times Howe is concerned with the violence permeating the history and landscapes of her heart and with the rampant displacement of the Irish. Hers is a "dispeopled kingdom" (160), emptied out by occupation forces and policies, by the dispossession of lands, by famine, poverty, pestilence, and by the resulting exile/emigration of the people.[16] Birds and beasts, those with "Hide. Shell. Wings. Fins. Scent. Claws. Horns" (194) seem to have a better chance than humans—particularly than women—of surviving the emotional, geographic, and historical landscapes of *The Liberties*.

In addition to actual birds, Howe's work repeatedly evokes mythological winged figures—a "small boy-bird" early in the text (163), a female spirit that "flew in feathers" (187), Lir's children who were turned into swans (172), and the six brothers and one sister of Grimm's fairy tale, also transformed into swans (197). *The Liberties* is a text of beating wings, of attempts to take flight beyond the constraints of known history, beyond the boundaries of traditional poetry. Indeed, in the first landscape represented in section one of the poem, natural borders are defied as "the sea rose and sheets clapped at sky": just as the water-birds so prominent in the text bridge two such separate realms as sea and sky, so do the sea and sky themselves in this storm image reach for each other and merge.

Swift's voice intervenes again in the parenthesized lines, "Say, *Stella*, feel you no Content / Reflecting on a life well spent?"—extracted from his poem "Stella's Birthday March 13, 1726." The patronizing tone of the lines is emphasized by Howe's only revision of the original, her placing of the name Stella in italics. The name "Stella" originates in the Latin *stella* (star), but Swift's Stella is entirely earthbound, and the italics seem to emphasize this, turning her name, the one he chose for her, into a type of taunt. Indeed, in the lines to follow, the reader's eye is drawn quickly down the page, down from the opening sky imagery to earth and below, from soaring voice to the silence of graves and coffins:

> Bedevikke bedl
> bedevilled by a printer's error
> the sight of a dead page filled her with terror
> garbled version
> page in her coffin. . . .
> Do these dots mean the speaker lapsed
> into silence?
>
> Often I hear Romans murmuring
> I think of them lying dead in their graves.
> (158)

The unidentifiable word *Bedevikke* may be a cross between *bedeviled* and *bedecked*, or an example of the type of printer's errors mentioned in the following line, while *bedl* is perhaps a reference to the archaic form of *beadle*, bedel. Stella the woman ("bedecked") is in the male role of scribe, or functions as the female equivalent of a university beadle. In either case, she is a minor character, one whose responsibilities are to keep order and facilitate the progress and accomplishments of others. *Bedevilled* together with the garbled *bedevikke* and *bedl* produces the stammer mentioned a few lines earlier ("wild geese in a stammered place") and introduces the sense of someone unsure of herself, unstable, perhaps—in a fashion—possessed. Lynn Keller suggests that Howe is speaking here of "the fears of the isolated woman writer," a fear of madness that induces, finally, "a lapsing into silence" (1997: 213). I believe that such a generalized reading, while valid, is secondary to the more specific concern with Stella. What remains of Stella but a "garbled version / page in her coffin"? What tale can possibly be told with so little known? Daunted by the difficulty of the task, the speaker lapses into silence. Nonetheless, with this lyric's final two lines, the speaker—who is firstly a listener—begins again, hearing as far back as "Romans murmuring," though they are long gone and buried.

"THEIR / *Book of Stella*"

The enigmatic heading of this section—"Their"—poses multiple questions due to its incompleteness. As a possessive form of the pronoun *they*, *their* first leads one to ask *who* are the two or more figures referred to? Does the *their* refer to Swift and Stella, or perhaps to Stella and Cordelia (who has yet to officially enter the text), or to Stella, Howe's mother, and Ireland as an extended chain of female figures in various states of exile and silence? Secondly, *their* leads one to ask: their *what*? Is the title referring to Swift and Stella's joint story, or perhaps to Stella and Ireland's common tale—their shared lifelong lack of certain liberties? It seems to me that the incompleteness of the heading speaks to Benjamin's concept of "the incompleteness of the past" (Tiedemann 1989: 183)—that the past is not over and done with but rather has "a claim" on the present, and "[t]hat claim cannot be settled cheaply" (Benjamin 1948: 254). The something that is missing cannot be ignored or easily replaced; the poet, like the historian, has to stand aware of the something missing and proceed from there.

   If *their* refers to Swift and Stella's joint history, the subtitle of this section—*Book of Stella*—seems a defiant rejection of such a traditional approach, a recognition that "joint histories" will, finally, serve the man and obscure the woman. Rather than being the object of Swift's tutoring attention and critical gaze, rather than being the listening ear for his letters or the silent subject of his birthday poems, here Stella will take an active role on center stage, here she will take possession of her own tale: this book is *hers*. However, from the first poem of this section, it is apparent that taking possession is no easy task, as access to the historical figure of Stella is all but blocked. Even in the use of the name Stella, Howe acknowledges that the only reason this early-eighteenth-century woman is at all known to the twentieth-century poet is because she was "inscribed in a male text" (Keller 1997: 197). The first page of the *Book of Stella* is a column of text describing in often disjointed words the architecture, the physical history, and the outside environment (stanza 2) of St. Patrick's Cathedral: "dilapidation at erected original / irish granite south was added" (159; see fig. 3.2). The rigidity of the perfectly aligned left and right margins of the text convey the absolute nature of certain boundaries: just as no word on this page can wander beyond the determined margins, so has the figure of Stella been severely bound by the historical literary narratives available until now.[17] More specifically, I believe that this column of words means to represent the "second column from the west entrance" of St. Patrick's cathedral under which the historical Stella was buried on a wintry midnight of 1728 (155). Like the historical Stella, the literary Stella of Howe's imagination is physically present—in some shape or form—beneath this word column, in the pages that follow.

In the lyric of the following page, the wandering speaker, "trackless near sea," is still bound by the borders of the preestablished margins, as though the weight of traditional history and poetry, the weight of the Cathedral's granite column, continue to bear critical influence and hold her back. There is some loosening in the rigidity of the form: line 4—"or whatsoever"—is indented, giving this column a slender and vulnerable middle, while line 7, the last on the page, stops short ("I halted") of reaching the right margin. The listening speaker hears footsteps, some trace that does not conform to normative retellings, something in the slight space that opens on the page (following "I heard footsteps") once conventional limits are avoided. What is heard is the "fearsad bell," the "evensong / the blue of sweet salvation" (161). Like the pealing of a bell—not the fearsome ringing of a cathedral bell but the "fearsad" sound of something more intimate and individual—the lines that follow swing across the page. In order to find Stella, the speaker— Howe—is returning to first places: an Irish landscape ("between the uplands / over the lowered cols / eden eadan"), a people who believe in miracles ("as many lives / as there are loaves / and fishes") and a maternal center that provides ultimate security:

THEIR

Book of Stella

dilapidation   at   erected   original
irish granite   south was added
effected   attempted   wintering
struck the bay's walls mathemati
cal   indicating   perfect choir
system   measuring from breach to
floor to roof the place tendered
ancient   famous   latin
external aisle or isle   eternal
ante pedes   the door opened em
braced   appeased
an ancient cliff or cleft   the
ende   recoiled   attempted

and quarreled in churchyard wall
surmising   that this drift
this treachery Lady East may use
the arms   and highbacked chairs
wattled dwelling on a thingmount
perpendicular structure walk and
purlieus   wall   perilous
rotten wood gives light   in dark
mouth of river   head of tide
poddle inlet pool   blue china sp
arkle of view If there be in the
land   Famine   wisdom is a fox
Liberties   unperceived

Fig. 3.2. The first page of *Book of Stella* (*The Europe of Trusts* 159).

and O
>her voice
>>a settled place
table spread   flesh and milk
>>in mystery
>in the room
>in the sunlight
about the dead
who come from west-the-sea
>raiment
>>shirt-clad and light-clad
>>>(161)

I read these lines as Howe's memory of her Irish maternal grandmother—Susan Manning—for whom Howe herself was named and to whom *The Liberties* is dedicated (147). In contrast to the "stammered place" Howe encounters at this journey's commencement (158)—the deathly silence of Stella, the doubtfulness of direction or success—Howe reaches here a female voice that is "a settled place," wide and abundant and nurturing. This voice tells her first wondrous tales, stories of " . . . the dead / who come from west-the-sea." Popular Irish belief held that "the dead inhabit a region situated to the southwest, where the sun sinks to rest . . . a wondrous realm where delights far surpass those of this world" (D'Arbois de Jubainville 1930: 15). Thus, immigration to America was equated with "earthly dissolution," resulting in the tradition of holding "American Wakes" for the emigrant on the eve of his departure from Ireland, wakes characterized by gaiety and grief both (Miller 1985: 557–559). However, Susan Howe the child, with her mother, Mary Manning, returns in 1938 *from* the west to visit her Irish family—"shirt-clad and light-clad," real and wondrous both as one's faraway family is. It seems that the grandmother integrates this change of directionality into her telling of the tale, and personal history and traditional mythology merge. One senses that Howe is recognizing at this moment that the road toward Stella may be through storytelling strategies first encountered as a child and through her own history and relationship with Ireland, its literature and its landscapes. Indeed, in the images of the pages that follow, Stella—as Howe imagines her—is a transformed, semi-mythical figure: first, "[s]he must be traced through many dark paths / as a boy" (162), then she is a "small boy-bird of the air" (163), and, finally, she is a woman in "a man's dress," with bleeding feet (164). Concealment through cross-dressing, liberation by taking flight, and the seemingly unavoidable suffering involved in all attempts to claim a place in the world ("her feet ble/d") are a few of the scenarios

Howe offers for what Stella's life might have been had she not stayed with Swift—all "guesswork through obliteration" (163).

The "small boy-bird" of page 163 returns us to the prominent motif mentioned earlier—bird imagery. I will quote this lyric in full as I believe the imagery here alludes to and rewrites a famous passage from an earlier Irish text:

```
           light flickers in the rigging
flags               charts           maps
to be read by guesswork through obliteration


           small boy-bird of the air


           moving or capable of moving
with great speed
rapidly running          flying              following
           flight of an arrow
known for the swiftness of her soul


and to swim with the dramatic uprise
           where a world of mountains begin
sudden              GUIDE          the plains
           alert
prompt in her youth and in her prime


her hair was blacker than a raven
and every feature of her face perfection


A PENDULUM SWUNG BETWEEN TWO COUNTRIES


the days are long now
                              a hard frost
see how fast ebbs out the night.
```

The boat imagery of the lyric's opening, in addition to the later references to Stella's youth, convey an image of the nineteen-year-old girl at sea, nearing the Irish coastline, about to begin an uncertain life with, or beside, a stern man fourteen years her senior—a man who, apparently, has promised her nothing. Swift's presence is declared in the two uppercase insertions— "GUIDE" and "A PENDULUM SWUNG BETWEEN TWO COUNTRIES"— "guide" being what Stella later calls Swift in her birthday poem to him (see p. 190) and the pendulum image an accurate description of Swift's lifelong back-and-forth movement between Ireland and England.[18] Swift of course is present in the text also through the reference to the "swiftness" of Stella's soul: Howe takes possession of his name and gifts it to Stella, as though countering Swift's own appropriation and erasure from history of Stella's birth name. The word *swift*, used mostly as an adverb, echoes through the text, particularly in *"God's Spies,"* the play of the middle section (pp. 176, 185, 188, 195, 197, 199, and 212), taking on new meanings in changing contexts.

The "small boy-bird of the air" also evokes Icarus and, through him and the Irish topography, the use of that myth made by Joyce in *A Portrait of the Artist as a Young Man*. The climax of that novella, Stephen Dedalus's moment of epiphany, occurs when he encounters a girl wading in the waters of the Irish coastline: "A girl stood before him in midstream, alone and still, gazing out to sea. She seemed like one whom magic had changed into the likeness of a strange and beautiful seabird. Her long slender bare legs were delicate as a crane's . . . Her bosom was as a bird's soft and slight, slight and soft as the breast of some darkplumaged dove . . . She was alone and still, gazing out to sea; and when she felt [Stephen's] presence and the worship of his eyes her eyes turned to him in quiet sufferance of his gaze, without shame and wantonness. Long, long she suffered his gaze" (171). Twice in this short passage the girl is described as "still," and indeed it is her inertness, as much as her birdlike beauty, that attracts Stephen. He can examine her as long as he wishes to and she will not fly off; he can depend on her to serve as the object of his gaze, subject of his art. The nameless girl is, at that moment and as Stephen sees her, Swift's Stella-like figure: silent, isolated, still, small, and, once her facilitating role is over, to be left behind. Though the girl is the one compared to a bird—seabird, elegant crane, and soft dove—it is Dedalus who flies: "his soul was in flight. His soul was soaring in an air beyond the world" (169). It is because of the girl, the *image* of her as it "had passed into his soul for ever," that he is infused with knowledge of his own godlike attributes and will now, as artist, "recreate life out of life!" (172). The *reality* of the girl is, of course, extraneous to Joyce's tale.

In contrast to Joyce's stationary girl-seabird, Howe's bird—in boy form but in fact a girl spirit, as conveyed through the female gendering through the remainder of the lyric—is in constant motion and is "known for the swiftness of her soul," as emphasized by five progressive, active verb forms in as many lines and three synonymous references to her speed. She is not the object of anyone's gaze, she is not the catalyst for another's self-enlightenment; she occupies the majority of the page on her own as subject and she is herself freedom and creation. Like Joyce's girl, Howe's girl is situated on the borderline between water and land; however, Joyce's girl is limited as to how far out she can wade and remains, finally, earthbound; Howe's girl is already airborne and hence traverses borders easily. Howe is steeped in the literary masters that preceded her, and a central strategy of her poetic project is to maintain an ongoing dialogue with those masters through the intertextuality of her works. In the search for the voice and image of Stella, Howe cannot help but wander through the literary and literal landscapes first claimed by four male Irish compatriots, perhaps the greatest Irish writers—Swift, Yeats, Joyce, and, later, Beckett.

To shift from the mythological to the biographical, as Howe is constantly doing, the "small boy-bird" may be read as an imagined memory of Stella in childhood, running wild, following no one or nothing but the "flight of an arrow," enjoying the freedom of movement she had and would later lose. Such a desire for and love of freedom might, in part, explain Stella's wholly unconventional decision to follow Swift to Ireland, which she might have conceived of as an escape from the confines of the life available to her in England. Thus, she flies/swims/journeys to "where a world of mountains begin"—only to discover there the authoritarian and limiting voice of the uppercased "GUIDE," Swift. "A PENDULUM SWUNG BETWEEN TWO COUNTRIES" refers, of course, not only to Swift but also to the uprooted Stella, to Howe's mother who lived a lifetime away from her homeland, and finally to Howe herself, whose Irish identity is deep and intrinsic to her sense of self (Keller 1997: 216). "One of the problems I have always had," Howe explains in her interview with Falon, "has been the pull between countries. A civil war in the soul" (1989: 37). And yet, the uppercase presentation of this line seems to me to represent a male voice—traditionally authoritarian and loud—calling attention to the specifically phallic nature of the image itself and linking it more directly with Swift than with the others. This line also serves as a visual border that may not be crossed—a representation, perhaps, of the limits Stella encounters in her Irish life. Thus, by the lyric's end, the action verbs in the progressive form ("moving," "running," "flying") are replaced by static ("are") or slow-moving ("ebbs out") verbs in the present simple, while the possibilities offered through incomplete syntax are closed off by restrictive, absolute statements—cold despite the summer days they describe: "the days are long now / a hard frost / see how fast ebbs out the night."

The remaining pages of the *Book of Stella* are formally and visually different from one another, with diverse page-space usage, shifts into italics and bolded uppercase letters, and the introduction of word fragmentation. The

attempts to reach Stella continue, with Howe admitting through the chang-
ing poetic tactics that every view of Stella's "drifting face" (168) is partial,
every rendering of her tale is as fleeting as a "memory written in meadows"
(167). At one point, Howe asserts boldly that "SHE DIED OF SHAME / This
is certain"—referring to the commonly held belief that Stella's health was
seriously damaged by her discovery of Swift's relationship with Vanessa and
by the scandal that followed the publication of Swift's letters and poem to
Vanessa. However, even this assumption is unverifiable, and Howe's certainty
and "hold" on the history are already slipping away in the lines that follow:
"This is mist— / I cannot hold—" (168). There is an encroaching sense of
madness in this tale and in the uncertainty and difficulty involved in its tell-
ing, a madness first Stella's and then that of other creating women.[19] It is the
madness of one driven to extremes to escape restraints, to name and claim
herself:

    she

    had a man's dress mad
    e

    though her feet ble
    d

    skimming the surf
    ace

    deep dead waves
    wher

    when I wende and wake

    how far I writ

    I
    can

    not
    see
           (164)

This imagined Stella, in man's dress, has run as far as she can, as far as the waterline, and there stops, is stopped. Similarly, the broken words, evoking not only the sense of a "bedeviled" mind, run into an invisible limit that stops them as they move toward the right margin and pulls a piece of them back to the left margin, back into alignment. I read the "skimming . . . surf / ace" and "deep dead waves" as a suicide fantasy/wish, as a recognition that there might be no other way out—a recognition that awakens Howe the poet from the dream-state of writing to the full horror of what she has written. The madness and the water-death here evoked seem to also allude to Virginia Woolf—a writer who, in Howe's words, could "make words sing!" (Falon 1989: 33), and who was of crucial importance in Howe's own evolution as a writer. As Howe recalls, when she was growing up, Woolf had already been "accepted into the male pantheon but [she] had to pay the price of otherness" (34). In this lyric, the very sparseness of the imagery evokes how Woolf was, again in Howe's words, "shut away . . . until she returned to her senses . . . shut up . . . forbidden to write," while the broken words and the waves evoke her madness and suicide by drowning.[20]

The inability to see mentioned at this lyric's end links Howe's figurative blindness to Stella's lifelong suffering from poor eyesight. As the *Book of Stella* draws to a close, it is this theme of sightlessness or dimsightedness that resounds. The language-cross on page 166,[21] evoking the four navigational directions as marked on a compass card, strives to attain a charted course— and fails. With mother to the east and horizon that draws Stella's squinting gaze to the west, the woman/child seems lost in the white space/emptiness in center page. Though she, with Howe, has "rowed as never woman rowed / through the whole history of her story" (168), the oar is broken and "[t]he real plot was invisible" (169). At this point, rather than abandon the project, Howe abandons only the attempt to document the historical Stella and *The Liberties* veers instead in "a fictional direction" (169). Though the plot *is* invisible, though eyesight is failing, Howe allies herself with the early-twentieth-century Swiss artist Paul Klee's insistence that "the fundamental point of artistic creation" is "not [to] reproduce the visible but [to] *make visible*" (Klee 1961: 76, 454—my italics).

"WHITE FOOLSCAP / *Book of Cordelia*"

In the final scene of *King Lear*, with Cordelia dead in his arms, Lear comes on stage howling with grief too great to bear. Though he sees and states clearly that his youngest daughter is "dead as earth," in his next words he negates his own perception by calling for a "looking-glass" to test if "her breath will mist or stain the stone / Why then she lives" (V.iii.263–265). In the final words Lear speaks before his own death, he *wills* Cordelia back to life by seeing what is not there—her lips moving: "Look on her," he proclaims, "Look, her lips, / Look there, look there" (V.iii.312–313). Characters and audience alike obey the four-time repeated command to "look" on still lips, to disbelieve their own eyes and entertain—for a moment—the possibility that those lips may yet move. With this fierce directing of our gaze, with Edgar's own echoing call three lines later to the dead Lear that he "[l]ook up, my lord," Shakespeare maintains a focus until the very end of the play on the fallibility and limits of human vision. The surface *look* of life is deceptive; the Cordelia of Lear's heart may live at play's end. Indeed, the artistic triumph of the play's closure rests in Shakespeare's ability to *make the invisible visible,* to show us how a heart too laden with sorrow does break, to show what this moment of break- ing *looks* like.

Howe's decision to shift her attention to Cordelia in her continuing quest after Stella seems a natural one. The possibility of a fictional character, or a "fictional direction," providing greater insight into the historical character than history's own misrepresentations has already been raised, and the mul- tiple concerns and motifs previously introduced—from various types of blind- ness, dispossession, and madness to the repeated use of water-bird imag- ery—are as central to the texture of the second book of this section—"WHITE FOOLSCAP / *Book of Cordelia*"—as they are to the first. In the final lyric of the *Book of Stella,* through her choice of imagery, Howe already signals several crucial links between Stella and Cordelia. The "veiled face / growing wings" image describes both women, one historical and one fictional, whose fea- tures are so little known. The attempt to paint an accurate portrait of Stella has already failed—or rather, Howe has dramatized the inevitable failure of such an attempt; as for Cordelia, she occupies the stage for the shortest time of any major character in *King Lear* and, as John Bayley states, "we know noth- ing about her" (1981: 59). Unfortunately, Bayley immediately undermines his own accurate and useful insight regarding Cordelia by adding that "there is nothing in her to be curious about," abandoning at the outset any investi- gation into the character's hidden depths and relegating Cordelia to a con- tinued state of enveilment. As Stephen-Paul Martin notes in his book *Open Form and the Feminine Imagination (The Politics of Reading in Twentieth Century Innovative Writing),* "[b]oth Stella and Cordelia have been deprived of full personhood by men . . . [and] exist in a kind of psychic limbo, a 'wilderness'" (Martin 1988: 169). Through this literary and historical "wilderness," a place of violence and hunting, Howe intends to search them out, to remove the veils from their faces, to restore to them "full personhood" and to facilitate the flight of freedom for these figures that are, in Howe's mind, already "growing wings."

The final line of the *Book of Stella* refers in uppercase letters to the "HALLUCINATION OF THE MIRROR"—a multidetermined and linking image. Firstly, I believe, together with Keller, that this image provides at section's end Howe's fervent and vociferous repudiation of "the illusion of realism that more mimetic art . . . leaves intact" (1997: 219). Any attempt to represent Stella through conventional poetry, through a dramatic monologue or a normative narrative, would add to the layers already obscuring her by their very presumption of knowing and by their preservation of the historical continuum which is the tale "of the oppressors" (Tiedemann 1989: 197). Stella's figure, face, and silence cannot be approached but through the most circuitous routes. Secondly, the "hallucination of the mirror" signals the motif of eyes failing and vision's lies, as already encountered in Stella's squint (166) and Howe's momentary inability to see (164), and which will surface again in Howe's description of Lear as a composite of himself and of Gloucester with "holes instead of eyes / blind(folded) / bare(footed)" (174). The mirror, of course, evokes also the aforementioned "looking-glass" called for at play's end and, with it, the grieving and self-deceiving Lear (hence, the hallucination) and the forever-silenced Cordelia.

Finally, the mirror of lyric's end and its illusions inevitably bring to mind Lacan's mirror stage, also translated into English as "the looking-glass phase" (Evans 1996: 114). At this early moment of identity formation, in the mirror image, the infant sees herself in the Other (the reflection) and sees herself *as* other. This tension will eventually give rise to a full identification with the mirror counterpart, which is, according to Lacan, what forms the ego (Lacan 1977). A general understanding of these primary narcissistic states and their evolution will be useful for a reading of Howe's later text *Pythagorean Silence;* here, my focus is only on the infant's perception of the adult/parent holding her in the mirror image. In the mirror stage, the infant lingers for a moment at the crucial juncture where the holding parent is still part of her, though already starting to be seen as separate. The separation will deepen, of course, accompanied by a sense of loss—an absence—that operates as a central component constituting identity. Earlier in this same lyric, Howe names Stella as "some sort of daughter," offering with this appellation a partial explanation of the role Swift must have played and the attraction he must have held for Stella, a fatherless woman fourteen years his junior.[22] The loss of or estrange-

ment from a father provides an additional link between Stella and Cordelia—
the daughter who expects her father to understand what she does not ar-
ticulate as though he were (still) part of her, the daughter whose father sev-
ers ties and abandons her. Fiction, history, and biography are intertwined as
Howe herself stands beside Stella and Cordelia to form a fatherless trio.
Howe's father left her family to fight in World War II and that early separa-
tion left scars on Howe's psyche. As she states in an early interview, "I had
been a frightfully homesick child. When my father went away for five years it
wounded me" (Falon 1989: 31). The "homesickness" Howe refers to is, at
this point, a longing not for a physical place but for an emotional one, a
place of safety and oneness with the parent, a paradise lost. Twenty-one pages
into her search after Stella—a search that takes her through the landscapes
of Ireland the motherland, her mother's land—Howe finds herself tracing
also the father. In the *Book of Cordelia,* against the backdrop of *King Lear,* a
play where the mother figure is all but completely obscured,[23] the father-
daughter relationship is foregrounded as a possible access route into lost
histories.

The nine-line opening and fateful exchange between King Lear and
Cordelia wherein the word *nothing* is repeated five times serves as the epi-
graph to the *Book of Cordelia* (170), establishing the difficulty of communica-
tion and the emptying out of meaning as focal concerns of the proceeding
text. Following this epigraph, the first page of the section presents language
that seems to have abandoned normative syntax altogether and images that
are fractured or encoded. This disjunction evokes the aforementioned diffi-
culty in speaking, with the "mouthed" words of the "heroine in ass-skin"
reduced to a "spittle," enacted on the page in the preponderance of *s* sounds
("ass-skin," "speak," "nonsense," "wainscotted," "sal salt sally / S," "nemesis,"
"scullion," and "salt" twice more repeated). Cordelia's choice of silence has
traditionally been interpreted as an assertive gesture wherein she acquires
greater dignity by rejecting her father's attempt to quantify love. I believe
that Cordelia's silence here is being presented as less of a choice and more of
the inevitable response from one who knows that she *has no language* that can
accurately represent her. The speaking "I," like Cordelia, feels herself to be
"maria wainscotted"—a person transformed into an objectified icon, a woman
paneled into the wall,[24] a speaking subject silenced by the structures of soci-
ety and language. The language of this first page seems to propose the only
possible alternative for Cordelia, Stella, and Howe, too: "a fundamental in-
version and undercutting" of conventional language usage to produce some-
thing from "the nothing" that normative language representations have left

them (Eagleton 1993: 85). Hence, the word rantings that follow:

cap o'rushes tatter-coat
common as sal salt sally
S (golden) no huge a tiny
bellowing augury

                    NEMESIS singing from cask
turnspit scullion the apples pick them   Transformation
wax forehead ash
shoe fits monkey-face oh hmm
It grows dark   The shoe fits   She stays a long something
Lent is where she lives   shalbe   shalbe
loving like salt (value of salt)

                                                        (171)

The White Foolscap of the book's title allies Cordelia at the outset with the Fool and Edgar/Poor Tom both, making her one of their disguised and seemingly deranged party on the cold and stormy heath.[25] The "cap o'rushes" and "tatter-coat" reinforce this unique image of the female fool who will speak wisdom in her wild speech and will see more than others do. This female fool doubles as the more familiar image of the witch, evoked through the highly inflammable "rushes" and the resulting image of the woman burned at stake, even as—or because—she is "bellowing augury." An amalgamation of fool, witch, common woman ("sally"), and common man ("sal"), this figure—this Cordelia—stands on the margins of the text and her tale has hitherto remained untold. The fairy-tale transformations—the "turnspit scullion" who will be princess once the "shoe fits"—are exposed as deception and the fairy tale ends not in the expected celebration and happy closure but in boredom ("oh hmm"), darkness, and lasting suffering and deprivation ("Lent is where she lives). The Christological images of hallowed long-suffering ("Lent" and "bleeding feet") and the iconography of "maria wainscotted" place the enduring and ever-faithful Cordelia within a long tradition of revered and silent/silenced women. Within this tradition, it is natural that Cordelia's most dramatic scene on stage is as a corpse—a silent, still, and beautiful body over which one may weep, to whom one may play out his own tragedy.

Indeed, in the pages to follow, the experiment of unsettling language to give voice to Cordelia proves a failure as Lear's own mental derangement dominates the text. Howe attempts to hold the focus and the link to Stella and Ireland by introducing an early source of the King Lear story—the Gaelic legend of Lir, the ocean god, whose three sons and one daughter were turned into swans by their jealous stepmother (Ellis 1987).[26] She even establishes a

connection between Lir's last child, Conn, and Cordelia through the follow-
ing sound map/image:

> Lir was an ocean God whose children turned into swans
> > heard the birds pass overhead
> > > Fianoula Oodh Fiachra Conn
> > > > circle of One
> > > > threshing the sun
> > > > [. . . .]
> corona
> Chromosphere
> Cordelia

(172)

"Conn," "One," and "sun" are linked as partial or full rhymes, while the circle
of swan siblings "threshing the sun" is the "corona"—a luminous ring around
a celestial body (*made visible* by the refraction of Howe's words). Moving ever
inward, toward the heart of the matter,[27] following the firm alliterative au-
ral-link of the hard c sound and the repeated internal r and o, "corona" leads
to the "chromosphere"—a layer closer to the sun—and "chromosphere" leads
to "Cordelia," the center around which this section is in orbit.[28] However,
Lear's voice intrudes immediately in the thrice repeated "no no no," lifted
from his famous final speech over Cordelia's body (V.iii.307), shifting thus
the course of the poem. The garbled and fractured words that follow, the
sudden shift into French (172), the childlike wild breath sounds, and the
strange word-compounds (173) all convey the madness of the man running
"unbonneted" in the storm. Lear the father has in his derangement regressed
back into childhood, "giggling in a whistling wind"; Cordelia the daughter
is forgotten. I believe that in this shift of textual focus Howe is foregrounding
the tremendous cultural weight and power of Lear's tale: Cordelia, like Stella,
is not easily brought to the fore. Cordelia, like Stella, dies quietly, offstage,
"reclasp[ing] her hands into obscurity" (175), and the very naming of that
moment as "heartrending" in a parenthetical aside conveys most forcefully
the incidental status of the character. Howe the poet retreats into momen-
tary silence, saying "I will go to my desk / I will sit quietly" (175), as though
defeated, as though to regather her forces.

"Can you not see / arme armes / give tongue / are you silent o my swift,"
asks Howe toward the end of the *Book of Cordelia* (176), addressing herself,
Stella, Cordelia, and reader, too, and admitting that her failure to give voice
to the silenced, her failure to expose the forgotten history, was a product of
her own narrow vision, her inability to see clearly enough the direct and rigid

connection between power structures and speech. The powerful, whether male or ruling class, *own* language and the tales it would tell through their authority and weapons ("arme armes"). Hence, the *Book of Cordelia* slips into the Book of Lear, with the weight of the Western canon proving this development all but unavoidable. However, even as Howe is attempting to read beyond the literary father, the literal father is constantly longed for, and the two figures inevitably merge. Indeed, within the context of a poem populated by daughters who find themselves fatherless at some crucial point in their lives, I also hear in the repeated reference to "armes" an evocation of a father's arms who would hold his child and through that secure embrace give to her the power of speech. This reading is supported, I believe, by the abundant use that Howe makes of legends and fairy tales—childhood stories that are among one's first exposure to language and the worlds it can create.

Howe foregrounds her concern with the relationship of the powerful to the powerless by repeatedly inserting hunt imagery into the *Book of Cordelia* in the innocent guise of the aforementioned childhood tales:

> Running rings
> of light
> we'll hunt
> the wren
> calling to a catch of thorn
> crying to announce a want
> [. . . .]
> Once again
> we'll hunt the wren
> says Richard to Robin
> we'll hunt the wren
> says everyone.
> (179)

The "running" game and the seeming innocence of "Richard" and "Robin's" play takes on an ominous tone through the repetition of the phrase "we'll hunt the wren," exposing the relentless nature of the hunt. The smallest and most vulnerable serve as society's natural prey, and the swift and violent chase serves as history's favorite theme. Howe's project is to halt the easy flow of lines down the page, to stop the hunt, to resist the lulling deception of the childhood ambiance, to challenge what Wilhelm Grimm named in his preface to the first edition of *Grimm's Fairy Tales* as "inherited patterns" (Grimm 1944: 833). In Benjamin's terms, Howe's project is to present "not only the flow of thoughts, but their arrest as well" (1968: 262), the individual and unmoving moment in place of "the ebbing actual" (178). Howe's project is to present woman, or women, "in the flight of time . . . framed" (178). Thus, a new fairy tale, a radical revision of the Rapunzel tale first introduced a page earlier, interrupts Richard's hunt at book's end and provides an escape route for the speaking "I":

> I can re
>
> trac
>
> my steps
>
> Iwho
>
> crawl
>
> between thwarts
>
> Do not come down the ladder
>
> ifor I
>
> haveaten
>
> it a
>
> way
>
> (179–180)

From the opening line, "I can re," the speaker boldly and defiantly announces herself, her re(turn), her presence, and her ability, claiming at the same time the right to speak differently: against the right margin, in fractured words, and with deviant orthography. The missing *e* on "trac" ("re / trac") leads one to read the word also as "track," linking this activity to her "crawl" and the "[d]o not come" through the repeated hard *c* sound and making the hunt associations of the word (that is, trackers) prominent. In addition, this missing *e* is paralleled by the missing *e* in "haveaten," as though the speaker has devoured—through hunger, rage, or necessity—not only the ladder, but pieces of the text, too. Of course, the arrangement of the words into a slender vertical line graphologically presents a type of ladder the reader descends as her eyes move down the page,[29] though the "other" addressed by the speaker may not. Finally, the haste of flight conveyed through words jammed together with spaces missing ("Iwho," "ifor I," "haveaten") stands in contrast to the deliberately slow pace of disclosure effected through the short lines, the abundant line breaks, and the wide space between lines. I believe that this slow pace of disclosure not only conveys the struggle involved in the escape and the arduous nature of all routes out, but it also is meant to claim and keep our attention—much as Lear's repeated command to "look" does at the end of that play. Unlike the closure of *King Lear* and in place of a female corpse, here we are asked to gaze on a woman framed in a moment of escape—she can retrace her steps, she does crawl between obstacles ("thwarts") put in her way,[30] though at the moment she is doing neither. The Rapunzel tale is inverted in that the Other—prince, traditional historicism, the Western literary canon—is the one in the tower, the one without the liberty to go. The ladder may represent the paths the speaker has already essayed—through the known figures of Swift and Lear, through literary and historical documents available—to reach Stella and Cordelia, paths that have not led to their destination. Now, by eating the ladder "a / way," the speaker provides for herself "a way"—an alternative route toward the lost histories.

"God's Spies"

The alternative route toward Stella and her lost history, the "way" Howe invokes at the end of *The Liberties'* lengthy and difficult first section, ultimately emerges from the meanderings of the text up to this point, through its various avenues and circuitous byways, its blind alleys and dead ends. "To understand something is to understand its topography, to know how to chart it. And to know how to get lost," writes Susan Sontag in her explication of Walter Benjamin's philosophy, adopting Benjamin's own geographic and navigational motifs to explain his thinking (Benjamin 1979: 13). Similarly, Howe—a poet of place—moves through her poetic topic as through an unknown territory, learning the features of the literary land, allowing herself to get lost in order to find and be found. Thus the attempt to lift lost female voices from the "dark side" of history leads Howe to consider Cordelia, which in turn leads to an extended intertextual relationship between *The Liberties* and the play *King Lear*. As a result of this relationship, the genre of drama provides a steady backdrop to the text, and one notes how through the *Book of Cordelia* the lexis and conventions of theater slowly gain in prominence. The phrase "pauses measures feet in syllables caesura" on page 173 links aspects of prosody with the blocking of movements across a stage, while the parenthetical asides on pages 174 and 175 double as stage directions. By page 176, Howe states explicitly that "we are left darkling / waiting in the wings again," punning on the "wing" allusion that has hitherto referred only

to birds. Now, the "wings" are also the unlit margins of the stage, the be-
hind-the-curtain place of the unseen and the silent, and the about-to-appear
actors. Utilizing this new denotation of the word and extending the use of
the dramatic format already introduced, Howe departs from poetic form and
presents in the second section of *The Liberties* a seventeen-page play entitled
"God's Spies," with Stella and Cordelia as its main characters.

The title of Howe's play is, of course, an allusion and a link to Lear, who
names himself and Cordelia "God's spies" in their captive state, embracing
imprisonment as an elevated, semidivine status in a world populated by
"gilded butterflies" and "poor rogues" (V.iii.8–19). In response to Lear's words
of elation, Cordelia—who wants to confront her treasonous sisters, wants to
take action—is eloquently silent, signaling her very different view of this sub-
jugation: she will not affirm Lear's idealization of captivity and passivity. In
The Liberties, Lear's phrase is appropriated to reflect what might have been
Cordelia's response to this new set of bars: she and Stella will not sit pas-
sively by, they will be forerunners, the first to search out the lay of the land
before claiming it. A biblical text alluded to in the phrase "God's spies"—
possibly in Shakespeare and certainly in its usage by Howe—is the story of
God commanding Moses to dispatch spies to bring back reports of the land
of Canaan; obeying God, "Moses sent [men] to spy out the land" (Num. 13:17).
As "spies" in their own wilderness, Cordelia carries a knapsack and the bibli-
cal prop of a shepherd's crook, while Stella holds a large book to which she
will refer throughout the play, *"filled with fold-out maps, alphabets, and pictures"*
(183). As female spies, Stella and Cordelia's task is all the more dangerous,
demands of them subterfuge, stealth, and disguise (hence their being dressed
as boys), but they are armed in the knowledge that the mission is sacred and
their quest is for a promised land. I read in Howe's choice of title also a refer-
ence to the first biblical tale, the creation story, through the allusion to fore-
runners, god's first messengers on earth. Stella and Cordelia as a new Adam
and Eve must not only discover the land, but must name it too—create lan-
guage that can describe their world (hence the alphabets in Stella's book).
Through naming their world, they are always attempting to name themselves,
which is to create themselves and each other: "Who can tell me who I am?"
asks Stella at play's end. "Swift, you are swift," answers Cordelia (199). This
interchange occurs on the seventh and final day of the drama, paralleling
the seven-day creation story.[31]

In the drama she is writing, Howe not only evokes the master tale of first
creation but returns to her own primary sites of self-definition. The shift to

drama must be read, in part, as a homage to Howe's mother, Mary Manning, who was a well-known actress and playwright in Ireland;[32] emerging from the father-laden *Book of Cordelia, "God's Spies"* is a return to the mother and the motherland. Long before vision develops, the infant knows her mother through the *sound* of her, and for Howe, the theater—place of the spoken word in general and her mother's spoken word specifically—represents such intimate first encounters, first havens. Not surprisingly, Howe names sound as "*the* element in poetry" (Keller 1995: 19) and "the core" of meaning (Falon 1989: 31), perhaps because sounds are "the echoes of a place of a first love" (Beckett 1989: 21). Furthermore, Howe locates her own original sense of her artistic self in the world of theater, stating that when she was young she was certain that acting was "what I would do with my life" (Falon 1989: 37). Thus, through the genre choice of drama in *"God's Spies"* in the continuing search for Stella, which is always also a search for self, Howe journeys back to a maternal arena and an artistic origin.

The full cast of characters in Howe's play is Stella, Cordelia, and the Ghost of Jonathan Swift. Stella and Cordelia hold the main parts, with the Ghost of Jonathan Swift playing a supporting role only. More crucially, the figure of Swift is but a ghost, while the women are fully bodied and present. Indeed, the shift to drama, I believe, is effected primarily to *flesh out* Stella and Cordelia, to *embody* them in a world that has consistently deprived them of voice, shape, and form, and through this newly acquired physicality facilitate access to the historical figure and her fictional partner. Even if this play is not intended for actual production—as may be indicated by such surreal stage directions as "*[t]he* GHOST . . . *walks through Stella"* (192, 193)—the conventions of drama are such that the reader reads the words on the page, all the while visualizing the three-dimensional representations of the play's landscapes and their inhabitation by flesh and blood people (the actors/characters) speaking their parts. As Pound, quoted by Paul Lawley, states: "The medium of drama is not words but persons moving about on stage using words" (1986: 325). This "moving about on stage," as minimal as it is in *"God's Spies,"* provides a certain liberty to Stella and Cordelia hitherto denied; hence, the move to drama provides the figures not only with voice and body but with some freedom—at least the freedom to explore themselves the ways they are not free.

The choice to present a dramatization of Stella's story is also an extension of the long tradition of Irish playwrights who retold the tale of Swift and Stella, in part, to unravel the mystery of that relationship (see note 17). Howe sees herself as a daughter of this literary lineage, even as she is subverting and challenging its assumptions and conventions. As previously noted, these dramatic retellings neglected to give Stella voice, consistently telling the tale from a male perspective. The closest Stella gets to speaking is in Yeats's famous play *The Words upon the Window Pane,* produced in the Abbey Theater in 1930.[33] Set in a lodging house that "in the early part of the eighteenth century belonged to friends of Jonathan Swift, or rather of Stella," a group gathers to hold a seance. In this seance and through the medium, Swift and Vanessa appear, though unsummoned, and they conduct a vocal and angry argument regarding the terms of their relationship. Upon Vanessa's unsignaled departure, Stella stands in place of her beside Swift; however, unlike Vanessa, she remains silent throughout the scene and we know of her presence only because Swift addresses her. Stella is, quite literally, the ghost of a ghost. Expressing his perception of her life situation, justifying all he has denied her, answering himself the questions he poses to her, and insisting on her continued silence, the character Swift speaks the following speech: "Have I wronged you beloved Stella? Are you unhappy? You have no children, you have no lover, you have no husband. A cross and ageing man for a friend—nothing but that. But no, do not answer—you have answered already in that poem you wrote for my last birthday [. . .] O how touching those words which describe your love . . . Yes, you will close my eyes, Stella. O, you will live long after me, dear Stella, for you are still a young woman, but you will close my eyes" (Yeats 1953: 614–615). His concern for her is fleeting; what preoccupies him most is his fear of dying alone, which indeed he does. As for Stella, her voice is represented only through the Ghost of Swift and another character, John Corbet (a doctoral candidate at Cambridge who is writing his dissertation on Swift and Stella), speaking these lines from the poem Stella wrote on the occasion of Swift's fifty-fourth birthday:

> You taught me how I might youth prolong
> By knowing what is right and wrong,
> How from my heart to bring supplies
> Of lustre to my fading eyes.

"Somebody cut some lines from [this] poem . . . upon the window-pane," states Corbet, "tradition says Stella herself" (600). No one on stage thinks to ask why Stella etched in glass the same words she wrote on the page, and the characters quickly shift their focus to a consideration of Swift and his "tragic life." However, the impact of this image of the isolated woman working her words into glass, shaving away slivers to shape sharp letters, remains. Like a madwoman shut away or a prisoner locked in a cell without paper or pen at her disposal, Stella utilizes her environment to transmit a message to the outside world, to convey proof of her existence to those who will come after her. And yet, the only words available to Stella are the ones taught her by Swift; hence, one must read the message despite, or through, the words themselves (as through glass). This image shifts one's gaze from Swift to Stella and empties the words of their original meaning; no longer a celebration of Swift, the lines stand instead as Stella's stark and limited declaration of survival.

Within the context of the extensive intertextuality of *The Liberties* with masterpieces of the Western canon in general and Irish works specifically, it seems likely that Howe means to invoke Yeats's play and have us reconsider its title and central image more closely. The connection to Yeats's play is made even more pronounced by Howe's insertion into her play of the entire text of the poem referred to in *The Words upon the Window-Pane*, Stella's "To Dr. Swift on His Birthday, Nov. 30, 1721" (190–191). The poem, recited in *"God's Spies"* by Stella in the posture of a schoolgirl speaking her lines (*"facing the audience, arms straight at her sides,"* 189), acts as the focal point of the play due to its placement exactly midway through the text, its length, which stands in contrast to the brevity of all the speeches until this point, and the unexpected violence immediately succeeding it. While Stella speaks her part, the Ghost of Jonathan Swift mouths the words, as though his voice is in her mouth and the words are actually his,[34] indicating how completely our encounter with her has been "mediated through male perspectives and expectations" (Keller 1997: 228). What is conveyed through this recitation is the impossibility of hearing the historical Stella; she is for all intents and purposes dead to us. Indeed, the recitation is succeeded by the following stage direction:

> *Pause six seconds.* STELLA *pulls a pistol out of her shirt. Points it at her left breast and shoots. Red blood spurts from the wound, the only color on the stage, it spatters the white ground.*
>
> GHOST *(On its knees):*
>   *Sobbing.*

I read Stella's suicide as an act of violent defiance directed at Swift, her "tutor," "guide," the one who "taught" her to write verses such as the one she has just spoken, he who gave "lectures" in abundance and, in the process, robbed her of all liberty (190–191). In shooting herself immediately following the recitation of the poem, Stella dramatizes her rejection of the words she has just spoken and kills Swift's creation; the pain of abandonment and betrayal is his and he is left bereft and sobbing. Stella, meanwhile, *"puts the pistol back in her shirt, and returns to her seat on the pulpit steps,"* indicating in this resurrection that a different Stella will now occupy the stage, one who henceforth will not necessarily "keep strictly to the text" (193), one who is not defined solely by her relationship with a man.

Of course, the defining relationship of *"God's Spies"* is the one between Stella and Cordelia, a relationship of mutual familiarity (as indicated by their tendency throughout the drama to finish each other's lines), of childhood intimacy (as enacted through the hopscotch/blind man's bluff game played, 185–186), of momentary merging into a single speaking subject (187–188), of separate styles and needs (as conveyed through the very different forms and contents of their "soliloquies," 194–195) and, finally, of care-giving and dependence. By placing two women and their relationship at its focus, *"God's Spies"* locates itself at the outset in an alternative landscape, a literary landscape little explored and barely known. In contrast, the tradition of literature that focuses on a pair of men is a long and familiar one. As Hugh Kenner describes, *"Robinson Crusoe,* a romance about one man rebuilding the world, becomes a different kind of book when his island proves to contain a second man, black Friday. A *pair* of men has an irreducibly primitive appeal. They can talk to one another, and it soon becomes clear how little either one is capable of saying" (1973: 23). How are we to describe the "appeal" or meaning of a pair of women trying to talk to each other, asks *"God's Spies,"* if we haven't any "primitive" archetype of this image to refer to? Inevitably, *"God's Spies"* struggles with this question by evoking and interacting with one of the best-known texts about a pair of men, a drama that is commonly recognized as "the presiding spirit" in contemporary theater (Graver 1989: 93)— Beckett's *Waiting for Godot.*[35] Thus, Beckett joins the list of other Irish expatriate writers with whom Howe is in dialogue throughout *The Liberties.* It is important to note that the Irish literature and Irish figures that claim such presence in *The Liberties* were the literary world Howe was first exposed to in childhood, and, consequently, they acquired for her the "mythic" nature of primary places (Foster 1994: 56). Hence, her evocation of *Waiting for Godot* and other texts previously mentioned is marked by intimacy and reverence in conjunction with rebellion and subversion.

The link between *"God's Spies"* and *Waiting for Godot* is established not only through the two women on stage paralleling Beckett's two men. Indeed, the central bond between the two texts is through their similar language usage. Both texts revolve around brief exchanges of stark statements and extensive repetition of specific words and word combinations:

> CORDELIA: The woods are on fire.
> STELLA: Let's rest.
> CORDELIA: Let's wade.
> STELLA: How deep?
> CORDELIA *(Marks a point with her crook):* This deep.
> STELLA: I am weary.
> CORDELIA: I am lame.
> STELLA: I have forgotten.
> CORDELIA: I must go back.
> STELLA: Don't leave me.
> CORDELIA: I won't.
>
> (184)

> ESTRAGON: Let's go.
> VLADIMIR: We can't.
> ESTRAGON: Why not?
> VLADIMIR: We're waiting for Godot.
> ESTRAGON: Ah! *(VLADIMIR walks up and down.)* Can you not stay still?
> VLADIMIR: I'm cold.
> ESTRAGON: We came too soon.
> VLADIMIR: It's always at nightfall.
> ESTRAGON: But night doesn't fall.
> VLADIMIR: It'll fall all of a sudden, like yesterday.
> ESTRAGON: Then it'll be night.
> VLADIMIR: And we can go.
>
> (Beckett 1954: 45–46)

The normative unit of thought and communication in both plays is the simple sentence stripped down to its barest components, much as the landscapes are characterized as nothing more than "a wilderness" *("God's Spies")* or "a country road. A tree" *(Waiting for Godot).* The characters inhabit worlds that have been scarred and stripped by violence, and they speak a language that knows it cannot convey the depths of destruction and hence says little. In Blanchot's terms, Stella, Cordelia, Estragon, and Vladimir "speak suggesting that something not being said is speaking: the loss of what [they] were to say" (1986: 21). "They murder each other," whispers Stella toward the end of

"God's Spies," to which Cordelia responds, "Of course. Always. Nakedness, murder, a great outcry" (198). The language, without the narrative markers of connectives or buffering qualifiers, sounds codelike, a language of spies wherein every word stands for itself and much more. The bareness of the language also evokes the danger of speech, as though both couples are wary of occupying too much space on the stage or page, aware that they are in potentially hostile territory. Thus, the full report, the history of an entire society, is encapsulated in isolated and few words and in the abundant silence surrounding those words.[36]

Additional language traits shared by the two plays are the repetition of the imperative "let's," the recurrent naming of one's individual's state of being ("I am weary," "I am cold"), and the reappearance of the simple question-answer format ("How deep?" "This deep"). These three traits enact the ongoing vacillation of the characters between clinging to their coupled state and attempting to define themselves as separate and individual. The question-answer format in particular seems indicative of a desire to communicate and to connect with the other—a desire that is constantly being frustrated. In general, the repetition structuring both plays establishes what Adam Piette names "memory-traces in a forgetful textual voice" (1996: 215). The fear of forgetting and being forgotten, the fear of being lost in forgetfulness, permeates both plays; as in a fairy tale, language serves as a crumb path that may lead back home. These word "memory-traces" not only signal key motifs but, through their rhythm and music, create a certain unity out of disparate parts and seeming incoherence. The "memory-traces" of repetition also serve to ritualize human communication, which has the paradoxical effect of concomitantly depersonalizing and elevating the exchanges.

Waiting for Godot and *"God's Spies"* are also connected through the linking "God" reference in both their titles and, possibly, through subtly shared characters.[37] Who and what "Godot" is of course remains a subject of ongoing debate, and Beckett's play leaves the question open. Nonetheless, the name of God is embedded in the name Godot, Godot's godlike omnipotence and saving grace are alluded to throughout the play, and the tentative description of Godot as a man with a white beard evokes a stereotypical portrayal of God. It is a minor character, a goat-tending boy who has a sheep-tending brother, who twice informs Estragon and Vladimir that Godot, once again, will not appear tonight. I believe that Stella and Cordelia—both dressed as boys,[38] one holding a shepherd's crook, acting as God's spies or messengers— may be read as that same boy and his brother from *Waiting for Godot.* In a technique made famous by Stoppard in his play *Rosencrantz and Guildenstern*

Are Dead (1967), Howe takes marginal characters and makes them major, with the double result of shifting the reader/audience's entire perspective on the action of the original play and also producing a new world/text in the process. The novelty in Howe's usage of this technique, of course, is the focus on gender. If we are meant to read Stella and Cordelia as the messenger boys from Beckett's play, then *Waiting for Godot*—a text inhabited solely by men, a world in which the female has no place at all—has in fact been infiltrated by women in disguise. They come like the biblical spies, to search out the promised land, only to find a place wasted by despair and violence. Furthermore, these women/boys have the crucial role of relaying long-awaited information, and they, ironically, are privy to Godot's realm as the men are not. Once one's perspective shifts, it becomes clear that their designation as minor players is misleading—much as Stella and Cordelia's relegation to the wings in their original contexts distorts and conceals entire worlds. The shift of perspective effected in *"God's Spies"* marks the sites of concealment, as an archeological tel is marked; the textual exchanges and inner explorations of the characters that constitute the play are pieces of the long, arduous, and uncertain unearthing process.

The archeological trope suits this drama well, for as in any archeological project what one may discover of Stella and Cordelia is unknown, and the work may in fact succeed in unearthing nothing. Certainly *"God's Spies,"* like *Waiting for Godot* and *King Lear* before it, is a text in which the word *nothing* resounds. However, the "nothing" which Stella and Cordelia evoke is an absence that doubles as a presence,[39] a nothing that is something. "[Y]ou have seen / *nothing*!" exclaims Cordelia at the close of the penultimate day: speaking both to herself (she is alone on stage at this point) and to the audience/ reader, she is naming that which has been raised to the surface and witnessed, the *nothing* which is available of these "storied" and "mute" women.[40] "Nothing is our own!" she states toward the end of the play, designating the "nothing" as something that categorically *is* and defiantly taking possession of the absence that has defined her and Stella. The ability to articulate this condition constitutes a liberation from the bonds of silence and from conventional wisdom that is, I believe, the characters' triumph. Indeed, immediately following the aforementioned exclamation, Cordelia tears off the blindfold Stella tied around her eyes on the fourth day of the play (making Cordelia like her father and Gloucester and foregrounding again the theme of blindness, which has been prominent throughout *The Liberties*), blinks in the light and, *"as if searching her memory,"* speaks the following monologue:

Come to the surface again true love, True.
You with the cradlegrave cords. Nothing can
estrange the tattling deep of summer hummed
in honeyed trees hmmm—a hush of homing
homeward rush of exile—flight—Liberty. (*Radiant.*)

Free from tangle our clipper flies. Billows—check the
chart! A flagstaff but no flag stands at the railings.
Not for nothing our going forth—lucky, into great
blue—bedecked with crowflowers and long purples—
Nameless abashing flame.

(197–198)

For a moment, and a moment only, something has surfaced: a vision of free-
dom in the birds flying overhead, an understanding that from the place of
nothing—once identified as such—*something* may grow. The passage is itself
generative, with words freely following where their sounds lead and, in the
process, creating an image of intense regeneration and sweeping liberty. The
deep and comforting *m* sound of the bees in "su*mm*er hu*mm*ed" becomes
the birds in a "hush of ho*m*ing" (linked also through the breathy alliteration
of hummed/honeyed/hush/homing and the long and steady assonance of
hon*ey*d/tr*ee*s/hom*i*ng) which, in turn, through rhyme (hush/rush) and allit-
eration (hush/homing/homeward), is transformed into the "homeward rush
of exile—flight—Liberty." The sounds of an open landscape, virgin territory—
perhaps as encountered upon first landings from sea—create the poetic lan-
guage Cordelia speaks and provide the epiphany that in some place as yet
unwritten—outside the established canon and recorded history—Stella,
Cordelia, and Howe too will find and identify selves. The flagstaff is without
flag, and the "abashing flame" is nameless, signaling this place of self-
identification and liberation as existing outside national boundaries, beyond
linguistic conventions and traditional gender roles. Thus the female imag-
ery implicit in the swell of "billows" is matched, even dominated, by the abun-
dant presence of the phallic in the "flagstaff," the lance-shaped leaves of the
"crow[foot]flower," the long spikes of the flame-like "long purples." I read
the phallic images as evoking also the pen and its powers—traditionally re-
served for men. Cordelia has in this monologue claimed the artistic preroga-
tive as her own and, in the process, has glimpsed liberty.

However, the insight of the moment and the elation it brings are Cordelia's
alone. Stella remains sad and confused to the play's end, terrified and asking

question after question, the final one—"Did we pass by?"—left unanswered (199). I believe that Howe is emphasizing at this point the distinction one must finally redraw between the historical figure and the fictional one: Stella/ Hester Johnson is indeed lost to us, she has indeed "passed by" and is irretrievable. Though Cordelia may take Stella's hand and speak of the "peace" created through their fictional bond, Stella is ultimately left behind in the gunshot sound and ensuing silence of the play's end. The desire to "brush history against the grain" that has propelled this poem is continually frustrated by the omnipotence of traditional cultural representations and modes of dissemination. "Let those who are gone rest—let them rest," says Cordelia, as though surrendering to the given state of oblivion. And yet Stella's desperate, unfinished, and self-obliterating proposal that perhaps "Truth is what always remains" sparks Cordelia to reinitiate the struggle for release from history's dark depths by remembering and vividly describing those who "lie— there—on the bottom— / tangle and seaweed—grinding on their teeth" (198), those who now

> . . . bite themselves fast in the tangle—
> grinding their teeth—listening in dread—the seamark
> (*Pause*): blotted out—shoved away.
>
>   (199)

The gruesome image of people tied at sea's depths trying to bite their way to freedom through seaweed fetters echoes the ending of the *Book of Cordelia*, where the speaker has eaten away the ladder cords to flee the tower of the Western literary tradition. The primal violence of the image also stands in contrast to the play's soft and gentle final words as spoken by Cordelia. "I knew a child," she says, longingly evoking Stella the eight-year-old, yet untouched and unclaimed by Swift, as though futilely willing a return to that innocent moment. The play's final words also evoke Howe the child, the one who listened to her mother's tales of Stella and Swift as to "another Grimm's fairy tale. But real" (Foster 1994: 56)—the one who continues to return to such primary places despite convention's continual thwarting, listening all the while for what and who have been silenced.

(Untitled)

In the final, untitled section of *The Liberties*, Howe takes greater poetic liberties than before: the fifteen-page section includes lyrics, a drama-fragment,

Formation of a Separatist, I

Crops

his horse

drew his sword

swung his sword

said he would slash and slay

1.	only	air	most	lovely	meath
longside	lean	soaring	in	mist	
matin	sky	breathing	longside	weir	
herd	naming	yew	colt	cottage	
lesson	laracor	aye	midhe	heron	
stirring	inlaid	( )	enclosure		
		stellar			
breach	boyne	churn	surely	blade	
pierce	side	clearly	meadow	my	
here	foam	pen	still	yew	1.

Fig. 3.3. The first "airy grid" of section III of *The Liberties* (*The Europe of Trusts* 204).

S

	churn	rebuke	boyne	bet	a	keep
1727	expose	alpha	broken			hid
		blade				

rebuke boyne

churn alpha bet a keep

1727 expose blade broken hid

pierce hang sum

clear hester quay Liberties 46

tense whisper here libel foam

print pen dot i still

hole yew skip 1.

Fig. 3.4. The third "airy grid" of section III of *The Liberties* (*The Europe of Trusts* 206).

words scattered across the page, puns, riddles, and other language games. Howe has abandoned the narrative approach altogether—Stella will not be found anywhere within conventional form. The solidity of lapidary representation as evoked in the first page of the section, opening with the upper-case reference to "(WHITE MARBLE)"—which certainly is an allusion to the white marble bust of Swift in a niche of St. Patrick's, just above where Stella was interred—is challenged and subverted by all that follows. Indeed, the bulk of section III is devoted to what Keller quite accurately calls "airy grids" of words (1997: 231; see figs. 3.3, 3.4). In these grids, words are extirpated from any linguistic structure, and the reader is forced to engage with each word first as its own individual visual/aural/semantic entity, only then establishing links between words. As a "Separatist"—what Howe names herself in the heading of the first grid—Howe separates words from their organizing systems and, in the process, separates herself from the literary tradition she has inherited to create a mode of expression that may succeed in representing what has hitherto remained unseen and unheard. Paradoxically, by naming herself "separatist," Howe is also placing herself *within* a patriarchal system—the Calvinist tradition of dissent that precipitated the first English people to cross the ocean and settle in the American wilderness, Howe's birthplace and home. Howe is forever swinging—like a pendulum—back and forth between the literary tradition she has inherited and the alternative literature she is creating, between the Irish sensibility of her mother and the Americanness of her father, between poetry and drama and the limits of both. The pendulum image, introduced in the *Book of Stella* and attached to the multiple figures in Howe's landscapes (that is, Swift, Stella, Howe's mother, Howe herself) who remain unsettled, not at home and not at rest, is re-evoked here in the twice-repeated word fragment "suspendu" (210). "In the swing of the pendulum," writes artist Paul Klee in his teaching notebooks, "new forces appear, which under certain circumstances shatter the domination of gravity" (1961: 387). I read Howe's unidentifiable and interrupted word as a compound creation of *suspended* and *pendulum*—Howe's neologistic linguistic enactment of the "new forces" uncovered in her continuing quest and her evolving poetics, "new forces" that may let figures and voices take light.

To return to the "airy grids" of this section, vaguely attributed to Stella or Cordelia by the signaling "S" or "C" at the top of the page, I see the suspended words on the page as visually evocative of birds soaring across white space. Doubtless, my perception of these words as bird-like is in part a direct result of the abundance of birds and bird-figures winging their way through *The Liberties,* representing the longed-for flight, freedom, and transformation. In addition, the first two grids in particular emphasize airy imagery in their repetition of such words as "air," "soaring," "sky," "light," "lovely," and "mist" (204, 205). The abundance of nouns from a pastoral landscape ("herd," "weir," "herd," "yew," "colt," "cottage," "heron," "churn," "meadow," "pen") seem to evoke a bird's-eye view of the countryside where each element is unqualified by modifiers, while I read the word-mergings of "estersnowe" ("easter snow" or "[h]ester's snow") and "homine" ("home mine") as the swooping view of a bird moving across space, blurring borders due to its speed. The words of these airy grids seem to *embody* the freedom the poem's characters fail to attain, much as the "generic restlessness" of this entire section enacts liberation in its movement across convention's boundaries.[41] However, through the inclusion in these word-scatterings of historic markers (the battle of "boyne," Stella's death at the end of 1727), society's restrictions and perceptions ("spinsters," "libel," "rebuke," "expose," "concept," "madhouse") and literary fragments from the canon, Howe reminds us that this language-freedom is partial at best; it is not easily preserved, nor can it ever be fully divorced from its greater context. Thus, what might be a reference to the midair location of the section's birds and words is twice misspoken as "midhe," with the male authority intruding on language's flight.

The separation of words in these airy grids, which may also be interpreted as an experiment in a revisionary portraiture of Stella and Cordelia (Keller 1997: 233), leads Howe to attempt naming herself also in alternative terms. Indeed, the personal and biographic have been integral elements of *The Liberties* from the beginning, and yet only toward the poem's end does Howe explicitly write herself into the text. On page 209, she poses the following nine-line riddle:

I am composed of nine letters.
1 is the subject of a proposition in logic.
2 is a female sheep, or tree.
3 is equal to one.
4 is a beginning.
5 & 7 are nothing.
6 7 & 8 are a question, or salutation.
6 7 8 & 9 are deep, a depression.

Obviously, in this riddle Susan Howe is dividing her full written name into its smallest units—letters—and extracting meaning from these word-atoms. Thus, *S*, the first letter of her name, stands for "the subject of a proposition in logic," while *U* is an ewe or yew (a tree four times repeated in the word-grids preceding, perhaps to evoke the letter or to address the reader through its sound-link to "you"). By riddle's end, Howe is not only the "subject" and pieces of the natural landscape, she also names herself as unique and non-representative ("one"), as the beginning (or at the beginning), as nothing (echoing the use of the word in *"God's Spies"*), and she is (to herself) a question, a salutation, and an unknown ("deep, a depression"). Finally, she is not the sum of these parts—hence, the need for the doubled decoding key that follows:

THE KEY

e n i g m a s t i f e m i a t e d c r y p t o a t h
a b c d e f g h i j k l m n o p q r s t u v w x y
z or zed
graphy
reland

I

The top-line letter-key, itself unwieldy and fragmented, names the uncovering and discovering process in which Howe is engaged as an "enigma," "crypt[ic]," and ever "stif[led]." In contrast stands the abc key of conventional language usage, though here too Howe reads multiple and unsteady meanings in the standardized key. The alphabet's final letter is pronounced as a z or a *zed*, depending on which side of the Atlantic she is standing and to which parent she is listening, while letters slip away to reveal other significations. The absenting of "geo" from "[geo]graphy" foregrounds how one's perception of place is thoroughly mediated by its graphic representation—hence, the Ireland Howe knows will always be mostly mythic. However, this mythic Ireland—represented here as divided, its opening letter *I* having slipped away from its lexical mainland of "reland"—is a place her psyche resounds to, a place she will inevitably return to (where she will always "re[-]land"), as it plays a constitutive role in the "I" that she is.

The mythic components are depicted again in the drama-fragment of section and poem's end. The drama-fragment, entitled "HEAR" (to rhyme with "Lear" and stand in contrast to Lear's "look"), is masque-like wherein the characters are society's archetypes, nameless and fulfilling set roles: Sentry, Scapegoat, Bride, Bridegroom, Parents, Heathen Performer, Sojourner, Bastard, and Fool. A literal and/or figurative sacrifice—of scapegoat or bride—occurs offstage as the play opens, once again establishing violence and oppression as society's dominant mode of being. The Sentry, he who is meant to guard others, states his fear, while the Heathen Performer speaks almost every line twice, as though his voice is returned to him, unreceived by another. The standard roles and lines have long outlasted their use and there is, finally, "only air hear" (217)—with the "hear" doubling as an imperative similar to Lear's "look" and as a description of the emptied state. The Sojourner, echoing words first spoken by Stella at the end of *"God's Spies,"* expresses sorrow and lasting bewilderment at what is lost in history's retellings:

> —if that definition of truth is correct
> that truth is what always remains—
> (Pause.)
> Peace at my tears for I am a stranger.[42]

"The good tidings which the [material historicist] brings with throbbing heart may be lost in a void the very moment he opens his mouth," writes Benjamin. So too the speaker/Sojourner with "throbbing heart" fears that all the alternative tellings of this long and difficult text will be lost in the void of convention the moment they are written. Still, "you've got to open your mouth to speak," insists Howe in the Keller interview, to tell the stories "that need to be told again differently" (1995: 30-31). And because of this "telling differently," at *The Liberties'* end something *has been* "set at liberty": perhaps it is Stella, no longer bound to the name Swift gave her and represented only by the letter *S* the Bastard carries in. Or perhaps it is Susan Howe, also represented by the *S,* who has claimed through the writing of this text a freedom of language and historical perspective whereby all society's marginal characters—Stella, Cordelia, Sojourner, Bastard, and Fool, too—may occupy center stage, whether with speaking parts or in silence ("speech" and "silence" being two more possible determinants for the Bastard's *S*—Keller 1997: 237). The final lines of the text are a command, to self and to reader, to "Tear pages from a calendar / scatter them into sunshine and snow" (217). The calendar as representative of traditional historicism will serve no longer; in an elegant return to the poem's opening image, the calendar's pages, thus thrown to the wind, are transformed by the agency suggested in the command into the soaring leafs of Stella's lost diary (158).

On the cover page of *The Liberties,* just beneath the poem's title, Howe has placed a reproduction of an old Irish postage stamp with the image of an angel of upturned face and wide-spread wings on it.[43] Across this angel's

THE LIBERTIES

for Susan Manning

Fig. 3.5. The cover page of *The Liberties* (*The Europe of Trusts* 147).

body flows a banner on which is written "Vox Hibernie" (the Voice of Ireland) (see fig. 3.5). This winged image not only prefigures the multiple airborne representations in the text to follow but also alludes to the central desire of the work to give voice to the voiceless. Ireland here stands for the oppressed, the marginal, and the forgotten, itself a land and people that have long been silenced, robbed of language, culture, and identity through centuries of colonization (Smith 1979). In the context of Howe's vigorous and ongoing investigation into history, the winged figure at *The Liberties'* opening also evokes Benjamin's famous "angel of history" as presented in the ninth thesis of his essay "These on the Philosophy of History." Benjamin writes:

> A Klee painting named "Angelus Novus" shows an angel looking as though he is about to move away from something he is fixedly contemplating. His eyes are staring, his mouth is open, his wings are spread. This is how one pictures the angel of history. His face is turned toward the past. Where we perceive a chain of events, he sees a single catastrophe which keeps piling wreckage upon wreckage and hurls it in front of his feet. The angel would like to stay, awaken the dead, and make whole what has been smashed. But a storm is lowing from Paradise; it has got caught in his wing with such violence that the angel can no longer close them. This storm irresistibly propels him into the future to which his back is turned. (1968: 257–258)

As Geoffrey Hartman writes in his analysis of Benjamin's angel-image, "[a]n angel is a messenger, but the image is the message here." With eyes fixed on the past in a disbelieving gaze, wings forced open by violent winds, self propelled backward—into the future—against its will, the angel is not only the symbol of history, as Benjamin has named it, but is also and most poignantly the embodiment of the individual's powerless position in the face of history's stormy and relentless push forward. The angel/individual "would like to stay rather than go into the future," argues Hartman, "not because he is happy but because his vision of the dead is unresolved: catastrophe and hope remain intolerably mixed" (1980: 76). Just as the angel/individual, in the grip of this conflictual historical consciousness, wants to stay and cannot, so does he want to speak, as though the articulation of the past will free him from its hold and allow him to turn away. However, speech is frustrated, both by the indescribable nature of the wreckage before him (in the past) and by the brute force of the winds that render speech impossible as they push him backward (into the future). The angel is an image of suspension and propulsion both, of body and soul leaning toward the past while moving into the future; the angel inhabits, in Hartman's words, " a written space of contradiction" (77), a place where opposing forces meet and merge, a borderline. Like this angel, the calendar pages "scatter[ed] . . . into sunshine and snow" of *The Liberties'* end and the soaring diary pages of the text's opening hover above the landscape, touching down nowhere, signifying "catastrophe and hope" both.[44] Unlike Benjamin's angel, the speaker of *The Liberties* does speak— in words that ultimately take flight like birds, as though the only relevant articulation is the one freed from the grounding fetters of literary conven- tion yet grounded in literary convention, and the only possible poetry is the one that "brings similitude and representation to configurations waiting from forever to be spoken" (*Europe of Trusts* 14).

The imagery of Benjamin's "angel of history" proves a useful entryway into the second text under consideration in this chapter, *Pythagorean Silence.* First published in 1982, two years after the publication of *The Liberties, Pythagorean Silence* may be read as the outgrowth of the earlier text. From *The Liberties'* preoccupation with a range of female figures and voices lost on "the dark side of history," *Pythagorean Silence* narrows its gaze to focus more closely on the child and her individual losses in the world. The personal and public realms are fully intertwined in all of Howe's works; nonetheless, I read *Pythagorean Silence* as Howe's most explicitly autobiographic work, with its depictions of the child's inevitable separation and resulting irretrievable loss most closely representing her own first experiences. Within the child-cen- tered context of *Pythagorean Silence,* Benjamin's imagery described above takes on an additional layer of meaning. The "open mouth" image (also used ear- lier in his essay, as noted on page 102 of this text) not only evokes the desire to speak but also represents the infant's opening of his mouth to suckle—a primary need that is left unsatisfied in the suspended image. Similarly, the "whole" which "has been smashed" may be read as the primary and forever lost union with the mother. For Howe, the individual losses of infancy are entirely interwoven with the general losses precipitated by historical events, as her earliest days and first memories are marked by the rampant violence and destruction of World War II. "For me there was no silence before armies," she declares in the first sentence of her introductory piece to the works col- lected in *The Europe of Trusts,* naming silence and speech both as inextricably bound for her to a place and moment of worldwide violence. "In the sum- mer of 1938," she continues, "my mother and I were staying with my grand- mother, uncle, aunt, great-aunts, cousins and friends in Ireland, and I had just learned to walk, when Czechoslovakia was dismembered by Hitler, Ribbentrop, Mussolini, Chamberlin, and Daladier . . . That October we sailed home on a ship crowded with refugees fleeing various countries in Europe. When I was two the German army invaded Poland and World War II began in the West [. . .] From 1939 until 1946 in news photographs, day after day I saw signs of culture exploding into murder" (9–10, 11). In *Pythagorean Silence,* through the ever-present mediation of "the presence of the now" (Benjamin 1968: 261), Howe returns to this place of origin, marked as it is by violence, displacement, and absence, to paint her own portrait, as she attempted in *The Liberties* to paint Stella's. In my consideration of this complex and multifaceted work, I will limit my brief analysis of *Pythagorean Silence* to an investigation into Howe's representations of the child's landscape of losses, within the context of Howe's specific historical consciousness.

Pythagorean Silence (1982)

The sixth-century B.C. philosopher Pythagoras is noted as having observed that "he who is called the wisest of all (i.e., Hermes) . . . was the inventor of names" (Fideler 1987: 69). While Pythagoras avoids wholly committing himself to this conclusion by utilizing the more evasive passive form in his recorded observation, his own attention to the importance of names is evident in his being the first to describe himself as a "lover of wisdom" (philosopher) in place of "wise man," the traditional and accepted Greek epithet for scholars. Pythagoras's use of the term philosopher not only insists upon the greatest accuracy possible in the naming of persons and things but also passionately embraces the unending *process* of acquiring wisdom (Fideler 1987). Indeed, the embracing of process and the rejection of stasis are apparent in Pythagoras's approach to language as well as to knowledge, two realms inextricably linked—as indicated by Pythagoras's insistence on the exclusively oral transmission of his teachings (Heninger 1974: 23). This refusal to engrave his thoughts and theories in the proverbial stone seems designed to ensure that the process of negotiating his philosophies not be halted by the (illusory) authority of a written text with its seeming evocation of the author's voice, that any attempt at mastery through language be frustrated and foiled at the outset. As he and his disciples left no writings behind, Pythagoras's teachings, as mediated and transmitted by others, revolve around a core absence that transforms the texts of his teachings into an ever-changing context.

Pythagorean philosophy maintains that there exists not only order but also "a dimension of *meaning*" in the cosmos (Fideler 1987: 67), and that the individual must go in search of this meaning. Language in general, and the tension between speech and silence in particular, inform this ongoing search for meaning, as partially indicated by the five-year vow of silence that was demanded of disciples in the Pythagorean School. Susan Howe's three-part poem entitled *Pythagorean Silence* considers this "[l]ong pythagorean lustrum"[45] and situates itself along this same fault line between speech and silence, between language and loss; in fact, *Pythagorean Silence* perches precariously on this fault line that is the language of loss. Howe negotiates this perilous place in her own search for meaning, what she terms "[t]he stress of meaning" (29)—referring to both the crucial importance of finding meaning in the world and the inordinate difficulty and emotionally and mentally disquieting impact of the search. Denoting also the phonetic emphasis placed on a sound or syllable, the word *stress* evokes the central role that language plays in the search—particularly for the poet who understands herself and is understood through this medium; particularly in this postmodern quest narrative wherein the nature of language itself is uncertain. Across the two planes of childhood and cultural perspectives where identity and meaning may be sought, the poem carries its speaker and its reader, speaking around—and within—an ever-encroaching silence.

The poem is preceded by an epigraph that carries a tone of aching nostalgia for the forever lost nonseparateness from the world and the Other, invoking that world and that Other to inform the creative process of the poem:

we that were wood
when that a wide wood was

In a physical Universe playing with

words

Bark be my limbs my hair be leaf

Bride be my bow my lyre my quiver

As printed in the original Montemora edition of *Pythagorean Silence* and reproduced here, the first two lines of the epigraph are as near to each other as they can be without overlapping, with the taller letters of the bottom line—treelike—jutting into and touching the letters above them.[46] These touching, almost mingling, lines visually represent the child's world of merging with her environment, a world doubly lost as the child is child no more and the "wide wood" has been scorched to the ground. Indeed, the scorched landscape image—the "after the disaster" historical consciousness that is Howe's—presides over the entire collection of *The Europe of Trusts* through the reproduction on the book's cover of German artist Anselm Kiefer's painting entitled "L'Ange Protectuer des Peintures." In this painting, an angel appears again, this time hovering over blackened ground, with one hand pointing forward toward an unseen horizon, the other hand gesturing toward the destruction below. The German words "des Malers Schutzengel" ("the paint-ers' angel-protector")—like the word *words* in the epigraph—also hover un-certainly in the gray area between earth and sky, suspended in space. The imagery of suspension is reinforced in the suspension of syntactic comple-tion of the epigraph's opening four lines: the main clause is missing and the "lost loss" is thus raised to the surface (Blanchot 1986: 41). As though the loss is too great to bear, the speaker shifts at this point from remembering to anticipation through the appeal/command for union: "Bark be my limbs my hair be leaf / Bride be my bow my lyre my quiver." However, violence intrudes even on this love imagery, resonant of the *Song of Songs,* as the bridal music-making bow and lyre become the weaponry of bow and quiver by the passage's end.

"Pearl Harbor"

Throughout the search for meaning, which Howe names the "dance" of the stress of meaning, the central relationship is that of child and parent. From Rachel "weeping for her children // refuses / to be comforted // because they *are* not" (21), through Hamlet and his restless ghost father (23, 42), to blind Oedipus wandering "backwards and forwards from reef / to reef Lost // to grief" (42) and Isaac overlaid with Iphigenia—both waiting to be sacrificed by their fathers (73)—the child/parent relationship is one of irretrievable loss and a resulting unrelenting grief. In *Pythagorean Silence,* child and parent do not simply drift apart but rather are wrenched one from the other. Indeed, the terrible societal violence explicit in these images seems to underscore a violence that is extrasocietal, a violence intrinsic to the process of "human-child" maturation (82)—a violence of premature separation and separate-ness. The search for meaning is, to no small degree, a search for a promised, longed-for, and unreachable wholeness. "Body and Soul[,]" asks the speaker in the closing moment of the poem's first section, "will we ever leave child-hood together" (32). The question has no question mark, knowing as it does its own answer—that promises of wholeness are illusory.

The mythical and literary child/parent relationships scattered through the text both frame and reflect the speaker's own child/parent separations: from her father off to fight in World War II; from her mother as mirrored by the speaker's separation *as* mother from her own child:

I lay down and conceived   Love
(my dear Imaginary)   Maze-believer

I remember   you were called
sure-footed
and yet off the path (Where
are you) warmed and warming   Body

turned and turning   Soul
identical soul   abandoned

to Sleep   (where
are you crying)

crying for a mother's help
                    (44)

The amazing "[m]aze-believer" child that was "Soul / identical soul" to the
mother, who merged with her in a symbiotic bond of filling each other's
needs, and who is now crying somewhere beyond the mother's reach; the
speaker who conceived and then lost the child is, through the separation
process, herself again a child, reliving her own first moment of loss. In the
repeated patterns of history, child and mother *merge* again even as the child
is *emerging* into a separate identity. For Howe, the child's (and mother's)
identification with the image of the Other is a frail illusion "stained with
mortality" (45). Indeed, the mother who was the child and the child who was
the mother "*are* not." [47]

This emphasized presence *("are")* in the face of absence ("not") at the very
opening of the poem is echoed later in the text in a passage that may be
understood in the framework of Lacan's mirror stage:

cataclysmic Pythagoras   Things
not as they are

for they *are not*   but as they seem
(as mirror

in mirror to be)
                (38; my italics)

In the mirror stage, the illusory mirror image wherein the child sees herself in the Other and sees herself *as* other—external image separate from her internal experience of herself—determines the formation of identity and "functions to establish a relation between the organism and its reality" (Lacan 1977: 4).[48] Reality refers here to a completely subjective context—things "as they seem" in the (child's) mirror and in the "mirror to be" (that is the grown child's own child "to be"). The foundation of identity that is a presence revolves around a recognition of absence, as highlighted by the text's crucially placed space after the words "are not"—a visual and spatial silence wherein nonexistence momentarily claims the text. Thus identity is shaped by conflict and contradiction, founded as it is on a mirror image that "symbolizes the mental permanence of the *I*, at the same time as it prefigures its alienating destination" (Lacan 1977: 2). Mirror imagery abounds in *Pythagorean Silence*, often in the guise of Narcissus, who enters the text unnamed but whose presence is signaled and recognized by the water images associated with him and the repetition of his final word, "farewell" (26, 31, 76). In the site of separation, by the mythological river now frozen into ice in the speaker's cold Buffalo, New York, landscape, the text becomes Echo herself, desiring the unattainable and doomed to forever repeat and relive the scene of loss:

> drawn and drawn together
> mirrors thaw
>
> only   Only
> what never stops hurting remains
>
> in memory
>
> In memory
> Errant turns to
>
> and away
>
> Farewel-
> twin half torn to pearl
>   (26)

The frozen river thaws, but the moment of loss remains, revisited by the "errant" speaker/poet on a quest in search of what cannot be found: a completion of self through a merging with the lost "twin half"—visually depicted here as the second and missing *l* in "farewel." This Narcissus-like "twin half" is a conflation of three images—the self, the mother, and the father—all evoked through the word *pearl,* all "torn" away from the speaker. The father is present in the word's echoing reference to Pearl Harbor—the event that precipitated his going off to war, his "plodd[ing] away through drifts of i / ce" (35), through drifts of a fragmented "I." The mother is present as "mother-of-pearl," that precious and protective inner layering of the shell, pulled off to make jewels. The self is the actual ice-image lost to the homonymous purling of the thawing river, the murmuring sound of rippling water. The ice-mirror's reflection and eventual thawing, the doubled merging and emerging moment, embody both the identification of the self as an other (itself) and the identification with the Other (the parent), and the inevitable tearing apart—solidity of ice into flowing water—resulting in a loss that "never stops hurting[.]"

It is important to note that childhood's pivotal moment of loss is also a moment of jubilation. The mirror image, "a drama whose internal thrust is precipitated from insufficiency to anticipation," promises the child an eventual self-mastery and sense of "totality" to replace its "fragmented body-image" (Lacan 1977: 4). "My bones are buffalo and shake their manes" (28), proclaims the speaker, gathering her frail bones into the complete and massive form of the ancient animal. Indeed, their "manes" becomes her "name" in an anagrammatic connection already established by the text (25). However, this totality is illusory, "an Ideal"

Slipping

forever

between rupture and rapture

soul
severed from Soul   drowned

Drowned

Mother and father
turn downward your face
(31)

Narcissus is again evoked, enraptured by a vision of himself—a vision that ruptures him from himself until he drowns in his own (alien) reflection.[49] From this narrow place between "rupture and rapture"—two words separated only by a single letter—identity emerges; at this same site remembered, the speaker of *Pythagorean Silence* reaches an uncertain and ever-threatened domestic calm, with "peace in the basement // all the dogs chained" and shadows (of parents, younger selves, and future selves as represented by children) "seated at the kitchen table" (32).

The introduction of the shadow motif at the end of the poem's first section foregrounds the centrality of the visual sense in the mirror stage. A shadow refers not only to an imperfect imitation of something else but also to the play between light and dark as perceived by the eyes. Elizabeth Grosz expounds upon the primacy of the visual in the mirror stage, explaining that "[o]f all the senses, vision remains the one which most readily confirms the separation of subject from object. Vision performs a distancing function, leaving the looker unimplicated in . . . its subject. [It is only the sense of sight that] directs the child to a *totalized* self-image . . . None of the other senses have the ability to perceive 'synchronically,' in a non-linear and non-temporal fashion" (1990: 38–39). This "Open // power of vision" (31) is primary to *Pythagorean Silence,* from the poem's abundance of sight-related imagery to the poet's ongoing endeavor to understand herself by looking forward and back, to see what is "invisible // and outside" (29). Indeed, the poem seems to revolve around the proposition that "to see is to *have* at a distance" (*Europe of Trusts* 12). However, sight is not only a theme of the text but is also central to its praxis, with words interacting on the page as images would on a canvas. Extending a strategy already encountered in earlier works, Howe "paints" her text, utilizing a variety of typefaces and the full range of the page's spatial possibilities—while exposing its limitations, a graphic expression of the text's central tension between speech and silence. The poem as visual entity is viewed synchronically, with chronology collapsing as images interact and words establish a physical (albeit fragmented) presence in a world of precarious identities and certain silence.

For a final word on the mirror stage as it informs our understanding of *Pythagorean Silence,* it is interesting to note Gallop's discussion of Lacan's original essay, delivered by Lacan at the Fourteenth International Psychoanalytical Congress in 1936, and his 1949 revision of this text, the version later collected in *Ecrits.* Gallop writes: "The war separates the two versions of 'The Mirror Stage.' Somewhere between the 1936 and the 1949 version, Lacan's thought, the thought we identify as 'Lacan's,' is 'formed.' The title of the 1949 version is 'The Mirror Stage as *Formative* of the Function of the I.' The essay is about the 'formation,' the forming of an 'I,' of an identity. And the text itself is formative of an identity we call Lacan" (1985: 77). This placing of Lacan's essay within its historical context parallels Howe's own historical contextualizing of her work in the introduction to *The Europe of Trusts* and her ongoing concern with and investigation into *"the cause"* that forms and informs history and her own identity (13). For both Howe and Lacan, World War II stands as a formative moment in their personal histories—a place of violence and loss around which their respective texts revolve. For both, this place of violence and loss evokes and leads both to reconsider the first loss of child/parent separation.

"Pythagorean Silence"

The internalization of self as other and identification of self with Other that characterize the mirror stage lead to the child's first experience of loss and lack. Howe's work speaks of the resulting mourning process wherein the grief is as unending as the absence is unfillable. A similar absence and loss inform the second and middle section of *Pythagorean Silence* (also entitled "Pythagorean Silence"), though here the speaker has moved from the child-hood plane most prominent in "Pearl Harbor" to an attempt to find herself within a cultural context. In a section of abundant allusions to the central canonic literary texts and philosophies of Western culture, from the Bible, *Oedipus Rex, The Odyssey,* and *Hamlet,* to Socrates, Plato, and their predeces-sors (Thales, Anaximander, and Pythagoras), the speaker considers the na-ture of her own words and their value in her ongoing search for meaning. "[A]ge of earth and us all chattering[,]" she writes at the opening of the sec-tion,

> a sentence   or character
> suddenly
>
> steps out to seek for truth   fails
> falls
>
> into a stream of ink   Sequence
> trails off
>
> waving fables and faces
> (36)

At the very outset, language is viewed as fallible, failing (falling) in its search for truth. The written word in particular is suspect, represented by "forger-ies" (36) and the "stray sheet" (37), by "Drafts," "Scraps," and "lost Origi-nals" (59), its authenticity at issue and its fleeting nature apparent. "We write in sand / three thousand proverbs and songs[,]" states the speaker, knowing that the inevitable winds will blow away these verses, too (45). In fact, language—and by extension literature—is the site of certain loss, founded as it is on "[a]bstractions of the world's abstractions" (28), revolving as it does around the forever absent.

Howe's engagement with language and its cultural contexts may be understood as an examination of the entry into what Lacan calls the Symbolic Order—"the social and signifying order governing culture" (Grosz 1989: xxii). *Pythagorean Silence* as a poem of quest perforce emerges from the Imaginary Order of images and immerses itself in the signifying chain, as "[a]nyone who goes in search of meaning at its source, or in its essential forms, has no choice but to travel by way of language" (Bowie 1990: 64). Language is necessarily the path of the poet/traveler but is also that which makes the traveler *what she is*—language "constitutes" her. The signifying chains of the Symbolic Order both "imprison" the traveler in an identity of its making and offer her the possibility of expressing that identity; the signifying chains hold the poet in a "paradise-prison" of sounds and symbols (54).

Within this labyrinth of language, "individual signifiers refer not to individual signifieds but rather to other signifiers under which the signified 'slides'" (Muller 1988: 56). In a similar movement and one evocative of the positioning of Benjamin's "angel of history," every myth mentioned in Howe's text reflects "backwards and forwards" (42), opening into another myth under which "meaning" slides. The Lacanian maxim that "the symbol manifests itself first of all as the murder of the thing" (1977: 104) is recast in *Pythagorean Silence* as the symbol manifesting itself first of all in the murder of the King—Oedipus sliding into Agamemnon sliding into Hamlet's father, all involving regicide that is also family homicide. Thus for both Lacan and Howe, the symbol revolves around absence and is ever in motion, ever in search of meaning in an "unfathomable visionary dream" (59), "[e]ver tolling absence homeward" (54). This absence or "constitutive lack" at the core of language not only leaves the individual "inevitably bereft of any masterful understanding of language" (Gallop 1985: 20) but also plays a crucial role in the formation of the individual's identity. Stated differently, the loss which is intrinsic to language is formative of the subject. "Their words are weeds wrapped round my head[,]" proclaims the speaker in *Pythagorean Silence,* referring to weeds as not only the resistant and durable plant but also as a mourner's garments, a widow's weeds (32).

Thus entry into the Symbolic Order wherein "nothing exists except on an assumed foundation of absence" (Bowie 1991: 93) is an entry into a world of loss. And yet, coupled with this loss, language allows the subject to speak of herself as subject and gives her a place from which to speak. The gain of the "signifying quest" rests in this knowing of self as subject: "if I dedicate myself to becoming what I am," explains Lacan, "to coming into being, I cannot doubt that even if I lose myself in the process, I am in that process" (1977: 165–66). Toward that place of process, the speaker of *Pythagorean Silence* goes "through the deeps of // childhood (afterglow of light on trees)" to emerge into the Symbolic Order:

Daybreak

by dying
has been revealed   Midday or morrow

move motherless

(Oh women women look) how my words
flow out

kindling and stumbling   Sunwise
with swords and heys

a dance of disguise
where breath most breathes   (Books

blaze up
my room is bright)World I have made

empty edge
Father's house forever falling

(40–41)

This now motherless speaker has passed into the uncertain realm of "stumbling" words, a realm of "twilighting" where light and dark contend with each other and shadows reign. The signifier is an uncertain entity, concealing and revealing at one and the same time, words kindling "a dance of disguise." The fire imagery is extended in the images of books that "blaze up"— a term that connotes both the light of inspiration lent to the speaker and the danger of burning (her) up in an auto-da-fé of books. The cultural context of these books and the language structures therein seem to lean out of the parentheses surrounding them, intruding on the speaker's creative claim of "[w]orld I have made" and typographically claiming even the speaker herself in a world *they* have made.

The perilous perch of this world made on an "empty edge" echoes the ice "edge of a hole" where father and daughter stand at the opening of *Pythagorean Silence,* singing before the impending and inevitable sundering apart. Indeed, the early parent/child relationship of absolute identification and eventual separation seems to inform all later losses. As Malcolm Bowie eloquently explains, utilizing spatial imagery that is both appropriate and resonant, "[e]ven in the heartlands of the Symbolic order, the Imaginary may retain a foothold" (1991: 93). For Howe, the Imaginary seems to retain more than a mere foothold in the Symbolic Order, as the image of mother and child torn apart intrudes into and disrupts language:

> R
> (her cry
> silences
> whole
> vocabularies
> of *names*
> for
> *things*
> (22)

Biblical Rachel's immense grief over losing her children not only silences the signifying system but she herself is half lost, her *name* torn in two. Language is visually marginalized, pushed as it is into the right margin, and white space (silence) dominates the page. The first loss retains a primary position in Howe's internal and textual landscape.

"Clay has fallen on my monologue / Clay on my coat," states the speaker toward the end of "Pythagorean Silence" (66), returning to the fallibility of language and frailty of self in this search for meaning—this search for "cause" that is the stated objective of the poem. And yet something *has* changed. By the end of this second section of the poem, the speaker is no longer motherless; she is now able to name that which parents her and her text.

> Poverty my mother and Possession
>
> my father
> Time to set our face homeward
>
> Shadow-emperor
> (68)

Poverty connotes lack and need, while *possession* evokes being owned or possessed as one is by madness or a demon. Both poverty and possession revolve around desire—desiring what is absent and desiring what is present (spirit or language) but uncontained and not ever owned. Bowie maintains that "[d]esire is the subject-matter of psychoanalysis" (1991: 1), and one may assert the same claim for poetry. Certainly *Pythagorean Silence* is a text born of desire, a "desire [that] is knotted to the desire of the Other but . . . in this loop lies the desire *to know*" (Lacan 1977: 184; italics mine). Desire for the absent is a desire generated and perpetuated by the absent—by the death that is intrinsic to the Symbolic Order. Surrounded by (and surrounding) death, as speech is surrounded by (and surrounds) silence, the desire "to know" establishes a creative life force in the text and in the speaker. The quest for meaning—the struggle through silence for speech as enacted on the page—*becomes* meaning, the only meaning available, valuable in and of itself.

(Untitled)

Hermes, the god of naming, was also the Guide to the Underworld—the "Shadow-emperor" who led the individual to his final home. This mythical combination of roles links language and loss, language and death, from the very beginnings of literature. Lacan argues that "psychoanalysis may accompany the patient to the ecstatic limit of the *'Thou art that,'* in which is revealed to him the cipher of his mortal destiny, but it is not in our mere power as practitioners to bring him to that point where the real journey begins" (1977: 7). In contrast, Howe seems to imply in the third section of her poem that poetry can carry the reader further, even to that "particular place fleeting / and fixed" (71) just beyond "the cipher of his [her] mortal destiny." Traveling from "Pearl Harbor" through "Pythagorean Silence," from memory through myth and culture to dream and back, the speaker (and reader) reaches a clearing—indicated by the third section's blank title page, a white threshold from which the woods of words will be entered. Having negotiated both childhood and cultural planes in search of meaning, having confronted the loss of the Imaginary Order and the absence of the Symbolic, speaker and symbol are now stripped bare in the face of meaninglessness and mortality. At this place ("at the back of the sky") where "biography blows away" (64), the poet leaves society's ordering structures behind, fallible as they are, in search of other means for making meaning out of the "fleeting and frail" self. At this silent threshold, the threshold of silence, "the real journey begins."

Like the first two sections of the poem, section III of *Pythagorean Silence* alludes to many literary genres, from ballad, fairy tale, and myth to the marginalia and commentary of the Scholiasts. However, at this threshold, these genres afford no comfort of context, and the overwhelming sense of the text and the speaker is of solitariness and impending, lasting anonymity:

O lightfoot

No spread of your name

no fabulous birth stories

no nations taken by storm

Moving in solitary symbols through shadowy

surmises

(74)

The hunt imagery central to this section, with the speaker as "gentle doe" chased by hounds that race all night (77, 80), recalls the hunt motif of *The Liberties,* though here there is no possibility of taking flight. From the aerial landscapes of the earlier poem, Howe has grounded herself and her imagery in *Pythagorean Silence,* foregrounding the proximity of danger and the isolation of the poet attempting to move beyond conventional language structures, into "solitary symbols through shadowy / surmises." The four word-grids of the poem's end, with their preponderance of wood references, stand on the page as "a row of signs / ordering sound // (sacred and secret tree systems)" (57), as though re-creating the forests burnt down by history's violence:

w

whortleberries   haw   pied   dun

unhired   churlheart   cress

rath   lintel   stag   hazel

slamon   blackthorn   bracken   wel

peak   furze   hut

(78)

Channelling into Echo's fading and disrupted (fare) "wel," standing on the edge of silence, the words claim no more than a momentary presence in the white spaces surrounding them. Conversely, extracted from any abstracting grammar or structure, their momentary presence bears a physical weight and authority on the page—as though the words *were* wood.[50]

The speaker and her double, the reader, together move through these words/woods—a place of the mourner's "clear cry" echoing (77); a place that means only *to be,* but, concurrently, is a place (of writing) that (like all writing) leads elsewhere (Gallop 1985: 34). Thus the wooded terms of trees, brush, and birds are slowly transformed into a place of religion and ritual:

cherubim   golden   swallow

amulet   instruction   tribulation

winged   joy   parent   sackcloth   ash

den   sealed   ascent   flee

chariot   interpret   flame

hot   arc   chaff   meridian

in the extant manuscript SOMEONE
has lightly scored a pen over
                    (84)

"The lure of all texts," writes Elizabeth Wright, "lies in a revelation, of things veiled coming to be unveiled" (1989: 112). Howe's revelatory closing diction seems to partly pull a veil aside, as though to provide a dramatic disclosure— a type of transcendence through the runelike word and the immortality of an unnamed "extant" manuscript, miraculously not lost or destroyed. Similarly, the poem's final image of Ophelia between water and weeds, her "clothes spread wide" (84/*Hamlet* IV.vii.175), seems to attest to the lasting power of the image, of the word and of literature, and to the concomitant need to be grounded in and freed of literary and cultural conventions—Ophelia's final fragmented speech stilled in the weeds of the stream where she drowns while preserved in Shakespeare's text. Meaning may be just there—in poetry's promise of transforming and perhaps lasting.

However, the dialectic of speech and silence remains unresolved in

Pythagorean Silence as do the tensions between cultural and individual voices, as the manuscript has been "lightly" penned over by "SOMEONE" and the final image is of a dead young woman. Clearly, Howe's poem resists any resolution or summary statement, inherently a text that is, like Lacan's essays, "difficult to enter and ultimately impossible to master" (Grosz 1990: 17). Mastery as a mode of reception is rejected by Howe and in its place comes an insistence on multiplicity of approaches, an acceptance of uncertainty and a foregrounding of the poem's aural and visual creations. When asked by Keller what her expectations of her readers are, Howe's single-word answer is "freedom" (1995: 31). I read this "freedom" as double, referring both to the freedom Howe must have to create as she will and the freedom readers must have to interpret her work from their own historical consciousness. As Hartman writes in his analysis of Benjamin's angel, "[c]riticism approaches the form of fragment, pensee, or parable: it both soars and stutters as it creates the new text that rises up . . . against a prior text that will surely repossess it" (1980: 78).

4

On Iconoclasts, Enthusiasts, and the Printed Text

A Reading of *A Bibliography of the King's Book or, Eikon Basilike* and *The Nonconformist's Memorial*

> ... I have
> assembled the scattered elements of a most violent beauty
> That I control
> And which compels me.
> —Blaise Cendrars, "The Prose of the Trans-Siberian" (1913)

> The sounds, these pieces of words come into the chaos of life, and then you try to order them and to explain something and the explanation breaks free of itself. I think a lot of my work is about breaking free. Starting free and being captured and breaking free and being captured again.
> —Susan Howe, *Talisman Interviews* (1994)

> Wayward Puritan. Charged with enthusiasm. Enthusiasm is antinomian.
> —Susan Howe, "Emily Dickinson and the Illogic of Sumptuary Values" (1993)

Without a doubt, Emily Dickinson is the poet whose work and life have had the greatest impact on Susan Howe, and Howe's readings of Dickinson offer her reader a key to Howe's own poetry. Dickinson is "a miracle," says Howe in the first exchange of the *Talisman* interview (Foster 1994: 48) and her writing is "my strength and shelter," she proclaims in the opening pages of her introduction to the essays collected in *The Birth-mark* (2), situating Dickinson in both cases as the threshold she crosses in all her creative and scholarly work. Indeed, Howe has devoted a considerable portion of her poetic essays—what Perloff has called "poessays"—to the study of Dickinson's work by investigating which writers were *her* primary influences, by considering the visual dimensions of her poetry in its original fascicle form, by tracing the transmission and printing history of her oeuvre, and by closely reading specific poems.[1] Particularly intriguing is the fashion in which Howe reads nineteenth-century Dickinson as continuing in the antinomian tradition of seventeenth-century Anne Hutchinson—and the unceasing misreadings and miseditings of Dickinson's work as a continuation of the antinomian controversy that resulted in Hutchinson's banishment. "Some keep the Sabbath going to Church— / I keep it, staying at Home," Dickinson states in one of her better-known poems, and certainly her refusal to join the Congregational Church during the wave of Calvinist fervor that swept through her hometown of Amherst in the 1840s and 1850s and her insistence on individual, unmediated, and, often unconventional worship qualifies as an antinomian stand. However, Howe has extended the meaning of the term antinomian to encompass the very form of Dickinson's poetry and prose, and to include Dickinson's choice not to publish—"a gesture of infinite patience," maintains Howe, and an enactment of the covenant of grace (*Birth-mark* 1). Dickinson's disruption of grammar and syntax conventions as a subversion "of the order shut inside the structure of a sentence" (*My Emily Dickinson* 11) and the visual strangeness of her poems—in fascicle form, before "normalized" and standardized by editors—are, for Howe, the antinomian's rebellion against the institutionalized "law" (in this case, literary law), while her manuscripts, meticulously sewn together in Dickinson's own statement of structure and kept private in her lifetime are an expression of faith and self-assertion and "represent a contradiction to canonical social power" (*Birth-mark* 1).

Howe's understanding of the term *antinomian* as "a contradiction to canonical social power" informs my own reading of Howe's *A Bibliography of the King's Book or, Eikon Basilike* (1989) and *The Nonconformist's Memorial* (1992).[2] Thematically, structurally, and—most crucially—visually these two works exhibit, I believe, this resistance to the hegemonic authority of the Western literary canon. "The poem was a vision and a gesture before it became sign and coded exchange in a political economy of value," argues Howe (*Birth-mark* 147), implying in this statement a greater legitimacy to the prior role of the poetic as visionary, *outside* the social exchange system that determines hierarchies of texts. Like Dickinson before her, Howe—a twentieth-century antinomian—"explore[s] the implications of breaking the law just short of breaking off communication with a reader" (*My Emily Dickinson* 11).[3] *A Bibliography of the King's Book or, Eikon Basilike* (here on to be called Howe's *Eikon Basilike*), posing as a bibliographic—hence scientific and authoritative—study of King Charles I's *Eikon Basilike,* sets out on a supposed "search for origins on paper" (Foster 1994: 63)—a search for the original text, original author, and original intentions of the seventeenth-century *Eikon Basilike*—only to uncover and set loose instead conflicting and multiple voices, clashes of versions, and radical visual violence. "What is found at the historical beginning," writes Foucalt, "is not the inviolable identity of the Origin; it is the dissension of other things. It is disparity" (1977: 142). In Howe's *Eikon Basilike,* a text of disparity and dissension, nothing is inviolable, most of all not the notion of the unequivocal literary canon and the authoritative master narratives. Indeed, the "master narrative" as sacred (and hence iconic) in Western culture is exposed as fallible, variable, and unstable, and antinomian Howe doubles in this work as iconoclast, shattering the image of the literary product as ever complete unto itself and closed. Within this iconoclastic strain, the breaking of form is always more than symbolic, represented in the visual rupturings of/in Howe's text. In addition, the materiality, or "textual condition" (McGann 1991), of that being broken—whether Howe's *Eikon Basilike* or Charles I's *Eikon Basilike*—is brought to the fore, examined, and charged with meaning. Finally, the "deep conviction" fostered by our print culture that "each work of verbal art is closed off in a world of its own, a 'verbal icon'" (Ong 1988: 133) is challenged and ultimately replaced with a similarly deep conviction that all poetry remains open in its complex and ever-changing network of relations with the poetry, poets and readers that both precede and succeed it.

Continuing and extending these themes, *The Nonconformist's Memorial* takes on *the* book of Western canonical power, the Bible—which Johanna Drucker has aptly named "the archetype of the unmarked [and hence closed] text . . . in which the words on the page 'appear to speak themselves' without the invisible intervention of author or printer" (1994: 95). Using as her point of departure a passage from the Gospel According to St. John—itself a text of uncertain authorship and origin[4]—Howe in effect *opens up* the New Testament by writing a text that could be called the "Gospel According to Mary Magdalene." The antinomian strain of this work rests not only in Howe's refusal, similar to Hutchinson's, to conform to "the communal consensus of scriptural interpretation" (Caldwell 1976: 351), but is apparent also in the thematics of her text: Mary's direct revelation of Christ is the pivot around which Howe's poem revolves, much as Hutchinson's direct revelation is the focal point of her story. Indeed, I see the image of Anne Hutchinson as enclosed in the figure of Howe's Mary Magdalene—a typological reading that seems appropriate to apply to the work of this late-twentieth-century Puritan. Some of the themes already examined in the previous chapters of this book reappear in my analysis of *The Nonconformist's Memorial*, as the New England Puritan sensibility of Howe's work (delineated in chapter 2) and Howe's commitment to "lift[ing] from the dark side of history" (*Europe of Trusts* 14) the silenced, forgotten, and often female voices (examined in chapter 3) come together in what may be considered Howe's most spiritually propelled work.

A final word to close this lengthy introduction: one may ask how this usage of the term *antinomian* is different from the avant garde, which is, in Richard Kostelanetz's words, art that, like the antinomian, "violates entrenched rules" (1982: 4). Specifically, the antinomian writer, as I read her, is situated firmly *within* a tradition as much as she is in defiance of that tradition. While Howe's work is avant-garde in the sense of being out front and "forging a path that others will take" (3), her work is also always moving backward, deeper into its own historical territories. This paradoxical position of concomitant "forwardness" and "backwardness" seems to me to be a pivotal trait of Howe's experimental poetics, as is her understanding of all historical territory as defined by the personal and the cultural both. By utilizing the term *antinomian* I mean also to evoke the particularly Puritan traits of Howe's traditional framework.

A Bibliography of the King's Book or, Eikon Basilike (1989)

In November 1637, in the town of Newton, New England, Anne Hutchinson was brought to trial for heresy, with Gov. John Winthrop presiding over the court. Just over eleven years later, in January 1649, in Westminster Hall, London, King Charles I was tried for "High Treason, and other Crimes and Misdemeanors" (Royston 1662: 446). Certainly, the differences between the two trials seem more apparent than their similarities, the former trial revolving around religious issues with a colonial woman of no special status and little power as defendant, while the latter involved international and internal political conflicts, with the sovereign ruler of England himself standing accused. And yet, on examination of the transcripts of the two trials, similar patterns of exchange emerge, leading one to consider the possible resemblances between these controversies. In the first four pages of Hutchinson's trial, over 50 percent of her responses to her accusers are not explanations or defenses of her deeds, as one would expect, but are rather questions directed *back* at her judges. Twice Winthrop finds himself pulled into a discussion with Hutchinson on a point of scriptural interpretations; twice he catches and attempts to extricate himself and set the trial back on course. By challenging traditional linguistic interrogatory roles—that is, that a question should be answered with an answer and not with another question—Hutchinson subverts the trial format, transforming the courtroom into a debating hall (Hutchinson 1768: 484–485). Similarly, Charles I also subverts the trial format by questioning the court. His unexpected response to the charges leveled at him is to ask "by what Power I am called hither . . . I would know by what Authority (I mean, lawfull; there are many unlawful Authorities in the world, Thieves and Robbers by the highwayes; but I would know by what Authority) I was brought [here]" (Royston 1662: 429). Incessantly throughout the four-day trial, Charles reiterates this same question regarding the court's authority, while the prosecutor, William Bradshaw—upon understanding that Charles will not offer a reply in his own defense—continues with the trial procedure of arguing the stated charges and sentencing the defendant. As in Hutchinson's trial, a conflict of language usage unfolds, with each man locked inside his own language system, unable—or rather, unwilling—to understand the other. Bradshaw himself identifies that he and Charles are in fact not speaking the same language, as is evident in his charge to the king that the latter is "not to have liberty to use *this language*" (434) and that he "may not be permitted to fall into *this discourse*" (439; my italics).

At trial's end Hutchinson was sentenced to banishment, which eventually led to her death;[5] the king was sentenced to beheading. After their sentences were read, as though attempting to stave off the severity of their situations and avoid the foreboding silence of their immediate futures, both defendants tried to reassert themselves in the courtroom through speech—only to have the privilege of speech denied them. Hutchinson's final recorded words were: "I desire to know wherefore I am banished," to which Winthrop replied curtly: "Say no more, the court knows wherefore and is satisfied" (Hutchinson 1768: 520). Similarly, Charles asks to speak to the court ("Will you hear Me a word, Sir?"), though Bradshaw disallows it with the following reply: "Sir, you are not to be heard after the Sentence" (Royston 1662: 446). To the end, the two conflicts revolve around differential language usages, and one hears in the two prosecutors' strikingly similar silencing tactics a desire to close the controversy in the only way possible—by eradicating the other's language altogether. By the same token, the prosecutors sought to eradicate what they interpreted as other representations of the antinomian woman and the "treasonous" king respectively: the stillborn, possibly deformed, baby to which Hutchinson gave birth after the trial and the book *Eikon Basilike*, some portion of which Charles penned between the time of his imprisonment and of his beheading. For their opponents, Hutchinson's and Charles's "issue"—baby and book both—were taken as material manifestations of their heresy and crimes. Thus the deformities of Hutchinson's baby were interpreted as "visible *figura* of [her] 'misshapen opinions'" (Kibbey 1986: 113),[6] while the vanity, hypocrisy, and literary inferiority that Milton and other Parliamentarians read in Charles's book were understood as representations of "[the King's] palpable faults, and . . . deformities" (Milton 1962: 341). The "monstrous" nature of baby and book needed to be exposed to public view: the former was dug up from its grave, while the claims of the latter were refuted point by point in an effort to expose its declared defects.

I open my consideration of Howe's *Eikon Basilike* with this lengthy analogy between the trials of Anne Hutchinson and Charles I, and the aftermath of those trials, for several reasons. Firstly, I mean to foreground the chronological coincidence of the New England Antinomian Crisis and the English regicide to provide a wider backdrop for the images unfolded in Howe's *Eikon Basilike* and to suggest the possible impact the two controversies may have had on their Old World and New World counterparts.[7] Secondly, the theme of language production—and reproduction—as multiple and unstable which emerges as central to our understanding of the Antinomian Controversy informs also Howe's reading—and rewriting—of the story of King Charles I and, more significantly, her reading and rewriting of the ensuing authorship controversy regarding the king's book. Finally, the tendency of the participants of the seventeenth-century Antinomian Controversy to fuse "the material shape and figurative image," as exemplified by their attitude to Hutchinson's baby (Kibbey 1989: 112), serves as a useful entryway into understanding both the seventeenth-century response to the king's verbal and visual image as presented in *Eikon Basilike, The Pourtraiture of His Sacred Majesty in His Solitude and Sufferings,* and Howe's twentieth-century version of Puritan iconoclasm in her *Eikon Basilike.*

Published within a few days—by some reports, within a few hours—of the king's execution, *Eikon Basilike* has been called "the most influential book of the [seventeenth] century," second only to the Bible and Foxe's *Acts and Monuments* (J. P. Kenyon qtd. in Loewenstein 1990: 164 n. 3). At first believed to have been penned by the king himself, the collection consists of "essays, explanations, prayers, debates, emblems and justifications of the Royalist cause" (*Eikon Basilike* 1). Thirty-five English editions of the work were reprinted in 1649, with an additional twenty-five issues published in Ireland and abroad—"an event perhaps without parallel" in publishing history, according to the bibliographer Francis F. Madan (1950: 2). Perhaps fueled by the guilt of a people who did little to save their sovereign,[8] the book transformed the image of the king from that of a controversial, at times corrupt, ruler into "a powerful icon of a martyred Charles I projected and fashioned with considerable visual and rhetorical art" (Loewenstein 1990: 51). The potency of the book was evident not only in the number of editions printed in a single year but also in the government's response to the work: attempts were made to censor it and control its circulation, in part by imprisoning the printers and publishers of the book. As these attempts mostly failed,[9] the government commissioned Milton to write a refutation of the claims set forth in the king's book, in an effort to expose it as fiction. In October 1649, *Eikonoklastes—* Milton's "longest and most sustained revolutionary polemic"—was published (51).

The publication of *Eikon Basilike* was notable not only for its popularity and impact on public opinion, but also for sparking "one of the most famous of English literary controversies" (Madan 1950): the dispute regarding the text's authorship. The *Eikon* was supposed to have been written by the king, but almost from the start the authenticity of this authorship was suspect. At the Restoration, the divine John Gauden claimed he had written the text; though his advancement to the see of Worcester "in recognition of this service to the Crown" (*Eikon Basilike* 2) seems proof enough that he was believed, the authorship controversy continued. In their bibliographic studies of *Eikon Basilike*, both Edward Almack and Francis F. Madan assembled pages of data, meaning to devote their work to descriptions of each material edition; however, "the vexed question of authorship kept intruding itself" (4). Basing their arguments on approximately the same set of data, Almack and Madan drew different conclusions, for "[i]n each case," writes Joel Kuszai, "their reading of the *Eikon* was mediated through what they already believed true."[10] What becomes most apparent in this authorship controversy is the high stakes involved and the desire on both sides to assign a *solitary* signature to the text. What in fact emerges from the controversy is a case for "dual authorship" and the notion of this text—and, through Howe's poetic use of the controversy, all texts—as "work freely adapted . . . from imperfect and scattered material" (Madan 1950: 132).

Many of the aforementioned details are laid out in Howe's prose preface to her *Eikon Basilike,* entitled "Making the Ghost Walk About Again and Again," where she attempts to provide a framework for the poetic "picture of violence" that she has "unleashed" and which she herself recognizes at composition's end as "so unclear, so random" (Foster 1994: 55–56). Indeed, in certain ways, Howe's *Eikon* is her most difficult and destabilizing work, confounding attempts to authoritatively name its intentions. Visually and thematically it is a tremendously *crowded* text—with words, ideas, and images vying for space on the page and in the book, abutting on and, at times, overtaking and obscuring each other.[11] Historically, the text is firmly and almost completely situated amidst the seventeenth-century events, though the three-page historical framework of the preface, while necessary, is—Howe implies—also beside the point, for dates, names, and claims pile up, contradict each other, and, in the end, prove nothing. It is, finally, the *material* text that Howe turns to—firstly, in the actual edition of Edward Almack's bibliography of the king's book that serendipitously ends up in her hands and, secondly, in embracing the bibliographer's role of engaging the text on its most material level: tracking watermarks, listing errata, describing bindings, spines, and all other physical aspects of the text. And yet, even as the bibliographer's role and talents are valued and, at times, adopted, by Howe, her *Eikon Basilike* means to disrupt such "analytic or systematic" approaches to writings, to question the very possibility of compiling "a set of authoritative texts" and to challenge the existence of that which the bibliographer searches for—"*the* original text" (*Eikon Basilike* 4). In the *Talisman* interview, Howe states that *Eikon Basilike* is "about impossibility. About the impossibility of putting in print what the mind really sees and the impossibility of finding the original in a bibliography" (Foster 1994: 63). *Eikon Basilike* is not just *about* impossibility; it is a visual and formal representation of this impossibility.

The "impossibility" of this poetic project is formally evident from the start, from the first fifteen pages of the text following the preface (7–21) which seem to me to be repeated efforts on the part of the poet to *enter into* her subject, only to have that attempt frustrated and to find herself still on the threshold. From and including the epigraph poem of page 7 through the restating of the book's title (in a revised form) and a renewed appeal to the reader of page 21, Howe's *Eikon Basilike* moves through rapid shifts in form, genre, thematic focus, and visual presentation, as though in search of its own starting point. This search leaves reader and writer on the margins of the text and, as such, these fifteen pages may be considered what Gerard Genette calls "paratextual"—"those liminal devices and conventions . . . that mediate the book to the reader: titles and subtitles, pseudonyms, forewords, dedications, epigraphs, intertitles, notes, epilogues, and afterwords" (1997: xviii). The paratextual elements, while not "*the* text," are—as Genette insists—"*some* text" (1997: 7), and the literary production can only be fully understood once these elements are also read closely. In the piling up of paratextual elements in its opening pages, Howe's *Eikon* suggests the possibility of a work composed entirely of the paratextual—the marginal made focal, with *"the* text" postponed or even absent. Genette argues that it is the role of the paratextual elements "to present" the text—that is, "to *make present,* to ensure the text's presence in the world" (1997: 1). Perhaps Howe's experimental use of the paratextual is meant as a double motion of both making the book present in the world while making present *the absence* of the single, authoritative text.

The epigraph poem that is the poetic beginning of this text rewards lengthy consideration, as many of the major concerns and techniques of Howe's *Eikon Basilike* are embedded in this opening page. The authorship controversy surrounding Charles's *Eikon,* the role of print in not only presenting a text but also in manipulating the reader's conception of *what a text is,* the notion of the text as a coded message and, finally, the function of the visually iconic in the original *Eikon* are all brought to the fore in this short opening poem. Indeed, I have named this text the "epigraph poem," as it seems to me to serve as a motto for the book as a whole, in addition to being situated on a prefatory page and including an identifiable—albeit fragmented—quotation in the form of Pamela's prayer. The debate surrounding the authenticity and, for Milton and other supporters of the regicide, the legitimacy of Charles's book is foregrounded in this religious supplication—"Oh Lord / o Lord"— that opens the text (see fig. 4.1). Pamela's prayer in Sir Philip Sidney's *Arcadia,*[12] said to have been "stolen" by King Charles I for *his* "Praier in a Time of Captivity," utilizes this form of appeal four times in twenty-four lines. This appearance of a prayer almost identical to that of the pagan shepherdess' among the Christian king's papers became, argues Howe, "a major issue in the ensuing authorship controversy. Scholars and bibliographers accused Milton of 'contrivance' in procuring the insertion of her prayer among the King's last devotions in order to ridicule the authenticity of the gathered notes and essays. The charge has been confirmed, and denied" (*Eikon Basilike* 3). By opening her text with an evocation of these prayers and, consequently, an allusion to the ensuing debate, Howe foregrounds the questions of literary "originality" and "ownership," and the reality of the "layered" text. In *Eikonoklastes,* Milton argues that Charles's *Eikon Basilike* is a reprehensible text in part because of Charles's repeated usage of words not his own, most pronouncedly in the case of "a Prayer stol'n word for word from the mouth of a Heathen fiction praying to a heathen God" (Milton 1962: 362). Making what seems to be an early appeal for some type of copyright regulation,[13] Milton argues that "every Author should have the property of his own work reserved to him after death as well as living," and that by using Sidney's text, Charles has trespassed "more than usual against human right" (365). This very notion of an author as "the originator and therefore the owner of a special kind of commodity, the work" seems linked to the print culture of the early modern period (Rose 1993: 1). As Walter Ong has argued, it was the sixteenth- and seventeenth-century shift from "manuscript culture" to print culture that gave rise to this perception of a text as "set apart . . . from other works . . . its origins and meaning as independent of outside influence." Manuscript culture, Ong states, "had taken intertextuality for granted. Still tied to the commonplace tradition of the oral world, it deliberately created texts out of other texts, borrowing, adapting, sharing the common, originally oral, formulas and themes, even though it worked them up into fresh literary forms impossible without writing. Print culture, [however], . . . has a different mind-set" (1988: 134). With Pamela's aborted prayer as its first words—a prayer that was, allegedly, reused by the captive king and that may be read as Howe's *own* appeal to spiritual forces before setting out on her writing project—Howe's *Eikon* opens with a challenge to this "different mind-set" of print culture, insisting that even the printed text is, at all times, pulling from and relating to works that preceded it, and that no word, poem, or prayer is "the possession" of an isolated writer. "What I put into words is no longer my possession," asserts Howe in her earlier critical work *My Emily Dickinson*. "Possibility has opened" (13). Howe's work is at all times committed to *enacting* the ongoing possibilities embedded in the creation—and reception—of poetry.

The role and impact of print is a crucial concern of Howe's *Eikon,* as might be expected in a poetic text that purports to be—in some fashion—a bibliography.[14] Clearly, Howe extends the concerns of the bibliographer by not only describing the material object created by print but also by considering print's manipulation of the reader's attitude toward that material object. Ong argues that in addition to fostering a sense of "private ownership of words," print culture also "encourages a sense of closure, a sense that what is found in a text has been finalized, has reached a state of completion" (132). Howe's *Eikon* is intent from the outset on countering that sense of the literary text as "closed" or "completed." Thus the epigraph page provides a wide field of typographic and orthographic deviations that result in an "incomplete" or open poem. The very strangeness of the poem's words—words which may be misspellings ("comand," "woule," "obwructions"), archaisms ("aud," "doe") and/or printing errors ("Mne," "envions," "nnfortunate," "un ust," "Futnre,")—transforms the printed poem into a text in process, with every word containing several possible readings within it. "[W]oule"—which seems most likely a

Oh Lord
o Lord
different from
Laws
zeal
transposed   OMne
                  envions   obwrucutions
beěng
                                 comand

nfortunate Man
                s

un ust
woule
Futnre
audPaged doe of Title-page

Fig. 4.1. The epigraph page of Howe's *Eikon Basilike*.

misspelling of "would"—has within it at least two other shadow-words: the "world," which has just been described as "un[j]ust," and the "wool," which Arachne weaves on the final page of Howe's *Eikon*, wool which is the material that leads both to her triumph as artist and to her downfall.[15] Similarly, "envions" may be read as "envious" (with the *n* turned over to make a *u*) and thus a reference, perhaps, to those who are envious of virtue (as in the case of those who hold Pamela captive), of power (as in the case of the Parliamentarians who capture Charles and bring him to trial), or even of the poet and her creative talents; or the word may be read as "environs" (with the *r* dropped from the text) and thus a reference of the captive shepherdess or captive king to her/his prison environment, to the "brazen" walls later evoked (14) and which stand in the way of freedom.[16] The strangeness of the word, of almost every word in this short opening poem, makes such doubled interpretations possible, even necessary, and results in a text that refuses to settle into a singular reading.

The sense of unsettledness is also emphasized by the placement of words and isolated letters on the page. As though the page itself were a slippery surface, letters tumble off line—as with the *s* that seems to belong on the line above it, as a possessive ("[u]nfortunate Man/[']s // un[j]ust / wo[r]l[d]") or as a "to be" contraction ("[u]nfortunate Man / [i]s"—with the modifier missing, indicated unfortunate man's absence or silence—both apt descriptions of the beheaded king), or drop off the page altogether, their absence marked by a telling gap between letters (as in "un ust," which I read as "un[j]ust") or signaled by a group of letters that have closed up around that which is missing but remain illegible and meaningless as they stand (as in "Mne," which I read as "M[i]ne"). A similar situational unruliness is apparent in the inverted and slanted placement of words on the page—a typographical deviation that obstructs normative, left-to-right, line-by-line reading procedures and transforms one's progress through the poem into a matter of individual choices and preferences.[17] Thus, the uniformity and stability commonly fostered by the printed text are challenged and, finally, undermined by Howe's epigraph poem, replaced by a sense of drifting letters and migrating words—a twentieth-century counterpart to the "drifting texts [and] migrating manuscripts" of preprint scribal culture (Eisenstein 1979: 124). In addition, the deliberate printing errors of this opening text reflect the workings and manipulations of the print-intermediary on the received literary text and expose the printer's fallibility. Howe may be suggesting here, and throughout the *Eikon*, that the bibliographer's—and canon-maker's—search for "the print-perfect proof of intellectual labor" needs to be replaced by a recognition that the essence of literary meaning may be found elsewhere, that the "heart" of the text "may be sheltering in some random mark of communication," among and within the text's "cancellations, variations, insertions, erasures, marginal notes, stray marks and blanks" (*Birth-mark* 9).

The unconventional spellings and word placements of the epigraph poem may also be read as a type of encoding, particularly as the motif of clandestine messages is a central thematic and formal thread of the *Eikon*. C. V. Wedgwood writes that King Charles I had always had "a taste for intrigue," and during his imprisonment he responded to the real dangers of his situation by capitalizing on this early propensity: "He became used to writing a feigned hand, to sending and receiving coded letters which were hidden in a laundry basket or slipped into the finger of a glove" (1964: 34).[18] Following Charles, Howe too seems to be sending encoded messages in her *Eikon*, utilizing various encoding strategies, which include the letter inversions and letter substitutions of the epigraph poem, writing between the lines (17), or superimposing text upon text (13–15, 18, 39, 45, 48). The reason for the encoding, I believe, is not only to evoke the historical reality and dangers surrounding the captive king, but to hint at the dangers (of hostility, of erasure, of misrepresentation) waiting for any writer choosing a mode of literary expression that fails to conform to expectations and conventions.[19] The encoding tactics are meant also to foreground the layered nature of every literary work and the impossibility of conclusively decoding a text. This impossibility is hardly seen as a limitation by Howe, since it is in each reader's individual engagement in the decoding process, and within each reader's willingness to withstand a certain degree of not knowing—to accept and even celebrate what Perloff calls the text's "mode of undecidability" (1981: 44)— that the transformative power of a text resides.[20] In the epigraph poem, I hear the reader being addressed—in code, of course—through the *u* (you) that is three times inverted ("envio[u]s," "[u]nfortunate," and "Fut[u]re"), more unruly than any other letter on the page and, as a result, set apart from the others. The authorial *i*/(I)—dropped from "M[i]ne—is absent, authorial intention unknown; the *u*/(you) is the reader who will, in the end, make the text, and remake it on each rereading. Indeed, the "doe" of the epigraph poem's final line, a seventeenth-century spelling of *do,* addresses the reader and the author both, enunciating the creation imperative that propels the text—a creation process that relies on the acceptance, even embracing, of the multiple, the varying, and the unexpected of a text.[21]

Finally, a word about the visual impact of the epigraph poem: Pamela's prayer intersecting the text at an angle from left seems a representation of the light beam touching the king's praying figure in the famous frontispiece of Charles's *Eikon Basilike* (see fig. 4.2).[22] The protrusion of lines toward the right margin of this page produces the effect of a profile to the right—the profile of the king kneeling in his chapel, his eyes turned toward heaven and his hands holding a crown of thorns. Potter points out that throughout his life—and death—Charles was "a king of images," preferring the visual self-presentation to the verbal (1989: 57), and this posthumously printed figure of the king-become-martyr became a fulfillment of Charles's self-fashioning preferences. In *Eikonoklastes,* Milton lambastes the frontispiece as a "conceited portraiture . . . drawn out to the full measure of a masking scene and sett there to catch fools and silly gazers" (1962: 343), and the very virulence of the attack indicates Milton's full awareness of the powerful effect of the portrait. Howe directly mentions (34) or alludes to this frontispiece five more times in her *Eikon* ("King in profile / to the right" [17]; "The King kneeling" [19]; "of Gold of Thorn of Glory," a reference to the portrait's three crowns [22]; "The exactly half-face" [32]), equally aware of and interested in the impact of that visual icon specifically and her own visual/verbal icons more generally. Thus, at poem's opening, Howe inserts this text that is meant to be *perceived* in addition to being read and that is, like all visual poetry, in some way "devoted to the cult of the image" (Bohn 1986: 5).[23] Paradoxically, this devotion to the "cult of the image" is coupled with the Puritan's zealous commitment to liberating oneself from this cult and its constraints; hence, Howe identifies also with the iconoclasts and, as her text proceeds, it is the shattering of images that is visually represented.

The shattering of images is preceded, however, by the breaking of formal conventions. Thus the epigraph poem, which serves as an introduction to central motifs and techniques and establishes an expectation that the body of the text will follow shortly thereafter, is succeeded by a title page (see fig. 4.3).[24] The highly unconventional placement of this title page *after* the prose preface and the epigraph poem radically challenges the norms of textual sequencing, exposing the degree to which the reader has internalized these norms and is, in fact, psychologically imprisoned by them, unable to consider other sequencing alternatives. The heterodox title-page placement is an antinomian gesture of rejecting the accepted doctrines of formal arrangement. As in much of her work, Howe is here intent on making the marginal and marginalized central, on focusing attention on the seemingly insignificant and the often overlooked (that is, copyright date, publishing house) in a commitment to considering how the literary product came to be in the world, and on claiming and integrating into her poetry every inch of textual

Fig. 4.2. The frontispiece to King Charles I's *Eikon Basilike* (1649).

space. "The invitation (and challenge)," writes Genette, "is to *read*, with vigilance as well as knowledge," these paratextual elements and "to become through this reading a collaborator in the ongoing literary construction" (1997: xvii).

Obviously, this title page is unconventional and striking not only due to its location in the book but also due to Howe's bold crossing out of Almack's name and publisher and inserting her name and publisher in their place. Howe is not content with just appropriating Almack's title as her own; as visually represented in this title page, she is *writing over* Almack's text. Instead of obscuring the written-over text, as one might expect, Howe's crossing-out technique keeps the primary text—and hence its influence—fully visible in her own. With Bloom's well-known notion of a writer's "anxiety of influence" apparently irrelevant to her, and with none of what he identifies as the twentieth-century writer's crippling sense of belatedness, Howe *foregrounds* her dependence on the texts that precede her, operating from a poetics wherein "books are not individually authored works of art but textual productions caught up in a web of quotation and rewriting" (Miller 1988: 6)—a poetics of the "matted palimpsests" (DuPlessis 1990: 126). Thus, Howe's self-proclaimed project of writing "*against* the Ghost" (*Eikon Basilike* 20; my italics) uses the preposition not in its standard sense of being "in opposition to," but rather in the sense of being in close contact with (as in "leaning *against*") or having as a backdrop (as in "dark colors *against* fair skin"). In similar terms, Pierre Macherey describes a book as "a figure against a background of other formations, depending on them rather than contrasting with them" (1978: 53). In all her writings, and in the *Eikon* in particular, Howe emphasizes this "leaning against" the ghost of previous texts—the ghost whom she first identifies as that of King Charles I but quickly recognizes as being also "the ghost of Hamlet's father, Caesar's ghost, Banquo's ghost, the ghost of King Richard II" (*Eikon Basilike* 2). Every image is *written over* earlier images, with the prior half crossed out by the new, though the old remains legible and present. "Dominant ideologies drift"—are temporary and unsteady—Howe writes four pages from the end of the *Eikon* (50), but literary and historical figures—and, by extension, literary and historical texts—continue repeating and reenacting the stories of their predecessors:

Charles I . . . is "Caesar"
Restless Cromwell . . . is "Caesar"
Disembodied beyond language
in those copies are copies.

A Bibliography of

The King's Book

or Eikon Basilike

BY ~~EDWARD ALMACK~~

(MEMBER OF THE BIBLIOGRAPHICAL SOCIETY.)

susan howe

LONDON

BLADES, EAST & BLADES

23, ABCHURCH LANE, E.C

1896

paradigm press
providence

Fig. 4.3. The title page of Howe's *Eikon Basilike*.

Howe's "poetics of the palimpsest" is, finally, a celebration of cross-genera-tional and cross-genre communication between writers—a joyful acceptance of the literary continuum within which every writer creates *and* a defiant resistance of canon-making critics who work to delimit the multitude of literary and historical voices available to subsequent generations of writers. The writer's individual context while in the act of creation—"This still House / An unbeaten way / My self and words"—and the writer's always unique perception of and engagement with what precedes her—"The King kneeling / Old raggs about him" (*Eikon Basilike* 19)—is what produces the new and the stimulating artwork. "One book overlays another book, one life another—a palimpsest," writes Blanchot, "where what is below and what above change according to the measure taken, each in turn constituting what is still the unique original" (1993: 289).

Though thematically operative throughout this work, the notion of the poem as palimpsest—a document that has been written on several times, with remnants of earlier, imperfectly erased writing still visible—is visually promi-nent in the opening, paratextual pages of the *Eikon*: including the crossed-out title page, six of these first fifteen pages have lines written over other lines, words superimposed on and intersecting each other, passages partially erased. The effect of these palimpsest poems is multifold: firstly, the writing-over-writing gives the page a sense of *depth* that affects reading strategies. Indeed, surface horizontal and vertical reading procedures prove inadequate as the palimpsest poem gives the page the semblance of three-dimensions and, consequently, asks the reader to look *behind* letters in addition to look-ing *at* them. This "looking behind" letters emphasizes the materiality of the literary product and the letters themselves become in these painterly poems an extension of the many other material aspects of the text—watermarks, paper quality, typesetting errata, bookbinding variations—which interest and engage Howe as poet/bibliographer.[25] The bibliographic and the linguistic are, in Jerome McGann's terms, "a double helix of perceptual codes," and for Howe—as for Blake and Dickinson, who are the subjects of McGann's imme-diate inquiry—"the physique of the 'document' has been forced to play an aesthetic function, has been made part of the 'literary work.' That is to say, in these kinds of literary works the distinction between physical medium and conceptual message breaks down completely" (1991: 77). The writing-over-writing of the palimpsest-poem transforms the "physical medium" of the page into a site of meaning and transforms the reader of the palimp-sest—like the poet/bibliographer who gathers "Driest facts / of bibliography

/ Scarce tract work" (*Eikon Basilike* 23) for the ongoing interpretative process and tracks down "water-marks / in the Antiquity / The Sovereign stile / in another stile" (24)—into a fervent "seeker" (23, 24) after the half-erased and the partially forgotten embedded in every written document. The notion of a text's depth and its three dimensionality is emphasized also on page 18 of Howe's *Eikon*, where the odd-angled passage starting "He bowed down" and continuing until "O make me / of joy" is, in fact, lifted from three pages earlier (15).[26] The effect of this verbal and visual repetition suggests the text as a physical imprint of what precedes it, as though the ink shapes from the earlier text have leaked through the intervening pages. Thus the reader needs to "look behind" not only individual letters but also behind the pages themselves. The text as physical object, written over and constantly being redefined, is emphasized also in the whimsical description on the penultimate page of Howe's *Eikon*, quoted from Charles Dickens's *The Personal History of David Copperfield*, wherein a manuscript about Charles I's beheading has been made into a kite that has "plenty of string . . . and when it flies high, it takes the facts a long way" (*Eikon Basilike* 52).

The writing-over-writing technique produces the additional and no less significant effect of *simultaneity* of voices—and of tales—speaking at once, cutting into each other and being, visually and aurally—as well as thematically—at cross-purposes. "In Howe's case," writes Craig Douglas Dworkin, "the political 'battle' becomes inextricably intertwined with the 'babble' of noise" (1996: 398). Thus, the Royalist voice likening Charles to Christ in the passage "crucified by ordinance" that opens the radically ruptured text of pages 14 and 15 is interrupted by a voice in support of the regicide, naming Charles as responsible for "[t]hat sea of blood" that characterized the civil wars.[27] Neither voice is given priority, and the reader must negotiate—and tolerate—the resulting cacophony. Indeed, the third effect of the writing-over-writing technique is to visually represent discord, disorder, and even violence on the page. For the tale of Charles I in particular, Howe states, "there was no way to express [the conflict] in just words on the page. So I would try to match that chaos and violence visually with words" (Keller 1995: 8). That "chaos and violence"—visually foregrounded in the aforementioned palimpsest poems—thematically permeate Howe's *Eikon*: "To walk side by side with / this chapter was Tumult" (*Eikon Basilike* 38), writes Howe halfway through her text, and "Arriving on the stage of history / I saw madness of the world" (40). In the poetic engagement with this violence, the visual and thematic complement each other, as is apparent in the palimpsest image of the be-

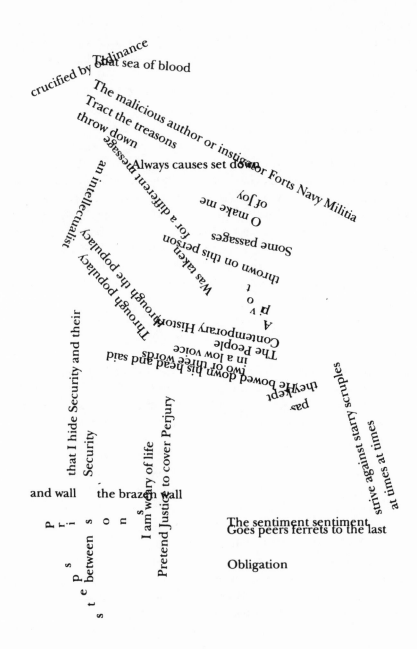

Fig. 4.4. Page 14 of Howe's *Eikon Basilike*.

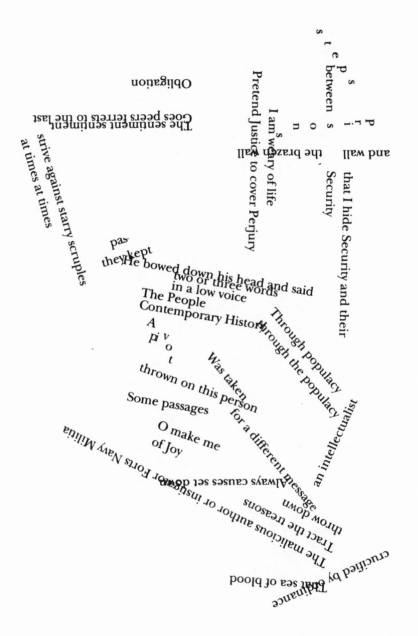

Fig. 4.5. Page 15 of Howe's *Eikon Basilike*.

headed Charles I figuratively written over the image of the beheaded Sir Tho-
mas More,[28] who is quoted and thus introduced into the text in what may be
considered an additional epigraph to the main text (12).[29]

The physical violence resulting from power struggles alluded to through-
out Howe's *Eikon* is coupled with a recognition of the force, sometimes vio-
lence, existent in words themselves. Charles's *Eikon* itself was described by
coauthor Bishop Gauden as "an army, and did vanquish more than any sword
could" (McKnight 1996: 39), and Cromwell is reported as having charged
his military council to "'keep a party of able pen-men at Oxford and the
Army'" as a crucial component in the continuing armed struggle (Cromwell
1647, qtd. in Achinstein 1994: 137). Achinstein herself writes that "[a]s the
volume of writings published during the revolutionary period suggests,[30]
books were prime ammunition in what was becoming a war of words" (137).
Utilizing the same metaphor as Gauden and Achinstein both, Howe calls
"Mrs Gauden's Nar- / rative"[31] regarding her husband's role in the composi-
tion of the king's book "a weapon" (*Eikon Basilike* 30) and, in the midst of
what should be a sedate search through a labyrinth of bibliographic and
linguistic data, Howe finds herself stopped short by "Blades Blades & Blades"
(23). Of course, the triple "Blades" not only allude to the pervasive violence
of the historical scene but are also a reference to the name of Almack's
printer—Blades, East & Blades—with the revision of the name foregrounding
the cutting, even killing, power of all that exits the publishing house and, by
natural extension, of the publishing house itself.

The theme of verbal violence also takes the reader back to Milton's fierce
rhetorical dismantling of Charles's *Eikon Basilike* and his breaking "to peeces"
the image constructed therein (Milton 1962: 343). David Loewenstein has
argued that Milton's iconoclasm was "a profoundly radical, creative, and lib-
erating response" (1990: 55), which meant for Milton, among other things,
"breaking the image of the past" (62). Loewenstein continues: "Leo the Icono-
clast is the prototype for this Puritan iconoclast who, however, realizes his
vocation not with the hammer but with the pen: his is a verbal iconoclasm
whose literary techniques of satire, irony, invective, and revisionary narrative
prove . . . just as powerful, disruptive, and liberating as the physical breaking
of icons and statues" (66). The radically disrupted and chaotic poems on
pages 14 and 15 of Howe's *Eikon* (see figs. 4.4, 4.5) seem to me to be not only
representations of violence, but also enactments of violence in this tradition
of Puritan iconoclasm.[32] Like Milton before her, Howe uses the pen as ham-
mer to dismantle an image that appears flawless, complete and deserving of
adoration; unlike Milton, whose target is the image of a martyr-king as por-

trayed in a book, Howe's iconoclastic target is the image of the book itself—
any book, any literary product—as complete unto itself without reference to
what precedes or succeeds it, as "closed" once printed and as containing
within it one authoritative meaning. Pages 14 and 15 are the image of the
poem broken "to peeces" and "filled with gaps and words tossed, and words
touching, words crowding each other, letters mixing and falling away from
each other, commands and dreams, verticles and circles" (Foster 1994: 63).
In place of the set image—the literary equivalent of the stationary statue—
shards of figures move across the page, movements that match the allusions
in the text to Charles's plodding steps from prison to scaffold, to the crowd's
insistent push to view the beheading ("Through populacy / through
populacy), and to the furtive fleeing from detection ("Goes peers ferrets")
and capture ("Was taken") of those still at odds with the forces in power.

On closer examination, and after accommodating the strange and unique
look of pages 14 and 15, one also notes that these two pages are, in fact,
mirrored and inverted versions of each other. Rotating around the "pivot" in
mid-page, the upside-down passages of page 14 are turned right side up on
page 15, and vice versa. This "mirroring impulse" is prominent in much of
Howe's work,[33] and Howe herself identifies the use of this technique as an
expression of her sense that these verbal reflections strengthen the impact of
the visual design on the page (Keller 1995: 9). However, I believe that every
usage of the "mirroring impulse" carries within it a meaning specific to the
thematics of its text, over and beyond Howe's general interest in the visual.
Thus I read the mirrored and inverted pages of Howe's *Eikon* as evoking the
two images of Charles reflected in the *Eikon* and *Eikonoklastes* respectively: in
the first, Charles is a martyr figure, emblem of all that is good and pious; in
the latter he is portrayed by Milton as tyrant, wherein evil and deception
reside. These two versions of Charles I are, of course, *inversions* of each other
and both, in their own ways, are icons, though the latter is what may be termed
a "negative icon"[34]—deserving religious revilement rather than worship;
Milton the iconoclast not only casts down an image but, as Loewenstein
notes, "radically refashions it as well" (1990: 67). "To break an image," states
Kenneth Gross (as quoted by Loewenstein) "is not necessarily to break away
from images [as we need also] to look closely . . . at the forms or fragments
left behind and at what was raised up in their place" (67–68).[35] By using this
mirroring and inverting technique in these poems of rupture and conflict,
Howe foregrounds the similarities between the political goals and rhetorical
strategies of the Royalists and the regicides, each side intent upon erecting a
single version of events, a single portraiture of the king. Howe also fore-

grounds the "ambiguity inherent in any dealing with icons"—negative or otherwise—as "both intention and interpretation [of an icon] are subjective, ultimately unknowable qualities—qualities not of the icon *but of the icon-user*" (Cable 1990: 135; my italics). Finally, by placing these two "versions" of the same text side by side so that they figuratively reflect each other, Howe counters the authority, legitimacy, and limits of the monovocal tale with a wild and open field of multiple readings.

Toward the end of her *Eikon* and re-evoking the animal imagery first introduced in the epigraph poem, Howe writes:

A poet's iconoclasm
A bestiary of the Night

I am at home in my library
I will lie down to sleep

A great happy century
A little space among herds
(*Eikon Basilike* 43)

The poet's iconoclasm—Milton and Howe's both—is identified here, in the calm tone of standard verse couplets, as "a vital artistic principle" (Cable 1990: 142) that produces strange, untamed, and illuminating shapes: "A bestiary" in the night sky. The poet's iconoclasm, for all its violence, is also recognized in these lines as leading eventually to an inner peace, the individual artist having created for herself something unique and new, "A little space among herds[.]" This "little space" is aurally echoed in the "*ace* of speechstone / Spelling surname" two pages later—these two lines written over each other and standing alone on the white page (*Eikon Basilike* 45; my italics). The alliteration of "speechstone" and "Spelling" leads one to hear the absent "sp" on "ace": the (sp)ace for artistic speech—small and hard as a stone, embedded within like a peach pit—is typographically intertwined with the poet's surname, a reference of course to "*Ikonoklastes,* the famous Surname of many Greek Emperors, who in thir zeal to the command of God, after long tradition of Idolatry in the Church, took courage, and broke all superstitious Images to peeces" (Milton 1962: 343). The antinomian poet as iconoclast recognizes the necessary dismantling of hegemonic structures as a clearing of space for her own "speechstone."

A final word on the notion and representation of creative space in Howe's *Eikon:* in the poem's opening pages, which I have identified as paratextual due to their prefatory nature, an obvious *absence* of space is apparent. In these pages Howe's *Eikon* moves through—at times lingers amidst—the visual, linguistic, and thematic crowds of multiple voices, numerous typographic experiments, and changing genres. Only on pages 20 and 21 does the work fully emerge from these crowds, into the open textual space of poems that I have marked as the last two pages of the paratextual. On each of these pages, three lines stand mid-page, amidst an abundance of white space and textual silence—space and silence that stand in sharp contrast to, but are also clearly a direct outcome of, the chaos, cacophony, and crowdedness of the pages that precede them. As prefatory statements, both pages enunciate through repeated imperatives how writer and reader are to proceed in their respective tasks of writing and reading the work in hand: the writer

> Must lie outside the house
> Side of space I must cross
>
> To write against the Ghost

I read "[t]he house" as representing the concrete structures of the Western canon wherein the master narratives reside; this house must be exited, and the "[s]ide of space" around it crossed, in order for the poet to write her poetry. However, the poet does not travel far from "the house" but rather lies outside it—that is, in close proximity to it—just as the "Ghost" of all the literature that precedes her is leaned "against" as a crucial and intimate part of her creative landscape. "The aim [of the avant-garde poet]," writes Perelman, "is simultaneously toward a lineage and a singular point of openness" (1996: 44). The radical iconoclastic poetry of *Eikon*'s opening pages is the visual representation of this poetic imperative to liberate oneself from the confines of "the house" in order to enter/create from a place of openness, even as the textual material used in these pages is, in large part, appropriated from within that house. The house image, and the poet's lying just outside it, also evoke the threshold motif utilized by Genette in his discussion of the paratextual (1997: xvii), though in this penultimate page of the paratextual, through this statement of personal poetics, one senses that Howe and her *Eikon* are no longer located *on* the threshold but have moved *across* it, into the clarity and calm of open textual space. Indeed, this sense of movement is apparent in the directive appearing on the following page to "STay Passenger / BE*hold* a mirror."[36] The reader is addressed as a passenger, aboard a text that is, perhaps, like the boat present in some versions of the *Eikon*'s famous frontispiece and alluded to later in Howe's *Eikon* as an "Oak cleft to splinters" amid "a sea raging" (*Eikon Basilike* 34).[37] Because the reader may feel engulfed by the abundance and unruliness of this poem's fluid materials, and because there is always the risk of drowning in a text as chaotic and unsteady as Howe's *Eikon* ("Eating our bread heads / we wonder under water," 34), the poet asks— in fact, demands—the reader's patience and endurance: "STay. . . ." With the phrase that follows ("BE*hold* a mirror")[38] the text may be promising that if the reader *does* persevere, she will find in this work not only multiple reflections of one tale, but a reflection of herself engaging with the multiple, the variant, and the unstable, and in that process liberated from the constraints of authoritative readings that support "the legitimation of power, chains of inertia, an apparatus of capture" (*Birth-mark* 46).

The phrase "BE*hold* a mirror" is lifted from Madan's bibliography, wherein it is recorded as an epitaph to miscellaneous poems relating to Charles's *Eikon* (Madan 1950: 100). However, the original phrase is "BEhold the mirror," and Howe's two simple revisions—italicizing *"hold"* and changing the definite article to an indefinite article—are telling. The italicizing of *"hold"* foregrounds the materiality of the text/mirror by emphasizing its tactility; indeed, at times the reader has no option but to physically engage with the book, to turn it upside down and at odd angles in order to read and decipher the text contained therein. This "holding" also foregrounds the sense of an intimate engagement with the work—that the work comes into being by figuratively and literally "being held" and, through this process, the reader is transformed "from a passive consumer into active participant in the genesis of the poem" (Richard Sieburth qtd. in Howe, *Birth-mark* 19). Howe's second revision of this short phrase stresses the singular and nonaxiomatic nature of the text ("<u>a</u> mirror" and not "<u>the</u> mirror") and of the individual engagement with the text. In fact, the shift in articles in this epitaph-like phrase prefigures the play of articles apparent throughout Howe's *Eikon*. "A First didn't write it" (*Eikon Basilike* 22), proclaims Howe on the first page following the paratextual, and the seemingly categorical nature of the statement (that Charles I didn't write *Eikon Basilike*) is undermined by the indefinite article at its start, which leads one to read more generally: whoever *did* write *Eikon Basilike*—Charles I, John Gauden, or perhaps some other ghost writer (Mrs. Gauden?)—was not "a first" but rather a "continuer"[39] of her/his literary tradition. Countering the paralyzing force of literary conventions that support the notion of "a first"—or the possibility of there being "*the* Truth" (32), which is, after all, only "*a* truth / Dread catchword THE" (32; my italics)—is, without a doubt, one of the prime objectives of Howe's *Eikon*.

A central trope of Howe's *Eikon Basilike* that deserves closer consideration due to its dominant presence in the text is that of the theater. Throughout this text, the world of drama, its conventions, components, and effects, are repeatedly evoked and utilized as an organizing motif; in fact, over one-fourth of the poems in the *Eikon* contain a theater reference, and already on the second page of the prose-preface Charles I is compared both to the "fictive ghost-king" in *Hamlet* and to Shakespeare ("writer-actor"), who acted that role (*Eikon Basilike* 2). I have previously discussed Howe's personal connection with the theater through her actor/playwright mother Mary Manning and her own early theatrical aspirations, and there is no doubt that the preponderance of these drama metaphors and allusions in her *Eikon* are bound up also in Howe's biography. However, I read the stage imagery in this text as directly emanating from specific concerns of Howe's *Eikon* and as particularly influenced by the manner in which the main players in the *Eikon*'s historical/literary drama—Charles I and Milton—themselves made use of the theater trope, in their lives and in their literature. "It is important to note," remarks Lois Potter, "how completely, until his death, Charles I was a king of images rather than words." She continues with the following explanation for this characterization: "Perhaps his speech impediment contributed to his preference for self-presentation through visual rather than aural means, but he made it a matter of choice as well as necessity" (1989: 157). In this "self-presentation through visual rather than aural means," Potter is certainly referring also to Charles's particular affection for, patronage of, and participation in the dramatic form of the court masque wherein dialogue was minimal, plot and action slight, while costumes, scenery, and other elements of pageantry were all lavish, meant to enrapture through visual appeal. A turn to acting, as metaphor and as mode of behavior, is also evident at crucial moments in Charles's life, most dramatically at his beheading: upon the "scaffold"—a word denoting also the stage for theatrical exhibitions—Charles most certainly had to be aware of his audience in his final moments when "He stood, with hands and eyes lift up, immediately stooping down [then] He laid His Neck upon the Block; ... bade [the executioner] 'Stay for the Signe.' After a very short pause, His Majesty Stretching forth His Hands, the Executioner at one blow severed His Head from His Body" (Royston 1652: 456). Charles's control until the end and his use of dramatic gestures (hands and eyes lifted upward as in prayer or prophecy, arms outstretched upon the block) that would be seen by "the populacy" even if his words were not heard made his execution, [40] as Howe herself notes, "a performance; he acted his own death" (Keller 1995: 8).[41] Bishop Juxon's comforting words to Charles on the scaffold that "[t]here is but one Stage more, this Stage is turbulent and troublesome, it is a short one" refer in the original to the "stages" of man's life; however, as quoted by Howe in her *Eikon* they are doubtless meant to conjure up also the performing stage, with the scaffold as the last one upon which Charles must perform.

John Milton, the second central player in the historical/literary drama surrounding the seventeenth-century *Eikon Basilike,* also turned to theatrical tropes as an organizing motif of *Eikonoklastes,* though his objective was not to dazzle with a performance but rather to "undeceave" (1962: III, 366) the thousands who had been "fatally stupifi'd and bewitch'd" (III, 347) by the king's acting in his final days and by the stellar posthumous literary performance contained in *Eikon Basilike.* The people are but "fools and silly gazers" if they are taken in by the "conceited portraiture" of Charles in that book, argues Milton, as "quaint Emblems and devices begg'd from the old Pageantry of some Twelf-nights entertainment at Whitehall, will doe but ill to make a Saint or Martyr" (1962: III, 342–343). As Loewenstein notes, throughout his polemic against the king's book, by interpreting the representation of Charles's image "in terms of its theatrical counterparts—role-playing and self-fashioning,"[42] Milton is suggesting that "the royal icon and text"—like theatrical performances in general and the court masque specifically—"are equivocal fictions," not to be believed and certainly not to be worshipped (1990: 55, 60).[43] Indeed, Milton's strategy in attempting to shatter the royal image so well crafted in *Eikon Basilike* is to repeatedly point out to the reader the text's scenery, costumes, and props that hide the "real" king, and his errors and faults, from view. I believe that Howe's use of theatrical tropes, like Milton's, is connected to her interest in which person(s) and whose voice(s) stand behind a text's "disguise" (24) or its "Mask Visor" (38); however, unlike Milton, Howe does not expect to find a single-hued person (not tyrant or martyr) or a consolidated voice behind that mask and costume. The truth for Howe, which is always "a truth" (32), is that "sowdayne" (sultan) and "sowter" (cobbler [12]), king and antic, canonized poet and marginal bibliographer, all share each other's roles in this diffuse and dense historical/literary drama. Thus, in this *Eikon,* Howe herself is "bewitched" by Milton (37), just as Milton felt seventeenth-century readers were "bewitch'd" by Charles I, and the "Real author of *The Lie*"[44] (Charles? Milton?) is always multiple, "fallible unavailable" (32). Naming Charles's *Eikon* "an imposture" (28) and Charles a "Personator" (32) is, for Howe, descriptive rather than judgmental: "Saying so[,]" she proclaims, "I name nobody" (28).

Two final points regarding the use of theater motifs in Howe's *Eikon*: firstly, theater may be considered a literary art form that provides a bridge between the oral and the printed and thus maintains more openness, fluidity, and self-awareness of its own protean nature than does the printed text. Because the performed drama is always, to use Walter Ong's phrase regarding sound, "an event in time" (1988: 76) and is to a large degree "receiver-dependent"—that is, in need of and contingent on its unique and always different audience in order to fully exist—it can never be "closed off," stable, or definitive, but is, instead, always subject to change within the "circuit of communication in which speech [and nonverbal exchanges] take place" (Culler 1975: 131). As Gerard Genette so aptly says of the paratextual, the performed drama is "always transitory because transitive" (1997: 408). It seems to me likely that Howe evokes the world of theater as extensively as she does in the *Eikon* in order to lend her printed word/world some of these "transitory" and "transitive" traits of theater. Instead of a text that presents itself as verbal icon—sacred and set (in this case, in print)—Howe's *Eikon* emphasizes its own flexibility and fluidity.[45] In addition, the reader of the text, like the audience of a performed drama, is named from the very beginning of the *Eikon* as the work's "object" ("To the Reader / the work" [*Eikon Basilike* 11]); from "the High Quire" (44), s/he surveys the scene and the staging, watches the unfolding of the drama on the page, and is left to make meaning of the scattered, sometimes shattered, pieces of the tale(s).[46]

Which brings me to my second and final point regarding the theatrical tropes in this work: one can read Howe's *Eikon* not as a rewriting of history but rather as "an attempt to 'restage' it" (Kuszai 3). Howe herself describes her craft in directorial terms, saying that "[s]ometimes I think what I'm doing on the page is moving people around the stage" (Keller 1995: 13). Using what McGann calls "performative typography" (1991: 155), Howe stages on the page the conflicts, confusion, and violence of the seventeenth-century historical drama and the ensuing literary debate. Thus, prosecutor Bradshaw and defendant Charles I face each other on page 13, their respective lines remaining in opposition as they vertically intersect the "normative" text that describes how "now nonexistent dramatis personae / confront each / other[.]" The line break between "each" and "other" of course emphasizes the gap that will not be bridged between the Royalists and the Parliamentarians. Similarly, the vertical lines separating the three words of "IN | HIS | SOLITUDE |" not only represent the printer's symbol for a line break but also enact Charles's solitude—the lines severing the words from their natural unit just as prison walls cut Charles off from the world around him—and represent also, I believe, the aloneness of the printer who left "No further trace" (*Eikon Basilike*

11). Obviously, the already discussed visual violence and chaos of pages 14 and 15 (see figs. 4.4, 4.5) ask to be read as a restaging of the execution scene, with the mid-page phrase "He bowed down his head and said / two or three words / in a low voice" on page 15 catching one's eye first and keeping one's focus; the reader, like the seventeenth-century scaffold audience, is transfixed by the figure of the kneeling king about to put his head on the block. The fashion in which the second line of this passage ("two or three words") crowds into and is partially obscured by the line preceding it enacts the manner in which Charles's final words were not heard by the people, were in fact lost to the executioners' stage-management. Obviously, such examples of "performative typography" abound in Howe's *Eikon Basilike;* however, I would argue that Howe's restaging of history—and her reflections on the relationship between history and staging—are not limited to the sections in her text where experimental printing techniques are utilized. Throughout the work, in the constant piling up of materials—bibliographic ("C * R and skull on covers / MADESTIE / . . . / King on the binding / 1 blank leaf" [31]), historical ("Milton described as 'late of Westminster,' is said to be hiding to avoid trial" [41]), and personal ("I feared the fall of my child / resting quietly with some hopes" [40])—Howe is re-presenting and, in the process, redefining as still evolving, the dramas of King Charles I and of the enigmatic king's book.

The final theme I want to examine in my analysis of Howe's *Eikon Basilike* is that of the gendered antinomian, represented by the female subject appearing midway in the text and, in multiple guises, hovering over the poem for a number of pages, only to disappear and then reappear more forcefully at the poem's close. Infiltrating the wholly male-dominated seventeenth-century historical scene and ensuing literary debate, this "she"—who is first many and finally resolves into the single figure of the weaving Arachne—slowly and subtly cuts through the text's preoccupation with the violence of that period and the chaos and futility of searching for "origins on paper," insistently shifting the focus of the poem toward the creative act itself. The female signature on this creative act, in isolated resistance to dominant ideologies and in defiance of social and literary hierarchies, again evokes the figure of Anne Hutchinson and, through her, the notion of the antinomian as gendered feminine. "She is the blank page / writing ghost writing[,]" explains Howe in her *Eikon* (31), and the reader is to understand that this nondesignated female pronoun—an amorphic "writing[-]ghost" and she who does "ghost[-]writing" both—is as much the "absent center" of this poem as is "the ghost of a king" (*Eikon Basilike* 4).

At the exact middle of Howe's *Eikon*,[47] on four consecutive pages and again one page later (28–31, 33), various female figures enter Howe's text, the presence of one inviting that of another. The first female entering the text ("In his sister's papers/ they often had discourse" [28]) is situated and identified by the male possessive pronoun "his," her unnamed existence entirely dependent on whose sister she is. However, while this sister's dependent state is grammatically emphasized, her identification is only partial, as *what* famous brother the text is referring to is not stated. From the context of what follows, the most logical inference is that the sister is Milton's; however, I was unable to uncover any record of papers in which such a "discourse" between Milton and his sister, Anne Phillips Agar, took place. Indeed, the indeterminacy of the reference and its resistance to clear resolution leads one to read it as multiple; thus the figure standing behind "his sister" takes shape not only as Milton's sister, but as Sidney's and King Charles's sisters also. The point of the possessive with no referent is that so little is known of these sisters, of their influences on their creating and/or powerful brothers, and of their own creative aspirations.[48] Within this framework, one is led to read in the figure of "his sister" a reference also to Virginia Woolf's famous fictive portrait of Shakespeare's sister, the "wonderfully gifted" Judith, who—despite her desires and talents—is destined never to write a word but rather, in shame and desperation, unable to support herself let alone create art, kills herself "one winter's night[.]" Buried "at some cross-roads where the omnibuses now stop" (1957: 50), the fictive Judith Shakespeare is resurrected through Woolf's insistence that "[s]he lives in you and in me, and in many other women who are not here tonight, for they are washing up the dishes and putting the children to bed. But she lives; for great poets do not die; they are continuing presences; they need only the opportunity to walk among us in the flesh" (117). This same "she" of unknown potential and untold desires, living her short life against the backdrop of a male relation's fame and achievement, walks through Howe's text in various shapes: she is sister of a famous man, she is the fictive captive shepherdess "out of a fictive legend" (29), and she is the faithful wife, Mrs. Gauden (30), who keeps her family safe by keeping her husband's secrets. Howe's representation of this female complicity is itself half buried, half encoded in a lyric appearing ten pages after the first reference to Mrs. Gauden, where Howe writes:

Opposers or despisers
Night page torn word missing

The family silence

gave up the ghost[49]

I feared the fall of my child

resting quietly with some hopes

as a bird before any
                    (40)

In the face of the violence surrounding the publication and authentica-
tion of the king's book—"Opposers or despisers" of the king fiercely attempt-
ing to first suppress and then deligitimate the book and thus short-circuit
its impact—"the family silence" alone keeps the Gaudens safe. I read the enig-
matic shift in focus away from the literary debate and onto a child "resting
quietly with some hopes"—together with the abrupt appearance of the first-
person pronoun—as Mrs. Gauden's strained voice entering the text, recog-
nizing the danger to the family of the beheaded king's ghost-writer and nam-
ing her maternal fears. Of course, this version of the tale is nowhere repre-
sented in the history narratives or the bibliographies, and even in Howe's
retelling the account remains fragmented, like the visually fragmented "Nar-
/ rative" from ten pages earlier (see note 31). With the final line on this page
incomplete, the modifier *any* left dangling and the simile disrupted, Mrs.
Gauden's voice fades out, perhaps to suggest that as long as she is in the tale
with no identity of her own, her ability to tell this tale, or any other, is partial
at best, and she herself is destined for oblivion and silence. Phrased differ-
ently, *our* ability to retrieve her lost voice can have only limited success, with
so few historical markers to guide our imagined re-creations.

Thus the desire to establish a female presence in her text by evoking the
historical women (Mrs. Gauden, Milton's sister, the Countess of Pembroke)
who figured (however slightly) in the drama surrounding the *Eikon Basilike* is
frustrated by these women's partial or complete inaccessibility: they are
mostly ghostlike, with little shape and practically no voice. Nonetheless, Howe
continues trying to "flesh out" and name the female figure present in this
work. From a "seeker / of water-marks / in the Antiquity" (24), Howe be-
comes a seeker of female tracks marking her literary landscape. On page 33,
she writes:

Face toward the Court silence

Scope of the body politic

Mock alphabet and map

Daniel's way was to strew ashes
Ashes strewn on his path

Daniel's way Daniel's way
Archaic Arachne Ariadne

She is gone she sends her memory

The confusing and multifaceted conflict between the Royalists and the Parliamentarians crystallized around the conviction of each side that they alone were truth-tellers and that they would "undeceive"—specifically through their literary endeavors—those deluded by their opposition. Thus this lyric's opening allusion to this conflict, as represented by the scene of Charles I on trial ("Face toward the Court silence // Scope of the body politic"), leads Howe to think of "Daniel's way" of "undeceiving." "Daniel's way" refers to the tale in the Apocrypha[50] in which Daniel exposes the deceit of the worshippers of the Bel, who claimed evidence of their god's existence in the disappearance of the abundant food nightly laid out for him. By strewing ashes on the floor, which later revealed the footprints of Bel's priests, their women and children, who entered the temple through secret doors in order to eat the food themselves, Daniel proved to the king that Bel was but an idol and his priests nothing but frauds. An early iconoclast, Daniel destroys the idol and his temple, while the king executes the lying priests. Howe repeats the phrase "Daniel's way" three times in as many lines, as though ruminating on these "undeceiving" tactics and their simple and certain strategy of literally making the truth visible by exposing the footsteps of the deceivers. However, Howe concludes that "Daniel's way" of reaching the truth is "Archaic," belonging to an ancient religious/mythological framework where absolute right as represented in the figure of Daniel is undisputed and, inevitably, triumphant; in the early-modern conflict surrounding Charles I, she is suggesting there is no absolute right, and the "Justice Justice" called out in the trial hall (33) could as easily be the voices of supporters of the king demanding his vindication and release as the voices of supporters of regicide calling for the king's punishment for crimes committed.[51]

In this lyric in particular, the reader witnesses Howe's associative and aural leaps and the way her poetry follows tracks laid by language: thus, the sound and look of the word *archaic* with its opening *a*, its rounded *r* immediately following, and its hard *c* sound in midword leads to *Arachne*—a word of similar aural and visual attributes.[52] The interconnection between these words also exists on the level of meaning: like Daniel, Arachne is archaic, belonging to the world of classical and founding myths; like Daniel, Arachne is proud, defiant, and uncompromising in her beliefs. The language links do not stop at *Arachne* but continue on to *Ariadne,* and one suspects that an internal logic of symmetry leads Howe to provide a threefold "answer" ("Archaic Arachne Ariadne") to the thrice-repeated "Daniel's way." Obviously, the figures of Arachne and Ariadne are linked not only through the half rhyme of their names but through the common material central to each woman's identity and tale: the thread or wool that both women use, Arachne to weave her tapestries, Ariadne to lead her beloved Theseus out of the Minotaur's labyrinth.[53] This thread may not uncover "the truth" as Daniel's dust strewn on the path means to do, but Howe seems to be suggesting that it can prove useful in leading one out of the labyrinths of artistic conventions, toward the freedom of one's individual creating impulses. Through the remainder of her *Eikon,* Howe points out literal and figurative threads that abut on the thematics of her text (the unclear reference to a "Threat[d] cord flung" in the famous frontispiece [31]; the "light blue silk / strings" binding the collected works of King Charles [51]; Mr. Dick's kite that has "plenty of string" so it may fly high with the facts [52]), as though establishing a threaded line for reader and writer alike to follow.

Though the thread metonymic of them both is repeatedly evoked, Arachne and Ariadne themselves disappear from Howe's *Eikon,* reappearing only nine pages after they are first mentioned. When they do reappear, they are no longer embedded between passages concerned with Charles and his conflict, but instead occupy a page and a landscape of their own. In addition, the force of their presence is amplified, I believe, by the addition of the goddess Athena:

> Election- Vocation-
> Justification-
> Cape of wind wreathe
> fame out laughing
> Seated on cloud
> Seacret drift
> seacretly behest
> the dear She
> comes to all Guilty
> all circling

Eye window soul body
Pride cannot bow
Ariadne's diadem
zodiac helmet belt
(42)

I read the "dear She" of this poem—echoing the unnamed "She" who is the text's "blank page" (31) and the Arachne/Ariadne "She," who "is gone she sends her memory" (33)—as a cluster image of Arachne, Ariadne, and Athena all, three separate stars that together compose a single zodiac unit. Thus the one "Seated on a cloud" is Athena on her Olympian throne, Ariadne whose "diadem" Bacchus sets in the heavens as compensation for Theseus's abandoning her (*Metamorphoses* VIII, 176), and Arachne, who is described as perched amid the "fleecy cloud" of her wool (*Metamorphoses* VI, 121). Similarly, the strange phrase "seacretly behest" can be read as referring to all three female figures: firstly, Ariadne is evoked as she who unravels the "seacret" of the labyrinth at the "behest" of her beloved, and within this "seacret" is inscribed her fate—to be abandoned at *sea* by this same beloved on his journey home. Athena comes in "seacret," disguised as an old woman, as though at the "behest" of some maternal instinct, to give the motherless Arachne advice and an opportunity to change her prideful ways. Finally, Arachne is alluded to, I believe, through the deviant usage of the noun "behest": positioned in the syntactic role of a verb ("seacretly behest") and interacting with the thematics of the *Eikon,* the word *behest* seems to serve as a shadow word for *behead.* While Arachne is not actually beheaded, her final fate carries some of the attributes of a beheading: in her transformation into a spider, her hair, nose, and ears fall off and "her head shrinks tiny" (III, 125).

The final three lines of this lyric provide some separation between the women, foregrounding a trait emblematic of each. "Pride cannot bow" is a clear allusion to the simple "girl of Lydia" Arachne, whose pride in her weaving skills could not be curbed or denied, though it would inevitably lead to her downfall. "Ariadne's diadem" is the double mark of both Ariadne's earthly royal stature and of her celestial "eternal glory" once her crown is placed among the stars, its gems "turned to gleaming fires" (VIII, 176). Finally, Ariadne's astral emblem evokes the zodiac sign of Athena, the warrior goddess, whose identifying props include the "helmet [and] belt." Howe may be suggesting that these three mythological female figures—in their defiance of norms and expectations, in their refusal to conform though they will be judged "Guilty" (Arachne of pride, Ariadne of disobeying her father, and Athena of the envy that led her to destroy Arachne's tapestry though it equaled

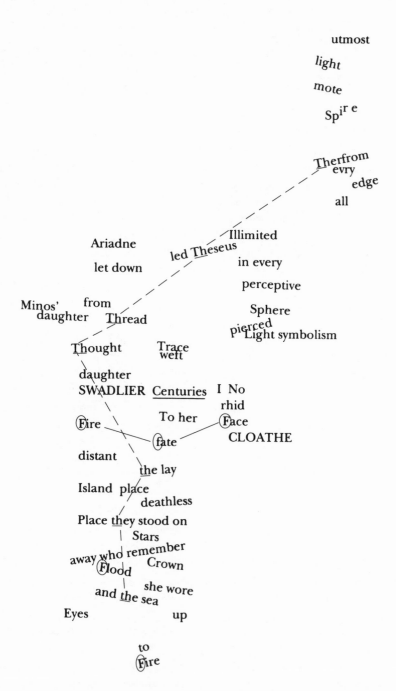

Fig. 4.6. Page 49 of Howe's *Eikon Basilike*, "Ariadne's Page" (with alliterative tracks marked).

Silk

symbolic

Praeparative

faith

Ariagne

Idman   satter

the   s e t
      Penned

stars
ARACHNE SUN'S
deft   ray

through

She   s h i e l

was   T shhr ieeal dd

winding trace

wool   weft

Cloud

soft

threada

twist

Fig. 4.7. The final page of Howe's *Eikon Basilike*, "Arachne's Page."

hers in craft and inspiration)[54]—represent the antinomian model central to the poetics and thematics of Howe's *Eikon*. Indeed, all three women "represent a contradiction to canonical social power" (*Birth-mark* 1) and each, in her own expression of refusal and defiance, is intent upon subverting the hierarchical order that in some way means to silence them. The pride and defiance of these female figures, and of Arachne in particular, evoke the antinomian Anne Hutchinson, described in her trial transcripts as being "a woman not only difficult in her opinions, but also of an intemperate spirit," whose words are proof enough of her "vanity and heat of . . . spirit" (Hutchinson 1668: 490, 511). Hutchinson's Puritan framework is evoked also through this lyric's opening reference to "Election," the Calvinist doctrine of predestination wherein only God's "elect" few will be saved. It seems likely that Hutchinson believed herself to be one of the elect; however, what resonates more forcefully for me is the sense that she seemed to have of herself as being chosen to *speak out*. Howe's own notion of the poet is not of one who chooses her art but rather she who—like the Puritan "Elect"—is "chosen," one whose artistic expression is both a sacred "Vocation" and "Justification" of self in the world. "Being a poet is a calling," explains Howe, "[y]ou are called and you must listen" (1995: 33).[55] I read the triple noun phrase at this lyric's opening—capitalized and linked with hyphens—as Howe's explanation of the unconventional choices made by Arachne, Ariadne, Athena, and Ann as expressions of deep-rooted faith (in their talents, in their god, in their desires): like clergy, they were called and they had no choice but to listen.

Two final pages of radical visual experimentation (49 and 53, the last page of Howe's *Eikon*) continue the exploration into the tales of Ariadne and Arachne respectively (see figs. 4.6, 4.7). While not inverted mirror versions of each other like the verbal images of chaos on pages 14 and 15 (figs. 4.4, 4.5), these two pages are similarly designed (both pages are organized around columnlike arrangements of words) and both revolve around similar thematic material; hence, I read these closing pages as a counterpoint to that earlier literary iconoclasm. Indeed, by the *Eikon*'s end, the need to shatter images seems to have subsided and in place of that violent "breaking to peeces" (Milton 1962: 343) is a calmer, always unfettered, movement of words down and around the page. On both these final pages, words are printed at a slant and upside down, in boldface or regular print, with their letters ascending or descending like a staircase ("Spire," "trace," "weft"), or spaced and encompassing within that space another word ("Thread / shield"); there is, however, none of the "writing over" or sense of words being cut up, and the pages are less crowded than earlier in this poem. Through the female figures of Ariadne and Arachne, away from the authorship debate and regicide drama—though emanating from them—Howe establishes a space for individual speech, as evoked (and concomitantly obscured) in the crossed-over lines of page 45. This space for speech is predicated on the principle of *not* bringing "[t]he production of meaning . . . under the control of social authority" and, most apparently, on *not* bringing "the line . . . into line" (*Birthmark* 140). Indeed, in the poem/picture of page 49, which I will refer to as Ariadne's page, there are no horizontal lines of text; instead, the page is roughly organized around three columns of words. The reader's eye is directed first to the upper right corner of the page, where the vertical arrangement of words suggests a towerlike structure, a "Spire" where "light" ascends and which provides a wide view of "evry / edge / all[.]" This "Spire" recalls the "High Quire" from five pages earlier (44) that kept the text's only communal "We" at a distance; seemingly, Howe is now inviting her readers, and compelling herself, to come down from a distant critical perch, down from the bibliographer and researcher's intellectualizing height, down to the multicurrented sea and site of Ariadne's inconclusive tale. The spire imagery also evokes the Tower of London, where prisoners were held, and Howe may be suggesting through this visual allusion that in the eye's descending movement down the page is embedded a promise of literary freedom.

The left column on Ariadne's page, with its semijustified left margin and uneven extensions rightward, can be read as the "historical" retelling of Ariadne's tale, with the major elements of the plot all in place (how she, "Minos' daughter," "led Theseus" with "Thread" out of the labyrinth; how she was then left "To her / fate" on a "distant / Island"; how she acquired a "deathless" stature through Dionysus's intervention and his placing the "Crown / she wore / up" in the sky, to be stars and celestial "Fire"). I read the middle column on this page, starting with "Illimited" through "Face," as evoking the emotional outcome of the left-column plot: by virtue of acting to attain her desired object, by virtue of refusing the limits of family bonds and expectations,[56] Ariadne—as imagined by Howe—experiences a sense of liberation and an ensuing surge of creative possibility ("in every / perceptive / Sphere / pierced / Light symbolism"). The cryptic lines "I No / rhid / Face" may be deciphered as "I nor hid [my] face"—perhaps Ariadne's declaration that the act of "provid[ing] the thread that unravels the maze" (Miller 1988: 92) is itself empowering and results not only in Theseus's freedom but in her own, as represented by her refusal to cover her face in conventional female modesty. This momentary freedom, however, is finally outweighed by the two uppercased words on Ariadne's page: "SWADLIER" and "CLOATHE." Both neologistic words evoke some type of concealment or restriction, the first through its relation to the notion of swaddling clothes and the second as an orthographic merger of "cloak" and "clothe." The weight of these words is, of course, obtained through their typographic singularity: they are the only uppercased words on the page and, hence, ask to be read as authoritative. Indeed, Ariadne's liberation is fleeting: she is soon trapped on the island where Theseus abandons her, and her revelation of self is quickly concealed by literary obscurity[57] as her tale of desire, maze-deciphering, and desertion is overwritten by Theseus's tale of male heroism.[58]

While Ariadne may, by the end of page 49, be partially "swaddled" or covered up by the weight of the male literary tradition wherein she figures slightly, Ariadne's thread as a trope of that which marks a trail into and out of the labyrinth is forcefully represented in this page's elaborate and musical sound map. The labyrinth that is the text may not yield to a single interpretation, but it can be engaged—entered—by following the thread of language links; thus the alliteration of the "th" sound leads the reader from the spire's "*Th*erfrom" through "*Th*eseus," "*Th*read" and "*Th*ought," down to the lower-page and lowercased "*th*ey" and "*th*e sea." The trajectory of the alliterative connection is from the height of light possibilities (how her tale might have unfolded differently), through the link Ariadne establishes between the thread and her beloved, down to her place of island captivity, surrounded by "*th*e sea" (see fig. 4.6). The alliteration of the *d* links "down," "daughter," "distant," and "deathless," as though painting in those few words the portrait of Ariadne (with its own mid-word *d* sound). An additional alliterative track is that of the *f,* which creates a mid-page triangular link between the sky's "Fire," Ariadne's "fate," and her "Face" revealed, which are all linked also to the "Flood" of island sea around her and to the again repeated "Fire" of her crown gems become stars. The repetition of the word *fire* suggests the two-sidedness of flames as concomitantly creative and destructive, and this doubled image may be read as emblematic of Ariadne, whose moment of creativity has embedded in it her own destruction. Other words which are twice repeated on Ariadne's page ("light," "daughter," and "place") may also be read as emphasizing the complex and conflictual aspects of her tale (the star "light" that symbolizes both triumph and defeat; the "daughter" role which—like the swaddling clothes—may provide safety and restriction both; Ariadne's "place," which vacillates between sea and sky). Other language links on this musically and visually labyrinthine page include the rhymes of "lay" and "away" and of "she" and "sea," the pararhyme of "let" and "led," and the alliteration of "I," "Island," and "Eyes." Finally, the language links lead the reader at the page's end back to the beginning through the rhyme of the final word "Fire" with "Spire" at the top of the page, and the circular direction of the word path represents the coiled nature of the textual maze.

The final three lines on Ariadne's page lead, I believe, to the figure of Arachne, to the final page of Howe's *Eikon Basilike* (Arachne's page), and to a closing illumination—if not resolution—of this difficult text. "Eyes / to / Fire[,]," writes Howe, alluding perhaps to how we can reconceive Ariadne by turning our eyes toward the only marker left of her, the firelike stars of her crown. However, this passage also evokes both Arachne, who in her defiant stance is described as having "blazing eyes" (VI, 122)—"Eyes" that have in fact turned "[in]to / Fire," and the poet herself, as Howe understands her, as "an animal charmed in one spot, eyes fixed to the light" (*My Emily Dickinson* 97). Indeed, this creating figure, transfixed by an internal light that compels her, *is* Arachne who *must* weave her tapestries, *must* create unfettered by norms of social hierarchies and, hence, *must* defy Athena, "female guardian of the [male] law."[59] Herein rests what Miller names as "the critical difference that separates, finally, Arachne from Ariadne: the making of a text" (1988: 95). Ariadne acts on desire but does not, finally, make anything, and she is remembered mostly as the facilitating and dependent female, deserted and forlorn; in fact, the misspelling of her name with a g ("Ariagne") on the final page of the *Eikon* can be read as the infiltration of a "*gyne*"[60] marker of female presence and Howe's foregrounding of Ariadne's inevitable submission to stereotypically female roles. Arachne, on the other hand, with complete "faith" in her craft and talent, whose "weft" she handles with "deft[ness]," whose boldness is represented both in the word-intertwining of "Thread" and "shield" and in the uppercased font of her name on this final page, is remembered as a maker. It is Arachne in the process of creating her "wondrous work" whom the nymphs come to watch, and it is this early image of her "winding / wool" that closes Howe's *Eikon*. The final eight lines of this page are extracted from the following passage in Ovid's *Metamorphoses'* telling of her tale: "And 'twas a pleasure ... to watch her as she worked; so graceful and deft was she. Whether *she was winding* the rough yarn into a new ball, or shaping the stuff with her fingers, reaching back to the distaff for more *wool,* fleecy as a *cloud,* to draw into long *soft threads* or giving *a twist* with practised thumb to the graceful spindle, or embroidery with her needle" (Ovid 1946: bk. 6). These isolated words—spare and solid crystallizations of the tale—wander vertically down the page, a thread of imagery that highlights the creating *process,* the "doe" of *Eikon*'s epigraph poem. Howe's own craft is evoked here with her insertion mid-page of the word *penned,* and one is to understand that the figure of Arachne, as Howe reads her, prefigures the antinomian Hutchinson, who is "Praeparative" for Howe herself. "My precursor attracts me to my future. Fixed purpose is the free spirit of fire," writes Howe (*My Emily Dickinson* 97), evoking again the sense of the poet as transfixed, not only by the internal fire of inspiration but by the creative/defiant "ghosts" of her past—against whose voices she is always writing, toward whose figures she is always moving (*My Emily Dickinson* 97).

The Nonconformist's Memorial (1992)

Poetry brings similitude and representation to configurations waiting from forever to be spoken.
—Susan Howe, *The Europe of Trusts* (1990)

It is the Word to whom she turns.
—Susan Howe, *The Nonconformist's Memorial* (1993)

The source text against which Howe situates *The Nonconformist's Memorial*— the subject of this chapter's final and briefer analysis—is the "nonconforming" and the last of the New Testament's four gospels, the Gospel According to St. John.[61] John's gospel differs notably, both in content and form, from the three synoptic gospels that precede it[62] and has consequently been the subject of extensive inquiry. Four verses extracted from John's gospel (20:15–18) and placed, epigraphlike, on the title page of *The Nonconformist's Memorial* (henceforth to be called *The NC Memorial*) set the scene for Howe's reimaginings of Mary Magdalene's tale, while the backdrop of the entirety of John's gospel, with its puzzling and unique nature, forwards the trope of the labyrinthine text of uncertain origin introduced and energetically examined in Howe's *Eikon Basilike*. Indeed, the obvious link between King Charles's *Eikon Basilike* and the Gospel According to St. John is that the appearance of both texts on their respective literary, historical, and theological horizons resulted in famous and fierce authorship controversies that inspired vigorous debates, ongoing textual investigations, and impassioned attempts to conclusively assign solitary authorship. Despite these attempts, both controversies have resisted resolution, forcing the reader to contend with multiple production theories and to engage both works within an open intellectual framework wherein the conventional Western understanding of a literary text as a discrete and closed product—and *not* an assemblage of scattered materials and myriad influences—is continually challenged. The question of *who* wrote John's gospel has been designated "the greatest enigma in the entire field of Christian history" and has been named an "insoluble" literary problem (Eisler 1938: 2), while bible critic George Beasley-Murray has argued that "[e]very-thing we want to know about [John's gospel] is uncertain, and everything about it that is apparently knowable is a matter of dispute" (1987: 376). By choosing John's gospel as *The NC Memorial*'s source text, Howe situates her work within this "field of uncertainty," which is, for her, not only an arena of fertile creative potential but also a site that allows, even encourages, the nec-essary rejection of "acts of uniformity" that characterize the canon-making process. The synoptical "act of Uniformity" that Howe refers to in *The NC Memorial*'s opening pages (5)—an "act" which "ejected" from the tradition Mary Magdalene's singular and intimate encounter with the resurrected Jesus in the garden—doubtless alludes also to "The Act(s) of Uniformity"[63] im-posed on the sixteenth- and seventeenth-century English population whereby only the liturgy of the *Book of Common Prayer* was allowed in all houses of worship. King Charles's attempt to enforce this ecclesiastical policy with the sword was one of the central causes of the Civil Wars, with all their bloody results. Emanating from an assumption of grave literal and symbolic dan-gers in attempts to regulate and standardize literary and religious self-ex-pression, *The NC Memorial* is a text committed to celebrating the noncon-forming spirit, first by uncovering the hidden presence of this spirit among the master narratives and then by testifying to its creative potency. In fact, by *The NC Memorial*'s end, one comes to understand that, for Howe, the "Non-conformist" of the poem's title is (also) the poet herself, and the poet *must be* a nonconformist, for the poem is an "immediate *act*" (23; my italics) that always draws its force from going "the obscure negative way," from "Turn[ing] again" and "Moving away" (33) from literary norms and expectations.

An additional link between the source texts of Howe's *Eikon Basilike* and *The NC Memorial* (Charles's *Eikon Basilike* and the Gospel According to John, respectively), and hence a link between Howe's two works themselves, is the figurative or literal "empty-tomb"[64] story at the works' centers. The posthu-mous publication of Charles's *Eikon* effected a type of resurrection of the king, with Charles rising from the grave to tell his own story and, in the telling, to refashion his image. Indeed, one of the central rhetorical strate-gies of the *Eikon Basilike* was to present Charles not only as *a* martyr but as *the* martyr of Christian tradition—as Christ himself, suffering and dying for the sins of others (Potter 1989: 173–174); hence, the powerful impact of the *Eikon* may be understood as intricately connected to this Christological framework wherein the voice speaking beside the "empty-tomb" serves as evidence of divine intervention and is thus endowed with sacred properties. Howe utilizes this same "empty-tomb" trope to describe the Puritan reaction to their part in the regicide: "the execution of Charles was a primal sin in the eyes of the Puritans who killed him. They tried *to bury their guilt.* As in the wonderful Hawthorne story 'Roger Malvin's Burial,' *the body would not stay buried*" (Foster 1994: 63; my italics). Howe seems to be suggesting in this passage that the earliest American sensibilities and, by natural extension, much subsequent American literature (her own included), are in some fashion marked both by an enduring guilt that walks among the people, despite attempts "to bury" it, and by a site of emptiness—or absence—at their core.

What is significant in this "empty-tomb" motif for my reading of *The NC Memorial* is the differential responses of Mary Magdalene and the Beloved Disciple (who is perhaps John and the gospel's author) to their first encounter with this "site of emptiness," as described in John, chapter 20 (in the verses immediately preceding those used by Howe as her work's epigraph). Responding to Mary's report that the stone covering Jesus' grave has been moved aside, the Beloved Disciple rushes to the site, enters the sepulchre (after an initial hesitation),[65] sees the shroud and head-band—"reminders of Jesus' presence, or rather of the presence of his dead body" (Ashton 1991: 506), and markers of the absent body—and infers, apparently, that the resurrection has taken place, as attested to in the verse "and he saw, and believed" (John 20:8). The disciple's response to the "empty-tomb" is a reaction of acceptance and of faith; in contrast, Mary's response is one of engulfing sorrow: "Mary stood without at the sepulchre weeping: and as she wept, she stooped down, and looked into the sepulchre, and seeth two angels in white, the one at the head, and the other at the feet, where the body of Jesus had lain. And they say unto her, Woman, why weepest thou? She saith unto them, Because they have taken away my Lord" (20:11-13)." Mary does not enter the tomb: through some combination of law, tradition, and choice, she stands "without"—on the margins of the site, an outsider looking in, a solitary individual on the fringes. It is her failure—or refusal—to apply an explanatory narrative structure to the "empty-tomb" phenomenon which also places her on the fringes, outside norms of comforting and cohesive interpretation; in fact, it is the repeated reference to her weeping that dominates the description of this scene, foregrounding her experience of the empty sepulchre as a site of sadness and loss.[66] I read Howe's *The NC Memorial* as utilizing this site of primary loss—which is the loss of a father/savior and of the absolute, singular, and authoritative "Word" he represents (John 1:14)—as its premise and point of departure: Mary, with the figures of antinomian Hutchinson and the nonconforming poet (Howe herself perhaps) enfolded in her frame, speaks, "suggesting that something not being said is speaking: the loss of what we were to say" (Blanchot 1986: 21). This "loss of what we were to say," however—painful and difficult as it may be—doubles as a site of liberation, as the speaking individual is situated outside ("without") the constraining limits of literary or theological norms ("what *we were to say*"). Within this context, Jesus' command to Mary in John's Gospel that she not "cling to me" (20:17)[67]—a command that opens *The NC Memorial*—may be understood as the spiritual and poetic imperative of moving *away* from dependence on set forms of literary or theological expression and *toward* the wholly individual, and free, act of self-expression and creation.[68]

Succeeding the opening quotation from John and a two-page poetic-preface that sketches in broad strokes Jesus and Mary's historical landscape ("Contempt of the world / and contentedness // Lilies at this season" [4]) and explains the gospel's textual formulation ("Citations remain abbreviated / Often a shortcut / stands for a Chapter" [5]), *The NC Memorial* is divided into three sections, a triadic structure that—while certainly resonant of the traditional triumvirate of the Father, the Son, and the Holy Ghost—seems more richly and relevantly read as foregrounding the poem's triangular relationship between the figure of Mary Magdalene, the speaking poet, and the reader. All three of the poem's sections, while constructed around different thematic foci and conveying disparate emotional tenors, are involved in repeated attempts to embody the ghostly "I"—who is both Mary and the poet—and to inscribe the listening/witnessing "you"—the reader—in these attempts and in the resultant poetic text. In fact, by the poem's end, one senses that it is *through* the poet's imagined fleshing out *of the reader,* through the immediate and intimate textual interchange between poet and reader, that the shadowy outline of Mary Magdalene—together with other named and unnamed silenced nonconformists that she represents—takes on shape and meaning. The poem is, of course, testimony to this half-erased scriptural figure who is concomitantly—and paradoxically—a disciple and a dissenter both, and, as "all history" is *not* "a progress" (6–7) but rather a repetition of images and reciprocal influences, biblical Mary, the poet, and the reader interact and are interdependent, their three names engraved in a netted pattern into this textual memorial.

I read the first section of *The NC Memorial* as a clustered collage of New Testament scenes involving—however marginally—Mary Magdalene, as though through a recapping of critical scriptural moments in which Mary participated, or which she witnessed, her features and identity may emerge. Naming this identity, however, is continually frustrated by the forceful and text-monopolizing presence of the gospel's male figures (Jesus, John, even the gardener); indeed, Howe's rendition of Mary's identity-seeking question "What am I?" (8; see fig. 4.8) is itself obscured,[69] appearing as it does at the bottom of the page, printed at an angle, half buried and all but illegible beneath surrounding words/pieces from the crucifixion drama. The severity of Mary's self-incognizance as expressed in her "What am I?" question is foregrounded through the sharp contrast between this question and the doubled subject assertion of the "I John" phrase (8–9)[70] and the absoluteness intrinsic to the thrice-repeated divine self-proclamation "it is I"[71] (10; John 6:20). In this latter formulation, the "I" (who is here Christ) in predicate nominative form stands definite and foregrounded by virtue of being situated in an object location, even as it is both in subject form and wholly identified with the sentence's subject. The Christ figure is, of course, the gospel's subject and its object/objective both; the always doubled identity of the savior figure who is concomitantly himself and the path to self-transformation is emphasized through the many material objects metonymically applied to Jesus in John (for example, "I am the bread" [6:41]; "I am the good shepherd" [10:11]; "I am the way, the truth and the life" [14:6]; "I am the vine" [15:5]), and listed in *The NC Memorial* in a breathless two-line rush ("the I is / the bread the light the door / the way the shepherd the vine" [10]).[72] Beside Jesus' abundance of identities stands Mary's spare, mostly silent, uncertain self; and while in another nonconforming gesture she goes alone on "[t]he first day of the week . . . when it was yet dark" (John 20:1) to Jesus' grave, she reports her discovery of the rolled-away stone in the plural form ("They have taken away the Lord . . . and we know not where they have laid him" [20:2])[73], as though she is not in possession of a singular identity. "We plural are the speaker" (11), states Howe, though this "we" carries no promise of companionship and in no way alleviates the severe isolation of Mary's fate (as Howe imagines it): her "solitude lies alone" (13) and "No community can accompany her" (15), her "[i]nner life led by herself" (26). In fact, this "we" has no meaning in and of itself but functions in the text only as a sign marking the site of Mary Magdalene's absent "I"—the "I" whose absence is again marked in the lines immediately following this "we" reference, wherein a list of verbs lifted from the opening of John, chapter 20 (where they describe Mary's actions), are placed subjectless on the page:

Came saw went running told

Came along

Solution continuous chaos

Asked told observed

Caught sight of said said

(12)

Reeled off uninterrupted by subjects, these subjectless verbs foreground the energetic, even frenetic, doings of the missing agent and the urgency of the scene, even as they emphasize the erasure of the acting individual. It is this absent "I" and not the absent body Howe encounters in *her* experience of the "empty-tomb," and it is this absent "I" Howe is interested in restoring to tradition.

The confusion of the dramatic scriptural events as experienced by Mary is conveyed in section 1 primarily (though not solely) through visual techniques, wherein the word is utilized "as a dual sign . . . compris[ing] two sets of signifiers and signifieds—one verbal, the other visual" (Bohn 1986: 5). Thus on the partially mirrored pages 8 and 9 (see figs. 4.8, 4.9), the angled or vertical arrangement of isolated lines over each other and/or intersecting the main text (which is itself printed upside down on page 8 together with the right-angle intrusion of a three-line verse fragment ("Where he says He . . . ")[74] on both pages depict a chaos of events, an unsettling of emotions, and the difficulty of formulating a coherent testimony to these events and emotions amidst the turmoil. *"Testimony"*—or bearing witness—is, of course, the objective of the gospel and *The NC Memorial* both,[75] emphasized on these pages through the foregrounding of the word *testimony* by situating it mid-page and by printing it in italics. In this poem with almost no punctuation and with almost no font variation,[76] the few instances of deviation from standard typeset into italics (*"Testimony,"* 8, 9; *"We,"* 11; *"Transfiguration,"* 16) carry extra force, words spoken in an insistent voice, signaling the urgent agenda of Mary Magdalene and of the poet who through *testifying* to that which they alone have witnessed will themselves be *transfigured*. That which has been witnessed is conveyed on these pages also through pictorial—or iconic—typography, the arrangement of lines in the upper-right quadrant of page 8 representing a crucifix, and the line starting at the bottom right of page 9 and intersecting the text in an ascending leftward diagonal representing the

Fig. 4.8. *The Nonconformist's Memorial*, page 8.

I John bright picture

dark background (Gardener

Must have been astonished

First anything so later

Testimony

More in faith as to sense

Having counted the cost

his hiding is understood

Mortal contained in

a state of separation

Where he says He

Upon the Cherubim

Baffled consuming doggerel

and in deep ocean

The soul's ascension

Fig. 4.9. *The Nonconformist's Memorial*, page 9.

ascension of the Christ figure. While the crucifix image dominates its page, it is tilted, implying perhaps that the "crucifying knowledge" (8) one extracts from this scene—contrary to convention—is anything but absolute and is, in fact, variable and unstable, shifting with each individual act of interpretation. Similarly, Jesus' ascension—traditionally read as a fulfillment of desired divine union—is represented here as involving also a dissolution, the definite upward movement of the single diagonal countered by the words of the line that state "[t]he soul's ascension [is] in a state of separation" (9). I read this "state of separation" as referring specifically to a separation from the known and the well worn, a willingness to "not cling" to conventions in order to set out on a wholly individual, most often isolated, creative path. Separation from scriptural consensus, from established doctrine, and, eventually, from the safeguards of communal life itself characterizes antinomian Hutchinson's life, just as separation from home and haven ("No abiding habitation / . . . / Settled somewhere" [26]; "Isled on all removes" [32]) characterizes Howe's imagined Mary Magdalene, ejected from the Scriptures, exiled from the land, telling her tale of direct revelation of Jesus in "a remote field / abandoned to me" (14). Indeed, this Mary Magdalene is to some degree even separated from self: so wholly absorbed in the truth and demands of her own composition, she discovers that she is "[a]s though beside herself" (25) and even "bereft / of body" (32).[77] "Creation implies separation," insists Howe in *The Birth-mark* (58) and, as such, together with transcendence (the "soul's ascension"), creation always involves a type of exile from known literary and emotional landscapes and a resulting element of loss inevitable and, perhaps, *necessary* in order to uncover the new.[78] "The work," writes Pierre Macherey, "has its beginnings in a *break* from the usual ways of speaking and writing—a *break* which sets it apart from all other forms" (1978: 52; my italics), suggesting (like Howe) that it is through rupture that the rapture of creation is made possible.[79]

The coupling of seemingly discrete, even opposed, forces—of creation and separation, of love and loss—is a central rhetorical strategy of *The NC Memorial* in general and of section 1 in particular. The motif of interconnected contrary states is announced already in the section's title: "nether John and John harbinger" (6). "[N]ether John" refers, apparently, to St. John, who was later exiled to the lower ("nether") island region of Patmos; "John harbinger" is, of course, John the Baptist, traditionally called "the Forerunner of Christ" and depicted in Greek art as having the wings of a celestial messenger. The pairing of these two Johns, representatives of lower and upper regions (and hence of contrasting landscapes), not only symbolizes the meeting point of the earthly and the divine as manifested in the coming of Christ ("And he said unto them ye are from beneath; I am from above: ye are of this world; I am not of this world" [John 8:23]), but also introduces the possibility of varied, even oppositional, narratives contained within each seemingly univocal and authoritative literary, historical, and theological tale. On pages 6 and 7 of *The NC Memorial* (see fig. 4.10), Howe extends this motif of contrasting images by writing the second line in every couplet upside down and by structuring the two pages as reflections and refractions of each other. The "as if" proposition ("As if all history were a progress") becomes the pivot or "the unmoving point around which a body [or text] / turns" (11), and the literal turning of the text around itself operates as material proof that history is not a progression, nor is it "A single thread of narrative," but it is rather a repetition of images, a constant negotiation of contending voices, and a function of reading strategies. *How* one is to read these two pages is unclear, and the reader is left to decide whether to first read the right-side-up lines, then turn the book and read the upside-down text, or to read every couplet as its own unit. Of course, the coexistence of alternative reading possibilities and the refusal to privilege one tactic over another is central to the poetics of this work, and indeed all of Howe's oeuvre.[80] A final word regarding these opening and interconnected pages of section 1: the fourteen lines and couplet structure of these verses encourages one to read this text as a type of sonnet, albeit a radically deviant sonnet. Through the presence of this alternative sonnet form, the love theme of this poem is foregrounded from the outset; indeed, Howe twice describes Mary as "some love-impelled figure" (21, 25), and it is in "the orbed circle" of love (25) that Mary wanders. Clearly, her love (and Howe's) is as much of the "love-impelled" act of narrative formation and self-identification through creation ("Love for the work's sake" [23]) as it is of the originary inspiration/compulsion represented in the figure of Christ.

Mary's embracing of her role as witness and testifier, together with her resulting submission of self to the demands of these word-centered tasks ("It is the Word to whom she turns / True submission and subjection" [30]) are, for Howe, an expression of the "courage to go to the brink . . . [where] love may save you and bring you joy. Love of language" (Falon 1989: 35). The Word—sacred and secular both—is attributed a humanlike presence, as indicated by the objective pronoun *whom* proceeding it ("the Word *to whom* she turns") and, as such, is itself always alive, vital, and subject to change. It is the Word, and Mary's turning to it, that also *effects* change—a transfiguration and resulting liberation represented on the final page of the first sec-

In Peter she is nameless
Actual world nothing ideal

headstrong anarchy thoughts
A single thread of narrative

She was coming to anoint him
As if all history were a progress

As if all history were a progress
She was coming to anoint him
A single thread of narrative
headstrong anarchy thoughts
Actual world nothing ideal

In Peter she is nameless
The nets were not torn

The Gospel did not grasp

Fig. 4.10. *The Nonconformist's Memorial,* pages 6 & 7.

tion of *The Nonconformist's Memorial* (see fig. 4.11). The word *Transfiguration,* printed upside down and cutting across the top of the page (which is also the bottom of the text), traditionally refers to Christ's momentary metamorphosis into a state of shining glory while still on earth (Matt. 17:1–9; Mark 9:2–9; Luke 9:28–36). The transfiguration referred to in Howe's text, however, is not of Jesus but rather of this poem's trinity: of Mary Magdalene, of the poet, and of the reader. It is through Mary's willingness (as imagined by Howe) to risk public censure and persecution in order to speak her own truth, through her finding a voice of her own "to cry out" (15), that she is transformed from a shadowy shape into a fully formed individual; it is through her faith in her own vision that she is freed from the limits of convention and the fear of repercussions. Like Hutchinson, Mary Magdalene may well have claimed that "having seen him which is invisible [and having found the voice to tell of it] I fear not what man can do unto me" (Hutchinson qtd. in *Birth-mark* 3). "Out of enclosure She / was out of enclosure," writes Howe at the end (which is the beginning) of this page: the enjambed first line foregrounds the independence (and isolation) of the "She," together with her precarious location at the edge of open undefined space, while the repetition of the "out of enclosure" phrase highlights the sudden wonder of the transfiguring freedom.[81]

The transfiguration experienced by the poet, I believe, is effected through her poetic commitment to lifting "from the dark side of history, voices which are anonymous, slighted—inarticulate" (*The Europe of Trusts* 14), accomplished in this poem by seeking out the figure of Mary Magdalene ("The motif of searching" [15]) amidst—and in spite of—the meager space allotted her in Scriptures. The poet invites the reader to accompany her on this particular quest, with the implicit promise that a discovery of the erased, external other will result in a discovery of the erased, internal other: "Come then!" writes Howe, addressing the reader, "Feet wrapped in hay / I stray to stray / her knowledge of Me[.]" The enigmatic image of "[f]eet wrapped in hay" may evoke individuals, especially women, through the centuries and particularly in the last years of seventeenth-century New England, burned at the stake for various acts viewed as heresy or dissension, hay "wrapped" around their feet to feed the flames. Through this allusion, Howe may be naming her lineage of dissenting women. However, as this speaker is clearly not bound nor are her movements restricted—she is, in fact, moving "out of enclosure" like her subject Mary (*through* her subject Mary), she is "stray[ing] to stray"—I am inclined to read the "[f]eet wrapped in hay" image as a reference to an actual hay-filled location, a field or meadow, perhaps, which the speaker figuratively was out of enclosure

Transfiguration

Out of enclosure She

So many stumble

going out of the world

Come then!

Feet wrapped in hay

I stray to stray

her knowledge of Me

Hearers of the Face Discourse

Happy to be in peace

know next to nothing

She drank a tumbler-full of water

Often singing

Her body trembled like a leaf

Fig. 4.11. *The Nonconformist's Memorial,* page 16.

crosses in her quest after Mary. "Love may be a stumbling // out on the great meadows" (14), writes Howe two pages earlier, and this "stumbling" in the world (as opposed to those who "stumble / going out of the world"—[16]) seems to be Howe's kinetic equivalent of "stuttering." The "stumbling" and "stuttering" both are the "sounding [or physical manifestation] of uncertainty" (Foster 1994: 67), which is, of course, a natural byproduct of venturing into new and unfamiliar territory. "Would never have stumbled / on the paved road" (14), asserts the speaker, but the "road" that this text traverses is not paved. The notion of "straying" is central here, with its denotations of "wandering . . . beyond established limits" and "becoming lost" (American Heritage Dictionary); for Howe, it is this "straying" that may lead one "out of enclosure." It is the act of writing, of course, that allows the poet "to wander . . . beyond established limits," or, in Emmanuel Levinas's terms, it is writing that "leads to the errancy of being—to being as a place of going astray" (1996: 134). The line "I stray to stray" may be read as standing on its own, so that the act of straying is both means and objective. However, one may also read the second "stray" as referring to the subsequent line: by "straying" into unknown thematic and visual textual territory in order to name, know, and embody Mary Magdalene, Howe hopes to name, know, and embody herself— "to stray" (which is "to wander in or through" obsolete form) "her knowledge of Me." Howe's writing of Mary is, of course, a reading of her, and, as such, it is, in Jefferson Humphries' terms, "immediately reflexive. That is, it reads itself [and its reader/writer] because it constitutes and becomes indistinguishable from its (virtual) object" (1983: xi). Thus the "Me" is transfigured (as indicated by its capitalized form), like Mary and Jesus both—transformed through the act of writing.

However, the transfiguration of Mary (and of poet and reader, too), like the transfiguration of Christ, is an unstable and ultimately fleeting state; one moves from the elation, promised transcendence, and possibilities that mark the end of section 1 to a state of disconnectedness and incompletion that characterizes section 2. The shortest unit in this poem, section 2 seems to hover over what it cannot say, piling up in the process sentence fragments that fail to complete their thought or intention and that contest with the encroaching page space/silence around them. One senses that the poet is stymied by her distance from the original scene and landscape and, despite her ardent desire to imagine forth Mary's tale outside of scriptural bounds, she is overwhelmed by the forceful presence of the master narrative of Western literature—the Bible—and by the numerous unknowns she must contend with in her revisionary writing. Indeed, section 2 is riddled with questions (six in as many pages), all of which linger in the text unanswered. In fact, even the most cursory examination of each question results in its deconstruction into a series of other questions; thus, in "What is our defense" (17) the reader is left wondering both whom "our" refers to (Mary and sister dissenters? nonconforming writers? poet and reader?) and about the exact nature of the implied threat from which they must defend themselves. Similarly, the question "Who will bear witness" (17) is baffling, as section 1 of the poem seemed to establish that Mary and poet both were taking on the role of testifier; in this fashion, previously understood premises are undone in section 2, as though "out of enclosure," beyond the guiding limits of Scriptures, "Thought has broken down" (17) and "courage fails" (18). Finally, the wholly enigmatic and pathos-propelled question "Oh when when" (18) reveals none of its intentions ("when" what?),[82] though its very incompletion, together with its breathiness (sound composed primarily of absence) in the open "Oh" sound and the repetition of the "when," fully convey the speaker's despair and her deep and desperate longing for that which is unnamed— that which, perhaps, was lost from the outset.[83]

The distance of the speaker from the biblical scene and her difficulty in clearly defining its forms is indicated in the imperative she gives herself, amidst the question-asking, to "Translate the secret / in lair idiom havoc" (17). Naming her task as translation, the speaker places herself at a remove from her own material, for translation, to borrow Walter Benjamin's terms, "does not find itself in the center of the language forest but on the outside facing the wooded ridge; it calls into it without entering" (1968: 76). The disconnectedness of section 2 may be read as a byproduct of the speaker/ translator's figurative distance from "the center of the language forest," standing as she does on its edges, calling into it. This distance from the language center is the result, I believe, of the nonconforming location of self outside of social or literary norms, on the margins of an established tale or a text. It is Howe's poetic project to foreground these margins, to make their textual material legible, and to shift the reader's focus from center page to "word flesh crumbled page edge" (13). There is, however, an ongoing negotiation of and relationship with "the center." Thus while calling into the "language-forest," Howe recognizes that the "secret" to be translated is in the dialect of the wilder realms ("lair idiom"), the chaotic nature ("havoc") of the unmade and the yet-to-be-named; that is, once outside the orderly and ordering "enclosures" that characterize convention and consensus, the nonconformist risks being engulfed by the turmoil of that wilderness landscape. "What ransom covenant," asks Howe, wondering, in effect, how high the price of a pact made with the figurative gods of dissension. The final page of section 2 makes no attempt to answer this question, but instead serves as Howe's liberating acknowledgment of the incomplete nature of her creation-from-the-margins:

> Stop clinging to me
>
> He hasn't left the earth
>
> The recognition scene
>
> These are thoughts
>
> This is not intention
>
> as to the sense of it
>
> To be a man of Sorrows
>
> the Person speaking
>
> For there is no proverb   ·
>
> Here is the depth of it
>
> (22)

"Stop clinging to me," says the speaker to the reader in a seeming reprimand, insisting that the reader's engagement with the text must be based on equality rather than dependence, that the "sense of it" is not, in fact, *in* the text but is rather located in the space *between* reader and writer. Howe seems to be insisting that the antinomian poetics of the work must be matched by the reader's radical autonomy from interpreting constraints or conventions: indeed, to the question "What are your expectations of your readers?" Howe's emphatic, single-word response is "Freedom" (Keller 1995: 31). A similar emphatic tone evident on this final page (with its four-time use of the definite present simple form of "to be") is coupled with an insistent foregrounding of what the text *is not*: authoritative ("These *are* [only one individual's] thoughts"), directive ("This *is not* intention"), or sacred ("there *is no* Proverb"). Clearly, Howe is not attempting to replace a master narrative with a countermaster narrative, but is rather proposing a poetics that revolves around, even celebrates, its own partial nature, challenging thus the literary or historical production that claims to say it all.

What produces a remedy and recovery from the disconnectedness of section 2 is the identification in section 3 of Mary's *act* of testifying, which doubles as the poet's *act* of writing, as the pivot of this poet's faith system. "I am not afraid to confess it / and make you my confessor" (23), states Howe

at the opening of the section, confessing that every "least coherent utter-
ance"—by being an honest *act of uttering*—contains its own intrinsic value.
"[T]ell lies and I will tell" (29), asserts the speaker midway through the sec-
tion, addressing herself as well as the reader and attaching to the literary
"telling" its only precondition: that it be the speaker's truth. Section 3 is
appropriately entitled "Immediate Acts," and revolves around the refrain (also
the closing words of this poem) "Love once said in her mind / Enlightenedly
to do" (26, 33). "Love" is, of course, not only the external figure of Christ but
also an internalized force that compels one to create; it is "Love for the work's
sake" (23). Thus "the work," which is a process, an action—a present-con-
tinuous "turning"[84] that characterizes the central movement of the text (and
that is the subtitle of this section of the book in which *The NC Memorial* is
collected)—is its own objective and raison d'être. The following statement by
Shoshana Felman regarding the nature of testimony seems to me also an apt
description of this poem's poetics: "In the testimony, language is in process
and in trial, it does not possess itself as a conclusion, as the constatation of a
verdict or the self-transparency of knowledge . . . To testify—*to vow to tell, to
promise* and *produce* one's own speech as material evidence for truth—is to
accomplish a speech act, rather than to simply formulate a statement. As a
performative speech act, testimony in effect addresses what in history is *ac-
tion*" (1992: 5).[85]

What Howe would add to Felman's definition of testimony, I believe, is
that in addition to being a "performative speech act" that "addresses what in
history is *action*," the act of testifying is always self-reflexive—that is, what-
ever one is testifying to, the testifying self is implicated and reflected in the
testimony. Thus the "*vow to tell*" Mary Magdalene's erased story, "to *promise*
and [then] *produce* one's own speech as material evidence for truth"—the truth
of how alone and in exile Mary "Lay at night on thorns / For the purpose of
self-concealment" (25), how she tells her own gospel-tale, "Arranges and ut-
ters / words to themselves" (24), how she is much later imagined as "matron
undone her hair / falling down" (28)—is a vow also to testify to the speaker's
own relationship to this tale. Indeed, the recovery from the disconnected-
ness of section 2 is effected not only by identifying the act of testifying as the
pivot of this poet's faith system but also by the poet/speaker's *naming herself*
in this act: "Reader if I told anything / *my* crookedness roughness" (25; my
italics), explains the speaker, elucidating that it is her own unconventional
and undomesticated shape that she is always (also) sketching in the telling.

The conditional form of the above passage is repeated in the penultimate
lyric of this work and it is with an analysis of this lyric that I will end my
reading of *The NC Memorial*. On page 32, Howe writes:

When night came on
Windows to be opened
so as to see the sky
She saw herself bereft
of body
would only seem to sleep
If I could go back
Recollectedly into biblical
fierce grace
already fatherless
Isled on all removes
When night came on

The intense isolation of Howe's Mary the disciple is conveyed through a soli-
tary night landscape and the appellation of Mary as "bereft" (with the al-
ready powerful word emphasized by its placement at the end of its line), as
though she sits alone, mourning for someone or something lost to her. How-
ever, what she is bereft of is her "body / would only seem to sleep," and one's
original reading may be revised in this completed description to understand-
ing the image as one of transcendence and release from material limits, as
though by obeying the imperative of "Enlightenedly to do" (33) Mary mim-
ics a Christlike ascendance. The poet inserts herself into the lyric at this point,
expressing her own longing for return (a re-turning) to a distant biblical land-
scape that is, in some fashion, first home to this late twentieth-century Puri-
tan writer; a return to a landscape of "fierce grace" that is, of course, lost at
the outset. The capitalized letter of "Recollectedly" encourages the reader to
read the next four lines not only as a description of where the poet would
return to but also as their own unit and thus, perhaps, a reference back to
Mary. Indeed, as the lyric and the work as a whole come to a close, Mary and
the speaker seem to have become their own self-referential unit—both of them
"already fatherless," both figuratively or literally "Isled on all removes" (Mary
reportedly ended her life on the island of Patmos; Howe's work is situated
outside literary and academic mainstreams). Similarly, with the lyric's clos-
ing line identical to its opening, the text becomes circular, turning in and
around itself. Thus the memorial text that is *The Nonconformist's Memorial*
bears witness not only to the lost figure of Mary but also to itself, to the act
of writing as its own value, intrinsically redemptive. Of the woman (unnamed
but identified as Mary Magdalene) who comes to anoint Jesus with a very
expensive "alabaster box of ointment of spikenard" and is attacked by the
other disciples for wastefulness, Jesus says: "Leave her alone; why trouble ye
her? . . . She hath done what she could: she is come aforehand to anoint my

body to the burying. Verily I say unto you, Wheresoever this gospel shall be preached throughout the whole world, this also that she hath done shall be spoken of for a memorial for her" (Mark 14:6–9). The memorial described above is for a nonconforming spirit and her extravagant act of love and faith; similarly, the memorial of *The Nonconformist's Memorial* is testimony to the creative force propelling her poetry, a creative force that is, for Howe, always nonconforming and that is, by definition, "Charged with Enthusiasm" (*Birthmark* 149): visionary, autonomous, and antinomian.

Epilogue

"The beginning is the end," states Howe in the *Talisman* interview, explaining her nonlinear and nonchronological procedures of poetic composition (Foster 1994: 55). I appropriate Howe's statement and invert it—as she appropriates and inverts texts—in order to use this ending to reflect, for a brief moment, on the beginning(s). Born in 1937, Howe spent her early childhood years in Buffalo, New York—a city of waterways and national crossroads, a commercial route for early traders, and a center of nascent American industrialization, later a haven for thousands of immigrants in search of work. I was born and raised in the same city, with its streets named for Indian tribes (Mohawk, Huron, Chippewa, Seneca, Delaware, Iroquois) and its frozen winters blanketed white. I discovered that I shared this early landscape with Howe long after I first met the poet and became engaged by her poetics and poetry.

In 1989 I had the opportunity of studying for a semester with Howe at Temple University, where she was a visiting professor. I had a weekly tutorial with her, during which she read my poetry and encouraged me to "open up" to the possibilities embedded within the language, and within myself. When I returned to Israel, where I had made my home, she sent me *The Birth-mark*, just then published, inscribed with the following words: "A book of essays about emigration and exile—from one border crosser to another—love—Susan Howe." Certainly, these points of personal convergence have influenced the ways in which I am involved and moved by Howe's work; however, biography aside, I know that through her work's fierce integrity, its music, and its exploration of literal lands and emotional landscapes to which she would belong, Howe has made something happen in her writing as has happened nowhere else.[1] For this poetry and the opportunity to study it, I am grateful.

Notes

Chapter 1

1. Etymological roots of *mark* are taken from *Webster's Third New International Dictionary*. See chap. 2, fig. 2.1.

2. Mark Antony DeWolfe Howe (1808–1895)—Howe's great grandfather, a bishop— was "the author of two antiquarian volumes: *Memoirs of the Life and Services of the Rt. Rev. Alonzo Potter, D.D., L.L.D., Bishop of the Protestant Episcopal Church in the Diocese of Pennsylvania* and *The Life and Labors of Bishop Hare: Apostle to the Sioux*" (*Frame Structures* 19–20). Mark DeWolfe Howe (1906–1967)—Howe's law professor father—spent a lifetime editing *Touched with Fire: The Civil War Letters and Diary of Oliver Wendell Holmes Jr., 1861–1864*, and writing the second volume of the authorized biography of Holmes, entitled *The Proving Years* (*Frame Structures* 17). Howe's grandfather, Mark Antony DeWolfe Howe (1864–1960)—referred to as "[t]he Dean of Boston letters"—was an antiquarian, though he "didn't write serious histories, his enthusiasms were indeterminate, he was a dabbler and a dilettante" (22). Howe also traces her writing heritage back to many of her female precursors, matriarchal and patriarchal, who were themselves writers (i.e., her mother, Mary Manning Howe, who wrote three plays and a novel; her patriarchal grandmother, Fanny Quincy Howe, who wrote two anonymously published novels; and her patriarchal aunt Helen Howe, who joined the ranks of Howe biographers with her volume *The Gentle Americans, 1864–1960: Biography of a Breed*). All of this familial information is provided in Howe's highly autobiographical prose preface to the works collected in *Frame Structures: Early Poems, 1974–1979*. Howe's younger sister, Fanny Howe, is also a poet and novelist.

3. With the term *investigations*, I mean to echo Paul Naylor's appellation of certain avant-garde poets as producers of "contemporary investigative poetry." "Like scientists or district attorneys," he writes, "they *investigate* the cultural conditions under which they write" (1999: 9). See Naylor's excellent analyses of the works of Susan Howe, Nathaniel Mackey, Lyn Hejinian, Kamau Brathwaite, and M. Nourbese Philip in his book *Poetic Investigations: Singing the Holes in History* (Evanston, IL: Northwestern University Press, 1999).

4. The significances of this work's title are outlined in chapter 2 of this book. However, within the context of this opening discussion, I am inclined to read the phrase "Secret History" as referring also to that which is the secret history of every poetic work: the personal history of its poet, as it is woven through the fabric of the text, in colors and textures more—or less—prominent, but always present.

5. This dedication appears three pages into the body of the text (*Frame Structures* 91). See chapter 2, p. 28 for a consideration of this subversion of literary conventions. For our present purposes, this placement of the dedication clearly conveys that the personal is central and intrinsic to the text and cannot be relegated to the margins.

6. The personal is a central strand in *all* of Howe's work. However, the texts that are most explicitly autobiographical and that provide the most specific data concerning Howe's life include "Frame Structures" (prose preface to *Frame Structures: Early Poems 1974–1979*), "There Are Not Leaves Enough to Crown to Cover to Crown to Cover" (prose preface to the works collected in *The Europe of Trusts*), the poem *Pythagorean Silence,* and the essay "Sorting Facts; or, Nineteen Ways of Looking at Marker" (printed in *Beyond Document: Essays on Nonfiction Film* [Wesleyan University Press, 1996]).

7. As Dworkin himself points out, he is adopting the term *grid* from Howe's use of it in *Thorow,* where she gestures toward her own objective of exposing and thereby unsettling the "European grid on the Forest" (45).

8. In her essay on the French documentary filmmaker Chris Marker, Howe considers Marker's assumed name: "Somewhere else I read his surname may simply be a reference to magic markers," she writes, "because they highlight or mark a text at the same time you can see through it" ("Sorting Fact; or, Nineteen Ways of Looking at Marker" 337). Similarly, the markers on/of Howe's text must both be *read* and *read through*—they call attention to themselves and to the poetic text beneath/beside/within them. The coincidence of Marker's name—with the word *mark* embedded within it—doubtless had a role in Howe's choice of this filmmaker for her essay's subject: "Marker collided with birth-mark," writes Howe, "the assumed name struck home" (329). Howe's keen attention to, and faithful following of, certain almost emblematic words establishes links within and between individual works.

9. McCorkle directs the reader to consider Howe's own various and variable interpretations of Dickinson's "My Life Had Stood—A Loaded Gun," which Howe lists as "Possibilities." See McCorkle, para. 8, and Howe's *My Emily Dickinson,* 76–77.

10. I am beholden to Paul Naylor for foregrounding this passage and its importance in understanding Howe's poetics. For an excellent analysis of Howe's feminist project and the similarities among Howe, Stein, and Dickinson, see Naylor's *Poetic Investigations: Singing the Holes in History* (Evanston, IL: Northwestern University Press, 1999), 66–69.

11. A small example of how Howe's text provides the terms of and tools for its interpretation is evident in the discovery I made that the particularly elliptical passage opening *Secret History of the Dividing Line* (see first epigraph on p. 3) was, in fact,

extracted from a dictionary passage at the word *mark*. This discovery was in no way remarkable, as throughout her work Howe is involved with the materiality of language—the word as word (separate, complex and changing with time)—and she herself is constantly investigating etymologies and word links. Reading a Howe text, one is led to reconsider one's understanding even—or in particular—of words whose meanings are seemingly self-evident: hence, my dictionary check of the word *mark*. See chap. 2, pp. 20–22.

12. The notion and rejection of "seizing" a singular meaning from a text, as one might seize hold of a beloved or a god, is particularly prominent in Howe's *The Nonconformist's Memorial*—the final work examined in this study. In that text, Howe uses Mary Magdalene's garden encounter with the resurrected Jesus (as presented in The Gospel According to St. John) and his negative imperative to her, "Do not touch me"—variously translated as "Do not seize me"—as its starting point. See chapter 4, p. 167 and note 67 on same page.

13. In "Artifice of Absorption," Charles Bernstein asserts that "any direct address / to the reader" breaks the absorption into the text, for in the absorptive text, the reader "must be ignored, as in / the 'fourth wall' convention in theater, where what / takes place on the stage is assumed to be sealed off from the audience" (1992: 31–32). Howe employs many such strategies that fall under Bernstein's rubric of "anti-absorptive" measures. See *A Poetics* (Cambridge, MA: Harvard University Press, 1992), 9–89.

14. See the Keller interview for a description of Howe's complete openness to varied interpretations of her work (1995: 31).

15. I am indebted here to Christopher Castiglia's provocative and stirring analysis of American women's captivity narratives. Castiglia (1996) convincingly argues that "in the experience of captivity, seemingly the most helpless and effacing of conditions, these [captive] women gain an agency [and voice] they would have found nearly impossible to claim in their native culture" (13–14). My thinking here is also influenced by Charles Bernstein's essay "Artifice of Absorption" and the link he establishes between his terminology and Howe's: "[Howe's] theme of 'captivity,'" he writes, "is an allegory for absorption: the fear of, and attraction to, being absorbed by Indian culture." See *A Poetics*, 25 n.

16. Umberto Eco's (1989) frame of reference in his fascinating discussion of what he terms the "open work" is the musical composition. Remembering Howe's insistence on the primacy of the acoustical in her poetry, I find his words all the more relevant to my reading of her work.

17. Henri Pousseur writes that "it is up to the listener to place himself deliberately in the midst of an inexhaustible network of relationships and to choose for himself." As with a Howe text, the making of the text/composition is dependent, finally, on the reader/listener's willingness to place herself in a field of possibilities, which is a site of promise and unknowing both, and to choose meaning from the "network of relationships" offered. Pousseur qtd. in Eco (1989: 10–11).

18. This ability to tolerate a degree of unknowing applies both to the reader and

writer and echoes Keat's famous term *negative capability*. In an 1817 letter to his brothers George and Thomas, Keats writes: "at once it struck me, what quality went to form a Man of Achievement especially in Literature and which Shakespeare possessed so enormously—I mean *Negative Capability*, that is when man is capable of being in uncertainties, Mysteries, doubts, without any irritable reaching after fact and reason" (*The Norton Anthology of English Literature* [New York: W. W. Norton & Co., 1968], 571).

19. The tract by Cushman is quoted in Avihu Zakai's book *Exile and Kingdom: History and Apocalypse in the Puritan Migration to America* (Cambridge, MA: Cambridge University Press, 1992), 128.

20. Howe has expressed her sense of being an outsider in relation to society's power structures in general and to the university (as holding a supposed monopoly on society's intellectual activity) in particular. Without any university degrees of her own and having worked for many years without an academic affiliation (Howe began teaching at universities only in 1988), she has named herself "an interloper and an imposter" (*The Difficulties* 17), and "a marginal person . . . outside the power structure" (Falon 1989: 36). In the Falon interview, Howe also discusses the advantages and disadvantages of being outside the university, with the outsider status, finally, more valuable to her: "For a long time I thought that this lack of a basic [university] education put me at a disadvantage, but now I think that maybe it's provided me with a certain innocence, and enthusiasm that hasn't been killed. I've been able to follow each path on my own and had I gone to college and majored in something then I would have had to write papers on people and issues I wasn't interested in. This is a slow, lonely way to go. It places you on the other side, you stumble. It's a weird melange of things you pull on, but you're free" (1989: 29–30).

In the last decade Howe's "outsider" status has significantly shifted as she has moved from the margins of the avant-garde to its center: she now consistently publishes her work with a major publisher (New Directions); she has been the recipient of various awards, honors, and fellowships; she is included in many major literary anthologies and her work receives widespread critical attention; and she holds a chair in a preeminent U.S. poetics program.

21. In her essay "Ether/Either," Howe describes her mother's wanderings thus: "even well into her eighties Mummy kept leaving in order to arrive either one place or another as the first step in a never-ending process somewhere . . . Throughout their married life her restlessness seemed to have puzzled my father" (1998: 119). The "restlessness"—as an inheritance—becomes for Howe a restlessness of language and ideas both, a vigorous curiosity and a rejection of the static.

22. Deleuze and Guttari assert that the nomad (and by extension the exile) is a threat to the authority of the state, for the nomad's path is established by principles external to and, at times, in conflict with, state interests. As the nomad threatens the state's objective of "striat[ing] the space over which it reigns . . . [and] establish[ing] a zone of rights . . . over all the flows traversing the ecumenon" (1986: 59), the nomad

is subjected to various types of state persecutions, including silencing and banishment. I am grateful to Hank Lazer for pointing out to me the relevance of Deleuze and Guttari's work on nomadism.

23. The figures of elusive nineteenth-century philosopher Charles Peirce and his mysterious wife, Juliette—the subjects of Howe's latest collection entitled *Pierce-Arrow*—must be added to this list of the banished, the exiled, and the lost. Early in his career, Charles Peirce was abruptly dismissed from his university position and, in effect, banished from the East Coast academic and social establishment of his day, pushed to the intellectual and geographic peripheries of his society. Juliette—a woman of unknown origins and multiple names—may have been "forced into exile by the French Third Republic for political reasons" (*Pierce-Arrow* 10), may have been disinherited by her family, may have been of French, German, or Gypsy heritage. Whatever her origins, she was a foreigner in America, an expatriate who never went home. While I do not devote a separate analysis to *Pierce-Arrow* in this book, many of the motifs and themes examined in other works resonate through Howe's beautiful, and deeply elegiac, recent work.

24. In her intriguing article "How Not to Erase(her): A Poetics of Posterity in Susan Howe's *Melville's Marginalia*," Megan Williams argues that Howe's "poetics of recuperation" is motivated to no small degree by her desire to secure the position of her own work in posterity. "I would like to suggest," writes Williams, "that Howe's poetics seeks to determine Howe's place in posterity by finding and writing Howe, the female poet, into the past and by removing the threat of historical erasure from that past" (107). "Like a 'sentinel,'" she continues, "Howe breathes life into past voices and guards her [own] work against death and erasure" (113). I find Williams's argument convincing and, in fact, in keeping with the sense of reciprocity of the engagement between Howe and the figures she pursues back into history. See *Contemporary Literature* 38:1 (Spring 1997): 106-132.

25. The voice and words of Herman Melville speak volubly throughout Howe's oeuvre. In addition to her work *Melville's Marginalia* (in *The Nonconformist's Memorial*), in which Melville obviously figures prominently, quotations from Melville are scattered throughout Howe's poetry. In the *Talisman* interview in particular, Howe speaks about Melville and his impact on her work at length (Foster 1994: 53-54, 65-68), stipulating that "[a] subject I would truly love to write on, but I know it's way too much and I never will, is the feminine in Melville. There has to be reason why his writing speaks so directly to me" (67). I have not proffered an analysis of *Melville's Marginalia* in this book, as I believe that the subject of Melville in Howe's work necessitates an entire book of its own.

26. See "There Are Not Leaves Enough to Crown to Cover to Crown to Cover"—Howe's prose introduction to the works collected in *The Europe of Trusts*—for her description of the impact that the outbreak of World War II had on her (1990: 9-14).

27. The poets most often named as part of the Language-centered poetry group include Charles Bernstein, Bruce Andrews, Ron Silliman, Bob Perelman, Lyn Hejinian,

James Sherry, Ray DiPalma, Carla Harryman, Rae Armantrout, Alan Davies, and Steve McCaffery. This list is partial and in no particular order.

28. See the entirety of Bernstein's essay "The Second War and Postmodern Memory"—collected in *A Poetics*, 193–217—for a wonderful and careful consideration of avant-garde poetry as a response to "the Second War." Hank Lazer rightly points out that for some of the Language-identified writers also preoccupied with issues of history and violence (i.e., Bruce Andrews, Ron Silliman, and Barrett Watten), it is the Vietnam War that serves as their frame of reference (personal communication). I would argue that while the violence and bloodshed of the Vietnam War were replayed nightly on TV screens in American living rooms, that war did not pose the same sense of existential danger as World War II did.

29. Howe's second husband—David von Schlegell—who was seventeen years her senior, served from 1943–1945 as a bomber pilot and armament-systems officer in the Eighth Air Force. In her essay "Sorting Facts; or, Nineteen Ways of Looking at Marker," she writes: "Until [David] died and was cremated he had a large scar on his left arm from where he was shot while piloting a B-17 in the fiery skies over Emden in Germany . . . It could be said this wound just above his left hand saved his life, because he was hospitalized for several months and then honorably discharged. But the war wounded him in ways he could never recover" (1996: 296). Thus the scars of World War II are not only psychological and childhood-based, but also manifest themselves in the literal and emotional markings on her life partner.

30. While I speak of the poets identified with Language writing as a group or groups, it is crucial to emphasize that every poet in this group is engaged in Language projects that are quite distinctive in intention and form. It is, obviously, well outside the scope of this introduction to discuss the significant differences between the Language poets, though, as Perelman states, it is clear that their "various writing needs to be read variously" (1996: 31). Perelman's *The Marginalization of Poetry* (1996) provides a useful introduction to some central tenets and figures in Language writing, as does George Hartley's *Textual Politics and the Language Poets* (1989). Key critical texts in Language writing include Bruce Andrews *The L=A=N=G=U=A=G=E Book* (1984); Charles Bernstein's *Content's Dream: Essays, 1975–1984* (1986) and his collection of essays in *A Poetics*; Ron Silliman's, ed., *In the American Tree* (1986); Paul Naylor's *Poetic Investigations: Singing the Holes in History* (1999); and Linda Reinfeld's *Language Poetry: Writing as Rescue* (1992).

31. I have appropriated this phrase from Howe's own use of it in her description of Futurist poet Vladmir Mayakovsky and avant-garde filmmaker Dziga Vertov in "Sorting Facts; or, Nineteen Ways of Looking at Marker" (297–298). In this same essay, Howe describes herself as working "in the poetic documentary form" (300). See *Beyond Document: Essays on Nonfiction Film* (1996), 295–343.

32. I am adopting this phrase from the following passage in Hank Lazer's *Opposing Poetries:* "The peculiar accomplishment of Howe's writing," he states, "is that while the marks of skepticism and intelligence are everywhere in Howe's poetry . . . her work equally retains and makes anew an exuberant spirituality" (1996: 68). My con-

sideration of the "opposing forces" in Howe's work is beholden to Lazer's own use of the term *opposing* and to his emphasis on the contradictory impulses in Howe's work.

Chapter 2

1. These dates are the years of original publication. *Secret History of the Dividing Line* was published by Telephone Books (New York); in my analysis of this work I will be referring to the later edition as reprinted in the collection entitled *Frame Structures: Poems 1974–1979* (New York: New Directions Books, 1996). The original publication of *Secret History* includes an additional six pages of poetry dispersed through the text and omitted from the reprinting. *Articulation of Sound Forms in Time* was first published by Awede Press (Windsor, VT) and was later reprinted in the 1990 Wesleyan University Press collection entitled *Singularities,* together with *Thorow* and an additional work. The original publication of *Articulation* does not include the two-page prose opening entitled "The Falls Fight," but starts instead with the letter extract. An equally significant difference between the original and reprinted versions of *Articulation* is the printing of two poems to a page through much of sections 2 and 3 in the reprinted edition, while in the original edition every poem stands alone on a page. With both *Secret History* and *Articulation,* what gets lost in the transitions from manuscript to original print version to reprinting—which is the transition from publishing with small presses to larger and more commercial ones—is *space* (see Keller 1995: 17–19). The ways in which the dissemination of poetry, and hence our reception of it, is mediated and often distorted by editorial choices, frequently economic and political in essence, is at all times a central concern of Howe's. In my analysis of *Articulation* and *Thorow,* I will be referring to the Wesleyan University Press edition.

2. For two extensive and enlightening discussions of the psychological makeup of the Puritans, see Kai T. Erikson's *Wayward Puritans: A Study in the Sociology of Deviance* (New York: John Wiley & Sons, 1966) and Charles Lloyd Cohen's *God's Caress: The Psychology of Puritan Religious Experience* (New York: Oxford University Press, 1986).

3. Of course many of these avant-garde poetic strategies may *also* be read as emanating from a postmodernist sensibility, and Howe names herself as working out of the modernist tradition (Keller 1995: 20). I believe that the modernist and Puritan influences coexist in Howe's work; however, this chapter means to limit its focus to the specifically Puritan nature of Howe's language usages.

4. The notion of a frame is central to Howe in her interest in the framing or positioning of oneself in relation to one's history and landscape. *Frame Structures* is also her chosen title for her 1996 book—a collection of early poems (1974–1979) that includes *Secret History*—and for its eponymous prose introduction.

5. Emblematic of both this arrogance and ignorance is the following example provided by Howe in her prose introduction to the poems collected in *Frame Structures:* "During the American Revolution when the British War Office issued a guidebook for troops who were coming over to bring the disobedient colonies to heel, its author

confused the Wampannoag sachem, Metacomet [sometimes called King Philip], with Spanish King Philip. 'Bristol is remarkable for King Philip of Spain having a palace nearby and being killed in it'" (22).

6. McGann adopts the term *black riders* from Stephen Crane's first published book, *Black Riders and Other Lines* (1895) and from Robert Carlton ("Bob") Brown's recasting of the term in his experimental poetry of the 1930s. In his collection *Readies for Bob Brown's Machine*, Brown writes of Black Riders as the "inky words" that "dash at full gallop across the plains of pure white pages." For a fascinating discussion of both Crane and Brown's works, see McGann's *Black Riders* (Princeton, NJ: Princeton University Press, 1993), 84–97.

7. My investigation into the etymology of the word *mark* led naturally to this "discovery" that the above passage was extracted from the dictionary. Indeed, Howe's work often leads her reader to the dictionary—specifically to the American *Webster's*—in her own interrogations into the origins and evolution of words. I believe that this source for the word-rectangles—which may or may not be uncovered by the reader—and its significance in no way takes priority, annuls or negates a reading of these words (such as the one I first offer) based solely on sound links and lexical associations.

8. The surveying expedition described by Byrd had to cross through a territory called "The Dismal"—a swamp of great density and darkness. The surveyors spent nine days in "The Dismal," barely advancing due to the thickets and underbrush, unable to see horizon or sky. Finally, the surveyors emerged from the swamp, abandoning their attempt to run the border line through it (Wright 1958).

9. "The Secret History of the Line" was finally published in 1929.

10. Howe does note her sources in the acknowledgments section at the opening of the collection *Frame Structures*. However, in the first edition of *Secret History*, the sources are unacknowledged, thus transforming Howe's original text into her own version of a "secret history"—a secret half disclosed only in the work's second edition. I am beholden to Hank Lazer for pointing out this intriguing parallel between Howe's editions and Byrd's.

11. "Trench letters do get used / eventually for poetry you / long history of nihilism," writes Howe in her latest book, *Pierce-Arrow*, reflecting thus on her own poetic strategies. I read these lines also as Howe's recognition that it is the soldier's self-documented words alone—as preserved in artifact and remade by poetry—that may truly represent war's arena, amidst the blurring of ethical borders and distinctions. Howe's interest in war letters is reflected also in her highly autobiographical 1996 essay, "Sorting Facts; or, Nineteen Ways of Looking at Marker," in which she uses letters her husband David von Schlegell wrote to his parents from the World War II front, where he was serving as a bomber pilot (309–310, 327). The personal in its multiple dimensions reverberates throughout Howe's work.

12. The entire passage from Holmes's 1884 Memorial Day Address, quoted in full in *Touched with Fire* (56 n), reads as follows: "I see another youthful lieutenant [James

J. Lowell, commander of Company E] as I saw him in the Seven Days, when I looked down the line at Glendale. The officers were at the head of their companies. The advance was beginning. We caught each other's eye and saluted. When next I looked, he was gone."

13. The "subterranean" image seems particularly relevant in relation to the Civil War—often termed the first modern war and the first war in which extensive use was made of trenches and field fortifications (Price 1961: 5). For the first time, masses of soldiers "dug-in" in order to survive and often found their death in these readymade graves.

14. Howe may also be mirroring in these letters marked by omissions and silences the military censoring of communications from the front that became the norm in later wars. "Each letter a soldier wrote home from the [World War II European] 'Theater' [of War] was inspected first by War Department censors," writes Howe in her 1996 essay. "On the march," she continues, "only a language of remains gets past" ("Sorting Facts" 310). *Secret History* is (also) a poetry of war's remains.

15. The notion of *translatio religionis* whereby "the progress of the Gospel [is] from East to West" was first introduced into Christian historiography by St. Jerome (c. 342–420 A.D.). Otto, Bishop of Freising, expanded the idea to include the transfer of power in his book *The Two Cities: A Chronicle of Universal History to the Year 1146 A.D.* (see Zakai 1992). The concept of *translatio imperii* was still a current and influential truism in colonial America, as evident in the writings of its most influential thinkers, including the following passage by John Adams, second president of the United States: "There is nothing, in my little reading, more ancient in my memory than the observation that arts, sciences and empire had traveled Westward; and in conversation it was always added since I was a child, that their next leap would be over the Atlantic to America." See Joseph J. Ellis's *Founding Brothers: The Revolutionary Generation* (New York: Knopf, 2000).

16. Within this ice context, Peter Middleton draws an additional and useful connection between Howe's work and Olson's, maintaining that "[c]ontemporary poets who write about glaciers and ice ages are working across a textual field designated by Charles Olson, for whom ice was a sign of the Pleistocene Era, in which we still live, whose inception was marked by the ice ages which have left behind the geographical conditions that form the ground, literally and figuratively, on which the history of Europe and much of North America depends. The new American economy of European invaders began with [the ice age] according to Olson." See Middleton's "On Ice: Julia Kristeva, Susan Howe, and avant-garde poetics" (1991: 87).

17. For an excellent analysis and comprehensive historical overview of the tradition of visual poetry, see Johanna Drucker's *The Visible Word: Experimental Typography and Modern Art, 1909–1923* (Chicago: University of Chicago Press, 1994).

18. The notion of suspension coupled with the frozen lake imagery calls to mind Mallarmé's famous sonnet "Le Vierge, le vivace et le bel aujourd'hui," which predates Duchamp's work by twenty years. The swan entrapped in the "white agony" of the

frozen lake—symbol of beauty and desires unfulfilled—may be hinted at in the per-
egrine falcon who wanders through Howe's ice-studded text.

19. For an analysis of a Howe text that I read as more crucially informed by Lacanian
theories, see the discussion in chapter 3 on *Pythagorean Silence*.

20. The inversion of initials in D. H. Lawrence and H.D.'s names seems to me
more than coincidental to Howe's choice of epigraphs. Already in her extensive use
of the name Mark in *Secret History*, Howe exhibits her attentiveness to the multiple
links that names make. Names, like words, lead where one must go.

21. One may read the final "sh" of *Secret History* as leading naturally to and com-
pleted—fleshed out—by the opening "She" in *Singularities'* epigraph. As Howe explains
in the *Difficulties* interview with Falon, meaning is often made through the connec-
tions sounds make (1989: 31), even between—I believe—discrete works.

22. The book in hand is composed of blank pages. See *Trilogy* (New York: New
Directions Books, 1973), 100, 103. H.D.'s blank pages call to mind the final exchange
in this Howe interview (Falon 1989: 42): "Q: If you had to paint your writing, if you
had one canvas on which to paint your writing, what might it look like? Howe: Blank.
It would be blank. It would be a white canvas. White."

23. The full title of Rowlandson's text is *The Sovereignty and Goodness of GOD, To-
gether, with the Faithfulness of His Promises Displayed; Being a NARRATIVE of the Captivity
and Restoration of Mrs. Mary Rowlandson, Commended by her, to all that desires to know the
Lords doings to, and dealings with Her. Especially to her dear Children and Relations*. A later
edition, printed in London, carried the following title: *A True History of the Captivity
and Restoration of Mrs. Mary Rowlandson, A Minister's Wife in New-England: Wherein is set
forth, The Cruel and Inhumane Usage she underwent amongst the Heathens for Eleven Weeks
time: And her Deliverance from them. Written by her own Hand, for her Private Use: and now
made Public at the earnest Desire of Some Friends for the Benefit of the Afflicted*. The edition
of Rowlandson's text referred to here is collected in *Classic American Autobiographies*,
edited by William L. Andrews (New York: Penguin Books, 1992, 19–69).

24. Between 1673 and 1763, 771 women were taken captive in New England, in
comparison to 270 men (Castiglia 1996: 199 n).

25. Captivity narratives dominated the list of texts published in the New World
between 1680 and 1716. Mary Rowlandson's narrative, first published in Boston in
1682 and reissued that same year in London and Cambridge, retained popularity for
a century and a half, and was reprinted in 1720, 1770, 1771, and 1773. Of the four
narratives that attained best-seller status in America between the years 1680 and 1720,
three were captivity narratives; the fourth was *Pilgrim's Progress*. See Richard Slotkin's
excellent discussion of the captivity narratives in his book *Regeneration through Vio-
lence: The Mythology of the American Frontier, 1600–1860* (Middletown, CT: Wesleyan
University Press, 1973), 94–145.

26. Christopher Castiglia develops an intriguing and convincing thesis regarding
additional reasons that may have accounted for the enduring interest in captivity
narratives, particularly among white female readers. Castiglia argues that the "plight
of the literal captive" in the captivity narrative offered the white woman reader "sym-

bolic form" to her own "less tangible form of victimization . . . : confinement within the home, enforced economic dependence, rape, compulsory heterosexuality, pre-scribed plots." No less significantly, the captivity narrative offered its female read-ers—a population subject to various forms of restriction and disempowerment—"a story of female strength, endurance, and even prosperity . . . a female picaresque, an adventure story set . . . outside the home" (4). See *Bound and Determined: Captivity, Culture-Crossing, and White Womanhood from Mary Rowlandson to Patty Hearst* (Chicago: University of Chicago Press, 1996).

27. I am adopting the term *deviant* as used by Kai T. Erikson in his fascinating discussion of social deviancy and its function in Puritan society. Erikson argues that "[d]eviance is not a property *inherent in* any particular kind of behavior; it is a prop-erty *conferred upon* that behavior" by the community (1966: 6). The deviant act or deviant individual performs a needed social service by creating "a sense of mutuality among the people of the community by supplying a focus for group feeling" (4). In a passage particularly relevant to Howe's investigation and reshaping of historical and literary boundaries, Erikson states that "[t]he deviant is a person whose activities have moved *outside the margins* of the group, and when the community calls him to account for that vagrancy it is making a statement about the nature and placement of its boundaries" (11; italics mine).

28. In his interesting article "Unsettling the Wilderness: Susan Howe and Ameri-can History," Peter Nicholls brings evidence that the words of the first six poems of section 2 of *Articulation* are extracted from George Sheldon's *A History of Deerfield, Massachusetts* (first published in 1895–96), a text Howe must have stumbled across while searching for information for her essay on Rowlandson ("The Captivity and Restoration of Mrs. Mary Rowlandson," *Temblor* 2/*Birth-mark* 89–130). Nicholls also convincingly argues that while uncovering the source-text for a Howe poem provides added interest and insight into her mode of composition, Howe does not mean for the source-text to stand in as an authoritative interpreter or master narrative of her poetry. Indeed, Nicholls shows how Howe's "selection of items" from the Sheldon text "tends to block [an] emergent narrative" and that she is at all times more inter-ested in the individual word, its sound and shape on the page. See Nicholls 1996: 595–596, and also Foster 1994: 57.

29. The multiple associations evoked by the word *Prest* include also "oppressed," "pressed," and "impressed" (Perloff 1990: 303; McCorkle 1999: sect. 11). Adamson has identified *Prest* as a Middle English version of *priest*—a direct reference, perhaps, to Hope himself, "minister of the gospel" (1997: 121). The abundant associative pos-sibilities of this section's opening word set the tone for all the poetry that follows, where every word contains within itself variable and coexisting meanings, frustrat-ing a reader's inclination to provide any single interpretation of the text as final or authoritative.

30. Perelman is obviously referring to and revising here Olson's notion of "Com-position by Field" whereby the poet places himself "in the open"—away from inher-ited "closed" forms—and composes solely according to the dictates of the specific

energy and perceptual trajectory of the verse at hand. See Olson's "Projective Verse" in *The Poetics of the New American Poetry,* edited by Donald Allen and Warren Tallman (New York: Grove Press, 1973), 147–158.

31. In her close reading of *Articulation,* Perloff writes: "In a sermon of 28 May 1670, reproduced in one of Howe's sources for *Articulation of Sound Forms in Time,* the Reverend Hope Atherton recalls that when, in his forest wanderings, he came face to face with the Indians, 'I spake such language as I thought they understood.' Was Atherton speaking English and assuming the Indians spoke it too, or was he assuming that whatever Indian language he spoke would enable communication with any and every Indian? In either case, Hope's tale is marked by assumptions of familiarity with and belonging to landscapes that are, in fact, foreign" (Perloff 1990: 302–303, 343 n).

32. In Puritan theology, the Covenant of Works refers to the covenant made with Adam whereby man's actions ("good works") could determine his salvation. When he ate from the forbidden fruit, Adam broke this covenant, which was later replaced by the Covenant of Grace, delivered through Christ. The Covenant of Grace emphasizes God's munificence, redeeming the Elect regardless of their deeds.

33. The first denotation of *aberrant* in *The American Heritage Dictionary* is "deviating from the proper or expected course." I am utilizing the word here with Erikson's interpretations of *deviancy* in mind.

34. Dr. John Clark's "Description of Mrs. Hutchinson's Hydatidiform Mole" in John Winthrop's *History of New England* is graphic, fantastic, and strange in choice of images. He writes: "I beheld first ... several lumps, every one of them greatly confused and ... altogether without form ... there was a representation of innumerable distinct bodies in the form of a globe. ... The small globes I likewise opened, and perceived the matter of them ... to be partly wind and partly water ... The globes were round things included in the lumps, about the smallness of a small Indian bean, and like the pearl in a man's eye" (Battis 1962: 347–348). See also Howe's multiple, far-ranging, and beautiful associations regarding the word *mole* in the *Talisman* interview (Foster 1990: 66).

35. Space limitations prevent me from discussing the highly flammable nature of the landscape in "Taking the Forest." Nonetheless, it bears mentioning that the text repeatedly refers to straw, tinder, hay, smoke, and contains within it an abundance of red and flaming images. The fire imagery returns us, I believe, to the soldiers mentioned in *Articulation*'s opening prose section who were lost in the woods after the Falls Fight. As Howe writes: "After hiding in the woods for several days some of them came to the Indians and offered to surrender on the condition that their lives would be spared. But the Squakeags, Nipmunks, Pokomtucks, or Mahicans, instead of giving them quarter, covered each man with dry thatch. Then they set the thatch on fire and ordered each soldier to run. When one covering of thatch was burnt off, another was added, and so these colonists continued running until, Indians later told the historian: 'Death delivered them'" (*Singularities* 4). The savagery of this scene resonates throughout *Articulation*.

36. Providing the always relevant historical backdrop to Howe's chosen landscapes, Paul Naylor points out that Lake George was "the site of William Johnson's 1755 victory in the French and Indian War" (1999: 52).

37. Hawthorne's sensitivity to names is evident in his own name change: to the family name of Hathorne he added the *w* so that the orthography may more accurately reflect the correct pronunciation. It is doubtless that Hawthorne—who was, like Howe, a writer prone to the use of emblematic names and name punning in his texts—must have also been pleased to evoke the hawthorn bush with his new name, linking himself thus with the natural and paradoxical (the hawthorn is a shrub bearing thorns and fruit together). In the context of Howe's return to landscapes marked by fences and borders, it is worth noting that the hawthorn bush was extensively used in the New World for hedges to divide properties.

38. It is interesting to note that the three women who are, for Howe, the mothers of American literature—Rowland*son*, Hutchin*son*, and Dickin*son*—all carry patronymic names that eradicate them by miscalling them "the sons of . . ." In Puritan sermons, writes Kibbey, "women and children were designated as the universal category of the renamed, as those who were 'called by the name of another'" (1986: 105).

39. Linda Reinfeld points out that "[m]uch of the language of *Thorow* is drawn from old journals and accounts documenting the history of the Lake George region" (1989: 98; qtd. also in Naylor 1999: 53).

40. In her essay "Submarginalia," Howe explicitly embraces this promontory position through her identification with the cormorants whom she defines as "strand birds [that] occupy cliffs by the ocean, where they perch upright on rocks, often motion-less for long periods of time, with wings extended" (26). The cormorants are "voracious," explains Howe, and are known for diving deep in search of what will feed them. Howe calls herself a "library cormonant" who—like Coleridge, the partial subject of this essay—"dives *deep* into books as if they were a sea" (32). See *The Birthmark*, 26–39.

41. I believe that Nicky Marsh's criticism of Howe for failing to raise to the surface of her poetry hitherto silenced Native American voices, and Marsh's corollary assertion that this failure is an outcome of Howe's inability to "acknowledg[e] the full implications of her own cultural positioning [within dominant white culture]" is misplaced (1997: 135). Howe is at all times aware of her lineage, her resulting cultural position, and her consequent complicity in the violence and violations of early American settlers. I believe that Howe's choice *not* to speak Native American narratives in her poetry emanates from her ethically charged recognition that those narratives are not hers, and speaking them would be an act of cultural appropriation.

Chapter 3

1. This essay was written in 1940; its first publication was in 1950, in *Neue Rundschau* 61, 3. The edition referred to here is collected in Benjamin's *Illuminations,*

ed. and intro. Hannah Arendt (New York: Schoken, 1968), 253–264. The title "Theses on the Philosophy of History" is not Benjamin's; the title he gave his essay was "On the Concept of History" (Tiedemann 1989: 205 n).

2. These dates are the years of original publication. *The Liberties* was first published by Loon Books (Guilford, CT) and *Pythagorean Silence* was first published by Montemora Foundation (New York). The editions of both works I will be referring to in this chapter are those collected in *The Europe of Trusts* (Los Angeles: Sun & Moon Press, 1990). In the Sun & Moon edition of *The Liberties,* many of the subtitles printed by Loon Books on separate pages are now tagged on to the poems following them, and additional space-saving devices are utilized (i.e., pages of text or graphics omitted in full). As a result, in the second publication of the work, the poem has decreased in length from eighty-three pages to seventy pages. More subtle, though no less significant, changes are in evidence in the second publication of *Pythagorean Silence* (see this chapter, note 46). In her 1995 interview with Keller, Howe speaks about what has gotten lost in her texts in the transition from manuscript to printed version to reprinting. Particularly with the larger and more commercial presses she has worked with in recent years, issues of space-saving have forced Howe to make unwanted changes in her texts. As a poet who is always concerned with the visual aspect of her work, Howe has consistently resisted and struggled with these demands (1995: 17–19). The ways in which our reception of poetry is mediated and often distorted by its editing and dissemination is a central concern of Howe's, as evidenced by her ongoing work on Dickinson's fascicles.

3. During World War II, Benjamin was a refugee from his German homeland. On September 26, 1940, while trying to escape from occupied France in order to emigrate to America, Benjamin committed suicide at the Franco-Spanish border. Upon hearing of Benjamin's death, Bertolt Brecht is reported to have said this was the first real loss Hitler had caused to German literature. For additional details regarding the circumstances of Benjamin's death, see Hannah Arendt's introduction to *Illuminations* (New York: Schoken Books, 1968), 2, 17–18.

4. My entire analysis of Howe's *The Liberties* is deeply indebted to Lynn Keller's lengthy and brilliant analysis of the poem in her book *Forms of Expansion: Recent Long Poems by Women* (Chicago: University of Chicago Press, 1997).

5. Edward Foster's interview with Howe was first published in 1990, in *Talisman: A Journal of Contemporary Poetry and Poetic* 4. The edition of the interview to which I am referring here is collected in Foster's *Postmodern Poetry: The Talisman Interviews* (Hoboken, NJ: Talisman House Publishers, 1994), 48–68.

6. In the interest of saving space and easing reading, I will keep the uppercase titles in uppercase only in headings and when first introduced into my analysis.

7. All of Swift's correspondences were addressed both to Stella and her constant companion/chaperone, Rebecca Dingley. However, once her service as a "beard" was fulfilled, Rebecca Dingley is erased from the tale, as evidenced by the title of the collected letters—*Journal to Stella.* With the twin "disadvantages" of being a woman and a member of the working class, Mrs. Dingley is positioned so deeply in what Howe

would term the "dark side of history" that perhaps even fragments or approximations of her voice and figure—what Howe hopes to provide of Stella—are irretrievable. It seems to me worth noting that this introduction to *The Liberties* is called "Fragments of *a* Liquidation"—indicating in the use of the indefinite article that Stella's erasure is only one of many and that Howe's project is self-consciously limited in scope.

8. Howe also reports—in straightforward and unembellished language—that on the night of Stella's death, Swift was entertaining guests in the deanery. The news of Stella's passing was brought to him at around eight o'clock, and Swift, apparently, "continued the party as if nothing had happened." See *The Liberties*, 154.

9. The 1976 *Supplement to the Oxford English Dictionary* provides the following addenda to the word *liquidation:* "[f. liquidate v.—after Russian *likvidirovat*]—the action or process of abolishing or eliminating; the doing away with or killing of unwanted persons."

10. Whether in Dublin or in the country residence of Laracor, Stella and Mrs. Dingley were free to use Swift's residences "only when he was away," writes Williams, the editor of Swift's *Journal to Stella.* Upon his return, the women "removed elsewhere." Williams's report of this arrangement whereby the women were constantly being uprooted according to Swift's itinerary and changing roles is matter-of-course (Swift 1948: xxix).

11. The entire passage reads as follows: "I am very weak but out of all violent Pain. The Doctrs say it would have ended in some violent Disease if it had not come out thus. I shall now recover fast. I have been in no danger of Life, but miserable Torture. I must not write too much—so adieu deelest Md Md Md FW FW Me Me Me Lele I can say lele yet oo see—Fais I dont conceal a bitt. as hope savd."

12. "MD" stands for "My dear"—Stella—or "My dears," while "FW" "serves both for Farewell and Foolish Wenches." "Me" apparently stands for "Madam Elderly"—Mrs. Dingely. As a rule, *l* is substituted for *r*--hence "deelest" is "dearest." This letter substitution and others, in addition to the repetition of the coded endearments, make Swift's "little language" much like baby talk. (See Swift 1948: lv–lvii.)

13. For discussions of Swift's role as a champion of Irish liberty, two useful books are Robert Mahoney's *Jonathan Swift: The Irish Identity* (New Haven: Yale University Press, 1995) and David Nokes's *Jonathan Swift: A Hypocrite Reversed* (Oxford: Oxford University Press, 1985).

14. Howe was significantly influenced by Robert Duncan and the mythological/ mystical nature of his work. Therefore, her mention here of the triumphant falcon, in conjunction with her reference to the outlasted "mother's hood" (166) seems to me an allusion to and telegraphic rewriting of Duncan's poem "My Mother Would be a Falconress." The subject of freedom from first binds is the subject of Duncan's work; at poem's end, his falcon/speaker remains bound:

My mother would be a falconress,
and even now, years after this,

I would be a falcon and go free.
I tread her wrist and wear the hood,
talking to myself, and would draw blood.

15. The "wild geese" reference reoccurs in the middle section of the text (196) and seems there to evoke also the following passage from *King Lear,* spoken by the Fool: "Winter's not gone yet, if the wild geese fly that way" (II.iv.45). Clearly, the wild geese are messenger birds marking the literal and figurative change in seasons.

16. The census population figure for Ireland in 1841 was over 8 million. The census population figure for 1881 was just 5 million (Foster 1988: 606–609). It is estimated that in the ten years of the Great Potato Famine, 1845–1855, 1.5 million Irish died of starvation or famine-related diseases. Massive emigration, particularly to America and Britain, followed. By the end of the nineteenth century there were 3 million Irish-born people living overseas (Miller 1985: 284–285).

17. The figure of Swift, and the enigmatic story of his connection with Stella and Vanessa (Esther Vanhomrigh—the other woman with whom he had a lasting though nontraditional connection) have been very popular subjects for Irish writers, particularly playwrights. From Arthur Power's *The Drapier Letters* (1927) to Ulick O'Connor's *The Dark Lovers* (1975), Stella has played a supporting role in the retellings, when she is remembered at all (in *The Drapier Letters,* Swift is saved from the English soldiers by a young harlot who gives her life to save him). The most famous play on the Swift story is Yeats's *The Words upon the Window Pane* (produced at the Abbey Theater in 1930), which will be discussed at greater length later in this chapter. For a complete discussion of representations of Swift in Irish theater (1930–1995), see Mahoney's *Jonathan Swift: The Irish Identity,* 140–169.

18. I discovered the pendulum image in Phyllis Greenacre's book *Swift and Carroll: A Psychoanalytic Study of Two Lives* (New York: International Universities Press, 1955). Her exact words are: "[m]uch of [Swift's] life was a pendulum swing between the two countries. He seems never to have ventured elsewhere" (17). I do not know if Howe adopted this image from Greenacre.

19. The madness also evokes Jonathan Swift, who in his final years had few lucid moments and spent the last three years of his life under care of guardians appointed by a Commission of Lunacy. In addition, the madness motif links the text forward to *King Lear.*

20. It is interesting to note that in her first novel, *The Voyage Out* (first published in 1915), Woolf combines the imagery of bird transformations favored in *The Liberties* and the theme of threatening silence and resulting obscurity lying in wait for the speaking/writing woman that so preoccupies Howe. As the heroine Rachel Vinrace lies dying, she sees herself "curled up at the bottom of the sea," and "while all her tormentors thought she was dead, she was not dead." In a tremendous and final effort to hold on to life through speech, she "pushed her voice out as far as possible until it became a bird and flew away"; however, "she thought it doubtful whether it

ever reached the person she was talking to." See *The Voyage Out* (London: Grafton Books, 1978), 348, 354.

21. Lynn Keller reads this "delicate cross" as a visual representation of the child Stella, "a squinting orphan" with thin arms outstretched (1997: 217). The cross, of course, can be read as the Christian icon, evoking—together with the bleeding feet, the skimming of the water surface and the mentions of loaves and fish—that archetypal tale of suffering. References to Christian tales and rituals beyond those mentioned here abound, as seems to me inevitable in a text located in a land so intensely defined, and torn apart, by its Christian identities.

22. The identity of Stella's father remains an open question. She was baptized a daughter of Edward Johnson, a steward on Sir William Temple's estate, but it was rumored from early on that Temple himself was her father. She was raised, apparently, with no father figure firmly in place, until Swift himself took on the role when he became Temple's secretary in 1689 and began also to tutor the eight-year-old Stella. It is interesting to note that Swift too was fatherless: his father died seven months before his birth on November 30, 1667. For further discussion of absent parent figures in Swift's childhood and its impact on Swift's literature, see Greenacre's *Swift and Carroll: A Psychoanalytic Study of Two Lives.*

23. There is no literal mother represented in *King Lear,* and the only figurative mention of the maternal is in the following passage, spoken by Lear:

O, how this mother swells upward toward my heart!
Hysterica passio! Down, thou climbing sorrow!
Thy element's below. (II.iv.56–58)

For a fascinating discussion of the missing mother in *King Lear,* see Coppelia Kahn's "The Absent Mother in *King Lear*" in *King Lear: Contemporary Critical Essays* (Hampshire: Macmillian Press, 1993), 92–113. Clearly Howe is aware of the completely motherless condition of *King Lear,* arguing in *My Emily Dickinson* that in this play Shakespeare has descended "into the violence of primal exile from our mother" (1985: 107). I am beholden to Lynn Keller for this point (1997: 333 n).

24. This image echoes the reality of Stella's burial beneath the cathedral floor, as though she too has been paneled, or paved, over.

25. In his final speech Lear calls Cordelia "my poor fool" (V.iii.307). The term *fool* here stands for the vulnerable, naked, and innocent, the one who is most like an infant, most in need of protection. It seems that here Lear rises above his own self-centeredness to realize, for a fleeting moment, how profoundly he has failed as father.

26. With the Lir story, Howe also links the *Book of Stella* and the *Book of Cordelia* through the motif of water birds. It is interesting to note that according to the legend, the children of Lir, once transformed into swans, were allowed to retain their power of speech. As John Rhys writes in his collection *Celtic Folklore, Welsh and Manx,*

the swan/children "used to converse from the surface of the water with their friends on the dry land" (1970: 93–94)—an image that evokes the hovering status of the small boy/girl bird in the *Book of Stella*. In contrast, an additional tale of children transformed into swans alluded to in *The Liberties*—Grimm's *The Six Swans*—emphasizes female silence and sacrifice. In this tale, six brothers are turned into swans by their stepmother, and their sister must weave them shirts of starwort in order to free them. During the six years of her labor, she must "neither speak nor laugh" (Grimm 234). Because she is silent, her children are stolen from her and she is nearly burned at the stake. In the second section of *The Liberties*, Howe speaks of "[w]hite swans—seven," attempting thus to revise the original and give the sister flight (197). However, the revision leads to "nothing," as though the weight of the traditional tales of the Western literary tradition keeps the sister grounded.

27. The meaning of the name Cordelia is not known for certain; nonetheless Hanks and Hodges in their *Dictionary of First Names* suggest that the name "may be a fanciful elaboration of Latin *cor* (genitive *cordis*)—heart." They also state that "it seems most likely [that the name has] a genuine Celtic origin" (1990: 71).

28. The planet imagery of course reminds the reader of the section's steady backdrop of Stella by invoking her astral name.

29. The ladder imagery and the need to escape (though this time by climbing *up* the ladder instead of down it) may connect to a primary and defining moment in Howe's own biography. In October 1938, with Europe on the brink of war and "bear[ing] the odor of death," eighteen-month-old Howe, in the arms of her mother, Mary Manning Howe, boarded the ocean liner *Transylvania* in Ireland in order to reach the safe shores of America. In her 1998 essay "Ether/Either," published in the anthology *Close Listening: Poetry and the Performed Word*, ed. Charles Bernstein, Howe writes: "that October at Cobh . . . ocean liners couldn't enter the harbor so they anchored beyond the Quay pronounced Key, somewhere in sea-fog. Boarding passengers were rowed out and climbed a rope ladder to get on deck. I was hardly talking had only learned to walk so I suppose a stranger took me up . . . many of our fellow passengers are sorrowful and frightened, they speak other languages, my mother says she can hear sobbing at night and lapping water level with where we lie confined, enclosed, self-enclosing, always moving" (119, 123). This literal tale of escape resonates in the figurative/fairy-tale flight described in the poem.

30. The noun denotation of *thwarts* is the seat across a boat on which an oarsman sits. I believe that Howe means to evoke both this meaning—as though her speaker has crawled beneath the feet of oarsmen to flee—and the verb denotation of someone putting an obstacle in one's way. The boat imagery connects back to the "riggings" and rowing ("as never woman rowed") described in the *Book of Stella* and already discussed. As Ireland is an island, escape by water is all the more relevant.

31. *"God's Spies"* opens on Monday evening and closes on Sunday at 9 P.M. in a scene that is described as "[n]ot dark, but not light" (198). The inability to distinguish between light and dark evokes the first day of creation when "the earth was

without form, and void," before God "divided the light from the darkness" (Gen. 1:2–4). I read this absence of distinctive borders at the end of the play's creation week as an indication that for Howe the self-creation process never ends but is always beginning anew.

32. Mary Manning continued her dramatic career also after immigrating to the United States at the age of twenty-nine to marry Howe's father, working then primarily as a director. For Howe's descriptions of her mother's involvement in the theater, see the Falon interview (1989), 30, the prose introduction to *Frame Structures* (1996), entitled "Frame Structures," 16, and the essay "Ether Either" in the anthology *Close Listening: Poetry and the Performed Word* (1998), 125.

33. Mary Manning, Howe's mother, apprenticed at the Abbey Theater, and while the exact dates of this apprenticeship are unavailable, it would have been approximately at the time of this premier.

34. One must keep in mind that Swift was Stella's tutor from a young age and had the most prominent role in shaping her style of articulation. There is much to indicate that Swift took pains to mold Stella in his own image and that he took pleasure in the creation that so resembled him. As John Irwin Fischer writes in his book *On Swift's Poetry*, "Swift was apparently so delighted with Stella's poem ["To Dr. Swift on His Birthday"] that he felt it necessary to assure those to whom he showed it that it was all purely Stella's and had not jot of his correction. There is no reason to doubt the truth of Swift's protestation, but we should note that he was pleasantly aware of much in the poem that *might have been his own*" (1978: 130; my italics).

35. Possibly, the intertextuality of *The Liberties* with *Waiting for Godot* and Beckett's other writings is signaled even before the opening of "*God's Spies*." The repetition of the name lucky Luck and the speaker's search for him in the final pages of the *"Book of Cordelia"* may be an evocation of Beckett's sometime mute, always abused character Lucky. In addition, Linda Reinfeld reads the final image of the section, "I can re/ . . . /way" as a reference to the "solitary attic poet" of Beckett's *Murphy*, who says, "Do not come down the ladder, they have taken it away" (Reinfeld 1992: 127, 127 n).

36. The image that comes to mind here is of each word as an island, with silence the immense sea around it. This image seems particularly apt for these texts, which are heavily influenced by the Irish island-landscape and its Irish sensibility. The word as island also recalls one of the denotations Howe provides for the word *mole*—"earth laid in the sea as a pier or breakwater." Writes Howe: "Thoreau calls a pier a 'noble mole' because the sea is silent but as waves wash against and around it they sound and sound is language" ("Sorting Facts; or, Nineteen Ways of Looking at Marker" 319). Thus poetry is created at the intersections of language and silence.

37. French philosopher Simone Weil's collection of essays and letters entitled *Attente de Dieu (Waiting for God)* was published posthumously in 1950. As Beckett's *Waiting for Godot* was written in 1949 and first published in 1952, there is no way Beckett could have been aware of Weil's title in choosing his own. Nonetheless, I feel the coincidence of two such similar titles bears mentioning. I am also evoking Weil

here due to her traits and biographic details that resonate with Howe's text: Weil's sense of enduring uprootedness, her struggle to claim "freedom from conformity," the "peculiarity" of her language, and, finally, her death by self-starvation. As Gabriella Fiori describes in her book *Simone Weil: An Intellectual Biography,* Weil's lifelong anorexia was caused by "*a fear of devouring*... This fear coincided with her fear of being devoured, of losing her own integrity" (1989: 302). Weil's refusal to eat and her resulting death stand in contrast to the speaker at the end of the *Book of Cordelia,* who saves her life by devouring the ladder.

38. In this reading of the messenger boys as cross-dressing women, the Renaissance norm of boy actors playing the parts of girls and women is subverted through inversion. Thus, the silence and invisibility of women is countered by their presence on center stage (albeit in disguise) and in speaking parts. A biographical link to this strategy of girl actors dressing as boys is established by the cover photograph on Howe's latest book *Pierce-Arrow* showing a ten-year-old Howe dressed as the boy Astyanax, son of Hector and Andromache, in a school production of *The Trojan Women.*

39. In his three-volume treatise on the effects of a parent's (usually mother's) absence on the development of a child, John Bowlby discusses the difficulty of pinning down the terms *presence* and *absence.* He argues that both terms "are relative and ... give rise to misunderstanding," and that "finding suitable language [to discuss these realms] is a problem." In an appendix to volume 2, Bowlby devotes five pages to "problems of terminology." See Bowlby's *Attachment and Loss* (London: Hogarth Press & Institute of Psycho-Analysis, 1973), 23, 404–408. Both *The Liberties* and *Pythagorean Silence* seem to me concerned and struggling with the meaning of a parent's absence and the lasting presence of that absence in the grown child's life.

40. Howe may be evoking Wallace Stevens's 1921 poem "The Snow Man" and his usage of the word *nothing* as a fierce and powerful presence. The final stanza of Stevens's five-stanza poem goes as follows:

> For the listener, who listens in the snow,
> And, nothing himself, beholds
> Nothing that is not there and the nothing that is. (Stevens 1972: 54)

In her interview with Keller, Howe names Wallace Stevens as "my favorite poet of the twentieth century," attributing his poetry with having "change[d] my consciousness" (Keller 1995: 23).

41. *Generic restlessness* is the term coined and applied to the long poem by Smaro Kambouli in *On the Edge of Genre: The Contemporary Canadian Long Poem* (Toronto: University of Toronto Press, 1991). Regarding this type of generic restlessness in her introduction to *Illuminations,* Hannah Arendt writes at length about the impossibility of classifying Benjamin's writings. "The trouble with everything Benjamin wrote," she argues, "was that it always turned out to be *sui generis.*" Howe is certainly working in this revolutionary tradition (a nontradition) of writing that "neither fits the exist-

ing order nor introduces a new genre that lends itself to future classification" (1968: 3).

42. The textual proximity between the name Sojourner and the twice repeated reference to "truth" in her speech evokes the mid-nineteenth-century American figure of Sojourner Truth (1797–1883). Born into slavery, sold three times before she was twelve, birthing thirteen children, and fleeing to freedom at the age of thirty, Sojourner Truth is well known as an early champion of women's rights, in addition to her ongoing struggle for emancipation. In 1843, after a mystical conversation with God, who told her "to travel up and down the land" to preach the sins of slavery, she shed her given name (Isabella Baumfree) and renamed herself Sojourner Truth. Because of the allusion to her, one is led to read Howe's ungendered Sojourner character as female. More crucially, her ultimate liberation tale provides an alternative at *The Liberties'* end to the bonded figures of Stella and Cordelia, and her renaming of herself speaks to the centrality of language in the liberation process. For further discussion of Sojourner Truth, see Tindall and Shi's *America: A Narrative History* (New York: W. W. Norton, 1993).

43. In his collection *One Way Street and Other Writings,* Benjamin speaks of the tales embedded in and the great appeal of old stamps. "To someone looking through piles of old letters," he states, "a stamp that has long been out of circulation on a torn envelope often says more than a reading of dozens of pages." The stamp, with its pictorial nature, speaks most directly to the child who "[l]ike Gulliver . . . travels among the lands and peoples of his postage stamps. The geography and history of the Lilliputians, the whole science of the little nation . . . , is instilled in him in sleep" (1979: 91–94). For my analysis of *The Liberties,* it is a wonderful coincidence that Benjamin should mention Swift's writings in his discussion of the stamp. Certainly, it is intentional on Howe's part to evoke the visual authority of a stamp, in addition to its function as a facilitator of communication across borders and nationalities.

44. See also Paul Naylor's discussion of Benjamin's "angel of history" in his excellent analyses of five "contemporary investigative poets" in *Poetic Investigations: Singing the Holes in History* (Evanston, IL: Northwestern University Press, 1999), 25–26.

45. This five-year span of silence in Pythagorean training parallels the five years of Howe's father's absence from their household during World War II—a period that marked for Howe the end of childhood. "[A]fter he came back from the war he didn't like me much," explains Howe in the Falon interview. "I was difficult. I don't blame him." Howe names *Pythagorean Silence* "a gift across space to my father" (1995: 36–40).

46. This effect of nearness bordering on merging is already partially lost in the edition I am working from here, the 1990 Sun & Moon printing of *Pythagorean Silence,* as collected in *The Europe of Trusts.*

47. Jerome McGann points out that the isolated capital letter *R* at the right margin on the following page—"R/ (her cry / silences / whole / vocabularies / of *names* for / *things*" (*Pythagorean Silence* 22)—"rhymes sonically with the copulative 'are' appear-

ing in the previous passage" (McGann 1993: 100), in addition to signifying the afore-mentioned Rachel at Rama propelled forward into the catastrophe of Pearl Harbor, a postmodern "day of lamentation" (98). Thus, from the very opening of this poetic text, issues of presence and absence are insistently foregrounded, even as the histori-cal spectrum is conflated. For McGann's excellent analysis of *Pythagorean Silence*, see his *Black Riders*, 98–106. For my analysis of the above passage, see p. 116 of this chap-ter.

48. All passages from Lacan's essays are taken from the English selection of *Ecrits*, translated by Alan Sheridan (New York: Norton, 1977). It is interesting to note that Lacan's essays, like Pythagoras's teachings, were primarily oral in nature, first deliv-ered as lectures. In fact, Lacan explains choosing the title "Ecrits" for his printed collection by stating that *"un ecrit* in my opinion is made not to be read" (Gallop 1985: 44–45). While this explanation is certainly ironic, and possibly playful, in na-ture, it is worth considering what Lacan is privileging in this apparent preference for an oral transmission of his teachings. Obviously, questions of Lacan's style enter here, as indeed his texts often seem designed "not-to-be-read." Finally, the sound element as primary echoes the conclusions drawn in *The Liberties*, where sight is always lim-ited and failing.

49. I am adopting here the version of the Narcissus myth, as presented in Bonnefoy's *Mythologies* (Chicago: University of Chicago Press, 1981), wherein Narcis-sus does not recognize himself in the water and falls in love with an image that is, for him, Other. Bonnefoy maintains that this version of the myth is the more universally accepted one.

50. Considering her ongoing and intense preoccupation with the roots of words and with their protean nature, Howe's linking of woods and words is charged with etymological meaning. In her fascinating essay entitled "Touch Wood: Coming to Terms with Bibliography," Caroline Blyth traces the "natural topography" intrinsic to every text by virtue of the wood- and woods-related linguistic roots of bibliographic words. Blyth writes: "The natural lexicon of Bibliography contains these words: *fo-lium:* the leaf; giving the leaves or folios of a book: *liber:* the inner bark of the tree, which gives our 'library'; *biblos/biblion:* the inner bark of the papyrus, from the Greek 'Βιβλος,' writing; which gives 'Bible' and BIBLIOGRAPHY; the Old English *boc:* beech tree: which gives book . . . ; and the Latin *codex/caudex:* the trunk or stem of a tree, then wooden tablet, and a bundle of tablets strung together, then a collection of parchment leaves; which gives 'codices,' or books of sacred writings, and 'code'" (67). With a Howe-like attention to the *materiality* of reading—and writing—Blyth argues that these wooded words "give shape to language, because . . . they *are* the shape of language" (67). In a manner resonant of Howe and her own interest in Thoreau (see chap. 2, pp. 50–52), Blyth's essay also highlights Thoreau's attentiveness to "the natu-ral forms" informing our literary world, and word, quoting at length from Thoreau's "extraordinary exfoliation of language" in *Walden, or Life in the Woods* (67–68). See *Word and Image* 9:1 (Jan.-Mar. 1993): 66–79. I am beholden to Craig Douglas Dworkin's

superb essay "'Waging Political Babble': Susan Howe's Visual Prosody and the Politics of Noise" for leading me to Blyth's essay. See *Word and Image* 12:4 (Oct.-Dec. 1996): 389–405.

Chapter 4

1. In addition to the entirety of *My Emily Dickinson* (Berkeley, CA: North Atlantic Books, 1985), see "These Flames and Generosities of the Heart: Emily Dickinson and the Illogic of Sumptuary Values," in *The Birth-mark* (Hanover and London: Wesleyan University Press, 1993), 131–153; rpt. *In Artifice and Indeterminacy: An Anthology of New Poetics* (Tuscaloosa: University of Alabama Press, 1998), 319–341.

2. These dates are the years of original publication. *A Bibliography of the King's Book or, Eikon Basilike* was published by Paradigm Press (Providence, RI) and *The Nonconformist's Memorial* was published by the Grenfell Press (New York) in a limited edition with illustrations by Robert Mangold. Both works were later collected—together with two other works—in a volume also entitled *The Nonconformist's Memorial*, published by New Directions Books in 1993. In my analysis of *Eikon Basilike* I will be referring to the original publication. As that book has no original page numbers, I have paginated it for easier reference, starting with the first page of the prose preface "Making the Ghost Walk About Again and Again" and continuing consecutively from there (including blank pages). In the New Directions publication of *Eikon Basilike*, the text, which is originally fifty-three pages is reduced to thirty-five pages, primarily by placing two poems to a page. For my analysis of *The Nonconformist's Memorial* I will be referring to the New Directions edition.

3. Patricia Caldwell has argued that in the 1637 Antinomian Controversy—"a monumental crisis of language"—Hutchinson both breaks the religious law of her community and, unwittingly, breaks off communication with her "readers," the New England founding fathers (1976: 346). The consequences, of course, were her banishment and eventual death. See chapter 2 of this book, pp. 45–49, for a discussion of this controversy. Some critics may argue that Howe, too, by so radically breaking literary conventions, finally breaks off communication with her reader. I would argue instead that in all her work Howe is redefining the notion of poetic communication. See my introductory chapter for a discussion of the density—sometimes termed "obscurity"—of Howe's work.

4. "The last of the four Gospels," writes George Beasley-Murray, "appears among the rest in a manner reminiscent of the appearance of Melchizedek to Abraham: 'without father, without mother, without genealogy' (Heb. 7:3). Everything we want to know about this book is uncertain, and everything about it that is apparently knowable is a matter of dispute" (1987: 376). One may assume Howe is attracted to this text for these very reasons.

5. Excommunicated from her community, Hutchinson moved first to Rhode Is-

land and later, after her husband's death, to an even more remote spot on the Long Island Sound. As Emery Battis describes her situation, "she was now alone with only her children about her and but 2 neighbors for miles around. For ten years she had been moving steadily toward this final isolation" (1962: 248). Isolated as she was, she became easy prey for a band of Indians who, in the summer of 1643, "intent on clearing all white settlers from their hunting ground," massacred her and five of her children.

6. For a description of the baby's deformities, as recorded by Dr. John Clark (and quoted in Battis 1962: 347–348), see chapter 2, note 34.

7. Obviously, the end of the English Civil Wars, the beheading of Charles I, and the Protectorate of the Puritan Oliver Cromwell had a direct impact on the American colony as it slowed the immigration of Puritans to the New World. The fact of the regicide, and America's reaction to it, also served to foreground for the colonialists—perhaps for the first time—their separateness from the English motherland. As Howe states, "[i]n America the regicides were heroes—in England, villains" (Foster 1994: 63). Conversely, the actual impact, if any, that the Antinomian Controversy had on seventeenth-century England is harder to determine, though we do know that the Old World was interested in all news from the colony and would most certainly have received news of this "most momentous event in the 1st decade of settlement" (Erikson 1966: 71).

8. In his comprehensive study of the trial of Charles I, C. V. Wedgwood maintains that "the majority of the English people did not want their King's execution," though "[i]t needs to be remembered that whether they wanted it or not, the majority of the English people were prepared to accept it." Indeed, "from the removal of the King from Newport until his death on the scaffold, not one of the King's subjects risked his life to save him." See *The Trial of Charles I* (London: Collins, 1964), 47–48. Howe speaks of the execution of Charles as "a primal sin in the eyes of the Puritans who killed him" (Foster 1994: 63).

9. Adopting a suggestion first proffered by Jeremy Taylor, Wedgwood has argued that the choice of a Greek title for the collection, printed in Greek letters, may in fact have been a tactic to "conceal the character of the book for the first few days of its existence, just long enough for it to capture the public imagination and give the printer time to cover his tracks." An additional tactic adopted to frustrate the censors was the publishing of first editions without the printer's name attached to the work (1964: 206). Clearly, the Royalists printing and circulating the *Eikon Basilike* were aware of both the potential impact of the book and of the government censors on their heels. Lois Potter has argued that even as certain restrictions on expression were lifted during the printing explosion that took place in the first half of the seventeenth century (i.e., the abolition in 1641 of the central literary licensing authority known as the Star Chamber)—or, paradoxically, *because of* this newfound freedom—publishers and writers often needed to adopt strategies of subterfuge, such as pseudonyms, encoded meanings, and "elliptical presentations," in order to avoid prison and/or censorship. See Potter's *Secret Rites and Secret Writing: Royalist Literature 1641–1660*.

10. I am beholden to Joel Kuszai's unpublished, excellent essay entitled "Prayer in a Time of Captivity" for its wonderful insights and for showing me possibilities for an analysis of *Eikon*'s complex and multilayered text.

11. The visual "crowdedness" of the text is experienced by the reader/listener also aurally—as a great "'noise emitted by the surface of the work of art'" (John E. Bowlt qtd. in Dworkin 1996: 402). The *noise* of Howe's texts is not only an expression of violence but also serves to unsettle what Bernstein has named "official verse culture" (1986: 247) and, as such, to provide "the potential for new social and political orders" (Dworkin 1996: 397). For an insightful and highly engaging discussion of the "noise" in Howe's poetry, see Dworkin's "'Waging Political Babble': Susan Howe's Visual Prosody and the Politics of Noise" in *Word and Image* 12:4 (Oct.-Dec. 1996): 389–405. See also p. 139 of this chapter.

12. The "tangled textual history" (Woudhuysen 1996: 317) of Sidney's *Arcadia* itself is worth noting, particularly within the context of Howe's preoccupation with the impossibility of "finding the original" text or of ever knowing authorial intention. There are three major versions of *Arcadia:* the first—*Old Arcadia*—was composed sometime between 1577 and 1582, then abandoned and lost, resurfacing only in the beginning of the twentieth century. The second version, now known as the *New Arcadia,* was Sidney's revision and expansion of his first text, though never finished (the *New Arcadia* breaks off in midsentence partway through the third book). The third version of *Arcadia* is a composite text edited by Sidney's friend and fellow poet Fulke Greville and his sister Mary, the countess of Pembroke, and printed in 1593. In this composite version—called a "broken-backed hybrid" by Woudhuysen (299)—the last two and a half books of the *Old Arcadia* were grafted onto the *New.* None of the above versions were published by Sidney himself. Three studies that provide useful discussions of the history of Sidney's *Arcadia* are H. R. Woudhuysen's *Sir Philip Sidney and the Circulation of Manuscripts, 1558–1640* (Oxford: Clarendon Press, 1996), Joan Rees's *Sir Philip Sidney and Arcadia* (London and Toronto: Associated University Presses, 1991), and Annabel Patterson's *Censorship and Interpretation: The Condition of Writing and Reading in Early Modern England* (Madison: University of Wisconsin Press, 1984).

13. The world's first copyright law—called the Statute of Anne—was legislated in England in 1710. See Mark Rose's *Authors and Owners: The Invention of Copyright* (Cambridge, MA: Harvard University Press, 1993) for an extensive discussion of literary proprietorship in eighteenth-century Britain.

14. Even in her choice of working in the bibliographic arena, Howe expresses her antinomian nature, for bibliography itself has been aptly called a maverick genre— prone to dissension and resisting easy categorization (Blyth 1993: 66). For a wonderful discussion of the subject of Bibliography—a "recognition of the mobility of [its] choreography and the unpredictability of its motive forces"—see Blyth's "Touch Wood: Coming to Terms with Bibliography" *Word and Image* 9:1 (Jan.-Mar. 1993): 66–79.

15. The role of Arachne in Howe's *Eikon Basilike* will be considered at greater length toward the end of this analysis. Suffice it to say at this point that with this "woule" at the poem's opening and the "winding / wool / Cloud / soft" at the poem's end (53), a

subtle though present sound frame is created for the entire text. While clearly a poet deeply involved with the visual aspect of poetry, Howe herself names sound as "*the* element in poetry" (Keller 1995: 13).

16. The captive king and shepherdess who wander through Howe's *Eikon* may lead one to consider how this text, too, like her *Articulation of Sound Forms in Time*, is some form of captivity narrative, though here within its very different Old World context. The motif of captivity and freedom surfaces in much of Howe's work and seems to be a crucial component of her poetics (as is apparent in the second epigraph to this chapter). With the literal captive king as its ever-present backdrop, Howe's *Eikon* engages the theme of literary freedom, whereby the text "liberates" itself and its readers from myriad poetic conventions.

17. The question of *in what order* one reads upside-down lines integrated into a normative text becomes particularly crucial in certain sections of *The Nonconformist's Memorial* (see pp. 6–7, 20–21 of the poem) and will be considered at greater length later in this chapter.

18. In her comprehensive and invaluable study of the printing press as "an agent of change," Elizabeth Eisenstein states that literary subterfuge was widespread in early modern Europe, suggesting a correlation between the ability to reach a wider audience as afforded by the printing press and an increased danger in printing one's views and opinions: the greater one's potential impact, the greater the risk of displeasing those in power. "The need to evade censors and to engage in clandestine activities was so common," writes Eisenstein, "that it characterized many 'normal' large-scale book-trade ventures in early-modern Europe" (1964: 142).

19. In the *Talisman* interview, Howe maintains that "form-breaking" writers attract more "ugly antipathy" and are in greater danger of their writing getting lost than avant-garde visual artists who, in fact, "enjoy wide popularity, are embraced by a critical establishment and sell their works for a tremendous amount of money." This difference in treatment, states Howe, "is because words are used as buoys, and if they start to break up . . . [t]hen everything goes" (Foster 1994: 65). Reaching a place where "everything goes" (conventions, structures, expectations) seems to be, in fact, a central objective of Howe's poetic project, with the resulting blank white canvas (as evoked in the Falon interview 1989: 42), the most fertile artistic site of possibilities and regeneration.

20. In his seminal book *The Open Work*, Umberto Eco proposes that "[p]erhaps we are in a position to state that for these [open and experimental] works of art an incomplete knowledge of the system is in fact an essential feature in its formulation" (1989: 15). I believe that "incomplete knowledge of the system" and, consequently, partial understanding of its meaning is not only "an essential feature" of the work's formulation but also central to Howe's antinomian position. Operating within an arena of "incomplete knowing," the reader—and, in some sense, the writer before her—depend only on their individual encounter with the work, forfeiting at the outset the notion of an "authoritative reading."

21. Obviously, the "doe" may also be read as a reference to the animal, a syntactically normative reading of the line. Joel Kuszai reads this "doe" as an evocation of Dickinson's poem "My Life Had Stood—A Loaded Gun"—a poem Howe analyzes in depth in *My Emily Dickinson,* devoting almost half of her book to a close, complex, and highly intertextual reading of the work (see *My Emily Dickinson* 75–120). Kuszai maintains that Howe identifies with both the subject (huntress) and the object (the hunted doe) and that the imagery involves "a rigorous empowerment." I read this "doe of Title-page"-ancient ("aud") and textual ("Paged")—as a metaphor for "the Poet," who is, Howe maintains, "an animal charmed in one spot, eyes fixed to the light" (97). The doe/poet as transfixed—and exposed—by the light re-evokes the aforementioned danger implicit in the writing project, though the possibility of enlightenment through the entrancement of the creating moment is no less palpable.

22. In the text of the prayer itself, there is mention of "some beam of thy Majesty so to shine on my mind" (*Arcadia* 336; *Eikon Basilike* 197). Thus, the original frontispiece engraving may be a representation of the verbal image, retranslated into the visual by Howe.

23. In his study of the visual dimensions of William Carlos Williams's poetry, Henry M. Sayre states that "the visual poem is an object to be perceived *and* read: the visual text does not dismiss 'reading.' The visual text is, rather, a dimension of the poem's experience which is parallel to its reading, an experience which in fact completes the poem" (1983: 7). This insistence on the equal importance of the visual and verbal and their completion of each other in the visual poem seems a useful, even crucial, framework for engaging Howe's poetry.

24. This title page is missing from Howe's *Eikon Basilike* as reprinted in the 1993 New Directions collection. In addition, the poems of pages 23–51 are put two on the page in the 1993 version, as opposed to being situated single and mid-page in the original printing. As Howe states in the Keller interview, "[a]s you [the poet] get more known, you tend to get anthologized, which means your work gets jammed together," and "[s]adly," in the process, "space always gets lost" (1995: 19). In many ways, Howe may be read as a poet committed to the retrieval of lost space; the 1993 edition of the *Eikon* seems to me less effective than the original as this "retrieval of lost space" is less apparent. Despite this sense of something missing from the reprinted version of the *Eikon,* and the unfortunate omission of the highly provocative crossed-out title page, I find it wholly appropriate that within the context of a poem concerned with the variant versions and the instability of a text, the two published editions of the poem itself should be different from each other.

25. In the *Talisman* interview, Howe states that the figures of two bibliographer/editors important in her life—her father and the then ailing George Butterick, editor of Charles Olson's work—were on her mind while writing *Eikon.* The role of the bibliographer/editor is one she values highly, as is evident in her naming Butterick's bibliographic scholarship and editing care as "heroic. In the fine sense of heroic. Unselfish and undaring, uncompromising" (Foster 1994: 63). For Howe, the bibliog-

rapher/editor is a type of pilgrim on the shores of a text and has, therefore, the great responsibility of providing a report of the land that takes all of the land/text's permutations into account. Howe's interest in the bibliographer/editor's role is apparent in her Dickinson scholarship and her enduring anger over the mis-editing of Dickinson's work.

26. Joel Kuszai has identified the passage "O make me / of joy" (and "No men / as expected / ever will be / Saviours," p. 25) as lifted from a table in Edward Almack's bibliography, which lists errata in the earliest editions of Charles's *Eikon Basilike* (Kuszai 23). As Kuszai notes, "this list reads like a poem" by actually giving portions of the list poetic form and significance, Howe foregrounds the sense and poetic value she sees "in the chance meeting of words" (*My Emily Dickinson* 24). Additional isolated words that may have been lifted from this list and that appear in a scattered, sometimes revised fashion through Howe's text include: "to Sea by a storme" (34, 42), "perpetrations" (39), and "populacy" (14, 15, 18). The passage "O make me / of joy" has the register of prayer and may be connected back to the "praier in a time of captivity." The speaker of the passage is also Howe herself, invoking what is for her the celebration intrinsic in the creation process.

27. Supporters of the regicide, Milton included, argued that Charles had to be held accountable for instigating the English Civil Wars (1642-1646, 1647-1648, 1649-1651) and that he alone was "guilty of the blood of thousands" (John Cook 1649, qtd. in Laura Blair McKnight in her interesting article "Crucifixion or Apocalypse? Refiguring the *Eikon Basilike*" 1996: 141).

28. More was taken to the scaffold in July 1535 for refusing to subscribe to King Henry VIII's Oath of Supremacy. While not king, he had fallen from the highest office in the realm, that of lord chancellor. For a discussion of More's "self-fashioning," his fondness for the theatrical metaphor—as is apparent in the passage quoted by Howe—and his "triumph and defeat" on the scaffold, see Stephen Greenblatt's *Renaissance Self-Fashioning: From More to Shakespeare* (Chicago: University of Chicago Press, 1980).

29. Almost every historical, and mythological, figure mentioned in the *Eikon* is subjected to some form of violence. Of the cast of seven characters mentioned in what I consider an additional introductory page (16), five were beheaded (Archbishop Laud, Charles I, the earl of Holland, John Capel, and the duke of Hamilton). Cromwell is also mentioned on this page and, while he died in his bed, after the Restoration his body was subjected to extreme violence and to a symbolic beheading whereby his head was reportedly stuck on a pole atop Westminster Hall and left there until the end of Charles II's reign. An additional central character in this poem is Milton, who was imprisoned and had his books burned.

30. Lois Potter marks 1641 as the beginning of the printing explosion in England and states that the record number of publications—particularly pamphlets—printed in 1642 was not matched in number until 1690 (1989: 1-4).

31. The virgule is present in Howe's text, at the end of the line, resulting in a doubly marked line break and a double fragmentation of the word *narrative*. This

emphasized disjunctiveness may be read as a representation of the general disman-
tling through ignoring of Mrs. Gauden's version of the authorship question.

32. For a useful overview of Puritan iconoclasm and its theological and historical
roots, see John Phillips's *The Reformation of Images: Destruction of Art in England, 1535–
1660* (Berkeley: University of Berkeley Press, 1973).

33. The following Howe works all make use of some variation on the mirroring
technique: *Secret History of the Dividing Line, Thorow, Articulation of Sound Forms in Time,
Eikon Basilike,* and *The Nonconformist's Memorial.* For a discussion of the mirrored pas-
sages in Howe's American work, see chap. 2, pp. 35–36, 53–56.

34. This notion of a "negative icon" first came to me while reading Ann Kibbey's
important book on the complexities of Puritan iconoclasm, where she notes that
"what historians and critics have misunderstood as a categorical opposition to im-
ages was actually a devoted, if *negative,* act of reverence" (1986: 42; my italics).

35. In her essay on the French documentary filmmaker Chris Marker, Howe names
Russian Futurist poet Vladimir Mayakovsky and Russian avant-garde filmmaker Dziga
Vertov (a pseudonym) "iconoclastic image-makers"—recognizing the contradictory
nature of the term and embracing the rhetorical trope of oxymoron as itself genera-
tive and instructive (1996: 297–298). Utilizing and inverting Howe's term, I would
name Howe an image-making iconoclast in the visually intricate, ornate, and charged-
with-meaning poetry of *Eikon Basilike.*

36. The capitalized first two letters of these lines appear to be based on an early
printing convention whereby the auditory unit (ST and BE) takes precedence over
the semantic. This capitalization of the opening two letters of a word is apparent in
the printing data recorded in Madan and Almack's bibliographies. The division be-
tween words as marked on page 11 of Howe's *Eikon* ("IN | HIS | SOLITUDE|") can
be explained in a similar fashion whereby some visual design and typographical en-
actment supersedes the organizing principle of a grammatical phrase. See Walter
Ong's *Orality and Literacy* (1982: 117–122).

37. In the 1662 edition of *The Works of King Charles the Martyr* housed in the rare-
books collection of the Hebrew University National Library, the frontispiece shows
beside the rock (see fig. 4.2) a ship being tossed about on a stormy sea, with the figure
of the king seated royally at the stern. This frontispiece shows a more detailed and
realistic portrait of the king's likeness, presents the king's full face instead of his
profile, and has the king facing left instead of right. Despite these differences, the
main symbolic elements of the original frontispiece—the three crowns and their lo-
cations, the tree with weights, the light beams—are all represented in this later ver-
sion.

38. Within the *Eikon*'s historical context, wherein the legitimacy of the sovereign
ruler is challenged and overturned, one cannot help but read in this mirror image an
allusion to Shakespeare's representation of an earlier deposed king, Richard II, and
his use of the mirror as a powerful prop. In the abdication/deposition scene of *Rich-
ard II,* the king commands a mirror to be brought forth "That it may show me what

a face I have, / Since it is bankrout of his majesty" (IV.i.265–266). After closely examining his face in the mirror and finding in it no resemblance of his former shining royal self "[t]hat, like the sun, did make beholders wink" (IV.i.283), Richard violently throws the mirror down on the ground, cracking it into "a hundred shivers" (IV.i.288). The motifs of royalty that are worn like a costume, of multiple versions of a single self, and of the violence intrinsic to the shattering of an icon expressed in this scene are, of course, germane to my reading of Howe's *Eikon*. In addition, like Shakespeare, Howe uses the traditional sun/king analogy, though Charles is for her an "antic sun" and thus as close to clown as he is to king. "Saying so I name nobody[,]" remarks Howe at the end of that lyric (28), implying that this characterization is not an indictment of Charles personally but rather of the power structures in general.

39. In her essay "These Flames and Generosities of the Heart: Emily Dickinson and the Illogic of Sumptuary Values," Howe poses the rhetorical question "What is writing but continuing" (*Birth-mark* 143). In my use of the word *continuer,* I mean to allude also to Virginia Woolf's statement in *A Room of One's Own* that "books continue each other, in spite of our habit of judging them separately" (1957: 84). On the penultimate page of that text, Woolf talks about the "continuing presences" of dead poets and their impact on the poetic creation unfolding in the present (117).

40. The original description of the execution scene states that troops were stationed around the scaffold to "hindred the approach of the very numerous Spectators, and the King from speaking what he had premeditated, and prepared for them to hear." The executioners were wary of Charles's unruly language usage and, continuing a strategy adopted in the trial and apparent in their fierce attempts to control the publication of his *Eikon,* remained intent on erasing his words from the political landscape. The king understood their staging of his final scene, as is apparent in his first recorded words upon the scaffold: "I shall be very little heard of any body here" (*The Works of King Charles* 452). As a king of images, however, Charles was able to perform also without words.

41. This "execution performance" was not unique to Charles I but was, in fact, mandated by the expectations of the time. J. A. Sharpe notes that public executions in seventeenth-century England "were carried out in a context of ceremony and ritual" and that they were "a theater of punishment," with those being executed as "willing central participants" (1985: 146, 153). What is particularly fascinating about Sharpe's informative article is its failure to mention the most famous English execution of the seventeenth century, that of Charles I. I imagine that one of the reasons for this omission is the absence in Charles's execution scene of an important element in the "set-piece execution" (158) and a particular focus of Sharpe's research—the scaffold confession. Charles's enigmatic final word—"Remember"—an imperative from the grave, may be read as his deviation from the generic conventions of this "theater of punishment" in order to accomplish his own performing objectives. For references to Charles's last word in Howe's *Eikon,* see pages 4 and 26.

42. Loewenstein's use of the phrase "self-fashioning" is certainly an allusion to Stephen Greenblatt's seminal work *Renaissance Self-Fashioning: From More to*

Shakespeare (Chicago: University of Chicago Press, 1980). In *Renaissance Self-Fashioning,* Greenblatt mentions that "the theatrical metaphor was [Sir Thomas] More's favorite," as is evident in the passage quoted from More in Howe's *Eikon* (12). "[T]he theater pays tribute to the world that it loves—or at least that it cannot live without," writes Greenblatt, "even as it exposes that world as a fiction . . . to conceive of kingship as a dramatic part, an expensive costume and some well-rehearsed lines, is potentially at least to demystify it" (27). Howe's *Eikon,* through its use of theater tropes, engages with this paradoxical relationship between the theater and the world, where each may, eventually, expose the other as false.

43. Loewenstein also notes that "the first unmistakably pejorative sense of the word 'theatrical' recorded in the Oxford Dictionary dates from 1649"—the year both *Eikon Basilike* and *Eikonoklastes* were published—and that the denotation given is of that which "simulates, or is simulated" and that which is "artificial, affected, assumed" (1990: 61).

44. *The Lie* may be an allusion to a 1641 anonymous pamphlet entitled *The Liar: or, a contradiction to Those who in the titles of their Books affirmed them to be true, when they were false: although mine are all true, yet I term them Lyes* (Potter 1989: 6). In this title, the writer has cross-dressed what he perceives as truth and lies in order to draw attention to the instability of the terms.

45. I am not using the term *verbal icon* as W. K. Wimsatt does in his book of the same name. Wimsatt refers to a verbal icon as "a verbal image which most fully realizes its verbal capacities . . . [through] an interpretation of reality in its metaphoric and symbolic dimensions" (1954: x). I am referring to a verbal icon in a more literal way as a text that, iconlike, is venerated as authoritative and hence worthy of worship and literary canonization.

46. The word *quire* is a variant and archaic form of *choir,* a section in the church where the congregation may sit, audience-like, and watch the ritual performances at the main altar. *Quire* also refers to "a set of folded sheets, as of a book, fitting one into another." Thus, in her careful choice of a word, Howe presents an intertwined image of the book reader and the theater audience that are, in the end, a single entity. The full phrase in this poem is "In the High Quire / We that are distant" (*Eikon* 44). It is interesting to note that this is the only instant of the plural first person *we* appearing in the entire text, as though toward the end of her *Eikon,* through the audience-oriented poetics of the text, Howe has created for herself a community.

47. I am marking the epigraph poem as the poetic beginning of the *Eikon.* Twenty pages from this beginning is the first mention of a female figure ("In his sister's papers" [28]). The end of the text is twenty pages from the final page in this midpoint five-page unit wherein the first mention of Arachne is made (33).

48. Of the three sisters, only the name of Sidney's, the countess of Pembroke, is commonly known, by virtue of her name appearing on many editions of his *Arcadia.* Sidney dedicated the *Old Arcadia* to her: in this dedication, he admits the centrality of her reading, perhaps editing, eye in the composition process, describing the work's composition as "'being done in loose sheets of paper, most of it in your presence, the

rest by sheets sent unto you as fast as they were done'" (qtd. in Woudhuysen 1996: 303–304). The countess of Pembroke also played a later role in shaping the *Arcadia*, offering revisions for the first printing of the text in 1590 and overseeing the second printing in 1593 (Rees 1991: 18–19).

49. The denotation of the idiom "to give up the ghost" is, of course, "to cease living or functioning; to die." However, within the context of this text's repeated references to the king's ghost, I believe that Howe is here deconstructing this idiom. Thus I read this line as meaning that the Gaudens's silence "gave up" or gave over, like a gift or a burnt offering, the ghost of King Charles as the sole author of the *Eikon Basilike*.

50. As Howe's *Eikon* is at all times in resistance to the notion of the closed and authoritative canon—literary or religious—Howe's choice of introducing into her text a tale from the *Apocrypha* is itself charged with meaning. The *Apocrypha* of course is the collection of texts that were excluded from the Hebrew or Christian canons because "they were secondary or questionable or heretical" (*The New England Bible with the Apocrypha* 1970: v). The word *apocrypha* originates in the Greek word for "hidden things" and "apocryphal" commonly refers to texts of questionable authorship or authenticity.

51. In the trial transcripts, there are two recorded instances of "the rabble of Soldiers" crying out "Justice Justice" as the king entered Westminster Hall (1652: 440, 448). However, not all interposed comments made during the court proceedings were in condemnation of the king; on the fourth and final day of the trial, an unnamed lady, responding to Bradshaw's demand that the king "Answer to the Charge of Treason and other high Crimes . . . [made] in the name of the people," called out "Not half the people," declaring thus her support of the king. She was quickly "silenced with threats" (441).

52. The sound links between these words may, in fact, be part of a larger aural trajectory, originating with *Arcadia*—twice mentioned in the opening pages of Howe's *Eikon Basilike* (3). The reverse rhyme of "Arcadia" and "Archaic"—together with the sound similarities between "Archaic," "Arachne," and "Ariadne"—establishes a lineage of fictive women submerged beneath the weight of male heroes saturating the Western canon—a lineage Howe is committed to naming. I am beholden to Cynthia Hogue for pointing out the presence of "Arcadia" in the sound map of "Archaic," "Arachne," and "Ariadne" (1999: 62).

53. My source, and Howe's, for both the Arachne and Ariadne tales is Ovid's *Metamorphoses*. As there are no line numbers in the edition I will be referring to (A. D. Melville, trans. [Oxford: Oxford University Press, 1986]), I will give book number and page number as references.

54. The relevant passage in *Metamorphoses* (125) reads as follows:

> . . . .Incensed at such
> Success the warrior goddess, golden-haired,
> Tore up the tapestry, those crimes of heaven,

And with the boxwood shuttle in her hand
... three times, four times, struck
Arachne on her forehead. ....

The "crimes of heaven" can be read as referring not only to Arachne's heretical initial challenge to the goddess but also as referring to Athena's violent and unjust reactions to evidence of Arachne's great talent. I am inclined to read Athena's "guilt" as resting also in her refusal of a traditional female role: as Nancy Miller notes, "Athena identifies not only with the gods but with the godhead, the cerebral male identity that bypasses the female" (1988: 82).

55. For extensive use of the priest/poet analogy in the American tradition, see Walt Whitman's preface to *Leaves of Grass* (*The Norton Anthology to American Literature*, 1:2033–2047). The notion of poets answering a sacred and spiritual calling is abundantly evident in Emerson's essay *The Poet* (1:1073–1088),which of course had a great impact on Whitman's writings and thinking.

56. It seems worth noting that Ariadne is not only in defiance of her father, but that she is willing to sacrifice her half brother, the Minotaur, for her beloved. The Minotaur was born of the union between Ariadne's mother, Pasiphaë, and "a wonderfully beautiful bull" (Hamilton 1940: 151).

57. Ariadne appears in a single line in Homer's *Iliad*. In Ovid's *Metamorphoses*, her name appears in the text only once and only in a subordinate and modifying role ("Ariadne's aid"), to describe the type of help Theseus received.

58. In Ovid's *Heriodes*, Ariadne predicts her own elision from the literary retellings of the tale that she in part authors when she writes to Theseus and begs "not to be stolen from the record of [his] honours" when he tells "gloriously" of "the death of the man-and-bull, and of the hall of rock cut out in winding ways" (1971: X, 131). I am beholden to Nancy Miller's article "Arachnologies" for pointing out that passage. See Miller's article also for a cogent and intriguing discussion of how "female desire," as represented in the tale of Ariadne, "becomes the enabling fiction of a male need for mastery" (1988: 94).

59. A discussion of the complex nature of Athena—virgin goddess deeply identified with male markers and social roles—is outside the scope of this chapter, though I have no doubt that an inquiry into the ambiguousness of her character would prove fruitful and intriguing.

60. Many thanks to Lynn Keller for honing this point for me.

61. It is, of course, wholly befitting that—like her Puritan predecessors with whom she is deeply identified and whose lives and "minds [were] saturated with the bible" (Caldwell 1983: 41)—Howe should turn to Scriptures as scaffolding for this poetic work. Indeed, as a latter-day Calvinist, Howe's intellectual framework may be described in the terms Walter Benjamin applied to himself: "My thinking relates to theology the way a blotter does to ink. It is soaked through with it" (qtd. in Smith 1989: xviii).

62. Wendy Sproston writes that "[t]he distance from the Synoptics to John's Gospel often seems not so much a step as a quantum leap," not only because of the

distinctive "Johannine language and style," but, more significantly, due to this gospel's presentation of a divine, rather than historical, Jesus from the book's very opening (1:1–14, most pronouncedly in the final verse, "And the Word was made flesh and dwelt among us"). See Sproston in *The Johannine Writings,* ed. Stanley E. Potter and Craig A. Evans (Sheffield: Sheffield Academic Press, 1995), 138–160. Similarly, John Ashton argues for the different nature of the Johannine Jesus, who is, in effect, "transfigured . . . from the outset" (191: 500). Within this context of an already transformed Jesus, one may read the fourth gospel as primarily the tale of those who come into contact with Jesus and *their* transformation. My analysis of *The NC Memorial* means to focus on just this—the transfiguration of Mary Magdalene.

63. The first Acts of Uniformity were passed in 1549 and in 1559, during the reigns of Edward VI and Elizabeth I respectively. Charles I's father, James I, authorized the Act of Uniformity of 1604, which Charles attempted to enforce. Following the Restoration of the monarchy (1660), the 1662 Act of Uniformity was executed, leading to the Bartholomean Exodus and marking the formal beginnings of what was then called Nonconformism: Protestant dissent from the Anglican Church (Cross 1997). The title of Howe's work, located within a New Testament historical landscape, refers *also* to this seventeenth-century group of religious dissenters, thus reading forward in history and conflating the time spectrum.

64. I am appropriating this evocative appellation from John Ashton, who applies it to the gospel's resurrection tale in his fascinating and exhaustive study *Understanding the Fourth Gospel* (Oxford: Clarendon Press 1991), 506.

65. The disciple Simon Peter, who accompanies the Beloved Disciple to the grave, enters the sepulchre first, even though the Beloved Disciple reaches the site before him. A literary analysis of the text's failure to mention Simon Peter's response to the empty tomb and of the Beloved Disciple's hesitancy to enter the tomb would doubtless proffer intriguing vantage points on the gospel's rhetorical strategies but is, unfortunately, outside the scope of this book.

66. As the personal is at all times a pivotal component of Howe's work, doubtless the loss of her husband, David von Schlegell, informs and propels the other losses—figurative and fictive, linguistic and literal—described in this text. One is led to read Howe's personal loss and love into this work as the New Directions 1993 collection entitled *The Nonconformist's Memorial* is dedicated to David von Schlegell, who passed away in October of 1992. The book's cover of a Percy Bysshe Shelley sketch of a boat stands as a visual memorial for her husband, who was himself a boat designer. For a partial documentation of von Schlegell's life and work, see Howe's elegiac "Sorting Facts; or, Nineteen Ways of Looking at Marker," particularly pp. 295–296, 309–310.

67. Jesus' command to Mary in the recognition scene (unique to John's Gospel) is variously translated as "Touch me not" or "Don't cling to me" (John 20:17). In *The NC Memorial,* Howe quotes from the former version (3) and refers to the latter (11). The Anchor Bible notes state that the verb in 20:17 includes meanings ranging from "touch" and "hold" to "grasp," "cling," and "seize" (1970: 992). In traditional biblical

exegesis, *why* Mary must not hold to Jesus is a subject of vigorous debate, particularly due to the fact that within what appears to be the same timeframe (and in the same chapter) Jesus instructs doubting Thomas to touch both his hands and side (20:27). Does Jesus ascend between the time of the garden scene and his appearance before the other disciples, or is a gendered difference at play here?

68. Obviously, I recognize that my interpretation of this passage is a radical departure from the norms of traditional biblical interpretations.

69. This query may also be read as Howe's rewriting of the question asked of John the Baptist in the opening chapter of John's Gospel, "Who art thou?" (1:22). John's answer is "I am the voice of one crying in the wilderness" (1:23). As Howe has transformed this question into a self-referential one, the "I" may be read as multidetermined and as referring also to the poet herself. In the Keller interview, Howe does not ascribe this "half-hidden phrase 'What am I?'" specifically to Mary, but rather describes the phrase in more general terms as a representation of "identity trying to come out of all this violence of knowledge" (1995: 11). The phrase "What am I?" also clearly resonates with Stella's question "Who can tell me who I am?" in *The Europe of Trusts*, p. 199 (see chap. 3, particularly p. 87).

70. The phrase "I John" extends the intertextuality of this poem by alluding to all three Johannine writings. "I John" may be read as a numerical reference signifying the *First Epistle of John* or as a reference to *The Revelations of St. John the Divine*, where the phrase "I John" is used as a framing device for the book's apocalyptic prophecies (see Rev. 1:9, 21:2, 22:8). For direct references to *Revelations* in *The NC Memorial*, see pp. 17, 25, and 28.

71. The "It is I" phrase resonates with a Melville passage from his Holy Land *Journal*, which Howe quotes and marvels over in the *Talisman* Interview (Foster 1994: 66). In this passage, Melville writes: "Saw a woman over a new grave—no grass on it yet. Such abandonment of misery! Called to the dead, put her head down as close as possible to it; as if calling down a hatchway or a cellar; besought 'Why don't you speak to me? My God—it is I! . . .—all deaf. So much for consolation." While all of Howe's work is deeply influenced by Melville's writings, an additional work collected in the book *The Nonconformist's Memorial* and entitled "Melville's Marginalia" explicitly evokes the nineteenth-century writer and his works.

72. See Kibbey's *The Interpretation of Material Shapes in Puritanism* for a fascinating discussion of Calvin's choice of metonymy "as the normative religious trope" and of the Puritan's insistence on the "unchanging materiality of the bread" and wine in the Eucharist sacrament (1986: 51–56).

73. This first-person plural form ("we know not") is traditionally read as evidence of the Synoptic tradition (where Mary is accompanied by at least one other woman on her early-morning visit to the sepulchre) influencing John and infiltrating his narrative (Byrne 1995: 33–34). While Howe is clearly aware of this interpretation, as is apparent in her line "Wording of an earlier tradition" (12), the "we" of course takes on added significance within the text's play of pronouns. I believe, however, that in

The NC Memorial Howe means for traditional biblical exegesis to coexist and interact with her own unconventional reading/re-creation of Mary Magdalene. Like Mary herself, Howe is at all times a disciple of the tradition and a dissenter both.

74. I identify the verse beginning with "I John" and ending with "Mortal contained in it" as the "main text" of pages 8 and 9 primarily because it is repeated on both pages and because it is the most sustained voice amidst the visual, aural, and thematic diffusion of these pages.

75. The notion of giving testimony or of bearing witness is made prominent from the opening chapter of John, where "bearing witness" is repeated five times (verses 7, 8, 15, 32, 34). Howe uses the word *testimony* three times in *The NC Memorial* and related words (to "bear witness" and to "confess") another eight times in the poem (pp. 11, 17, 23 [twice], 25 [twice], 29 [twice]).

76. The only two punctuation marks in the entire thirty-one-page poem are the question mark on page 8 ("What am I?") and the exclamation point on page 16 ("Come then!"). Capital letters alone identify the beginning of a sentence unit. The absence of punctuation marks gives the text the feel of a cleared field, or of the open "meadows" Mary crosses in her isolated wanderings and which constitute a central figurative and literal landscape of the poem (see pp. 14, 17, 18).

77. In the 1989 Falon interview, Howe describes her early days of writing in terms that are, for me, proleptic of this later depiction of Mary: "When you reach that point where no concessions in art are possible," she states, "you face true power, *alone*. Writing still seems more threatening to me than painting because it becomes so self-absorbing. I saw my desire [to write] as a threat to my children. Honestly, I nearly did go mad . . . This all really touches on the nature of the sacred" (34).

78. Within this framework of the creative force intricately connected to the theme of exile and the separation of self from the known, from that which is already made, the following wonderful discussion by Blanchot concerning Abraham as prototypical originator [author] seems relevant and worth quoting. Blanchot writes: "The origin is a decision; this is a decision of Abraham, separating himself from what is, and affirming himself as a foreigner . . . The Hebrew passes from one world (the established Summerian world) to something that is 'not yet a world' . . . ; a ferryman, the Hebrew Abraham invites us not only to pass from one shore to another, but also *to carry ourselves to wherever there is a passage to be made . . . the truth of the beginning is in separation*" (1995: 231; my italics).

79. I am echoing here Howe's phrase in *Pythagorean Silence* where she speaks of herself as "Slipping // forever // between rupture and rapture" (1990: 31).

80. For a description of how Howe imagines reading these pages aloud, see the 1995 Keller interview (9–11). What is particularly interesting in this detailed discussion of "the order" she has in mind is Howe's repeated validation of all other sequencing choices. There is no sense that there is a "right" order to these lines. What is important to Howe in these pages is her desire "to illustrate the process of [Mary's] interruption and erasure, and that she's continuing through these narratives . . . If I

read the poem aloud," states Howe, "I whisper all the upside-down words, and that way they sound like another voice—the hissing return of the repressed" (11).

81. The repeated word *enclosure* echoes Howe's earlier essay entitled "Incloser," in which she examines, among multiple other related themes, the New England conversion narratives as an instance of seventeenth-century women finding voice (however hesitant and riddled with contradictory impulses). In this essay, Howe provides the following narrative by the Widow Arrington, taken from Thomas Shepherd's *Confessions:* "Hearing Dr. Jenison, Lamentations 3— . . . it came as a light into me and the more the text was opened the more I saw my heart . . . And when I came I durst not tell my husband fearing he would loath me if he knew me. And I resolved none should know nor I would tell" (*Birth-mark* 49). What seems particularly relevant in the above narrative is the self-silencing tactics of the speaker—the sense of her "enclosure" in silence—and that only as a widow, alone in the world, is she released. As epigraph to this essay, Howe provides the following denotation for "Enclose" from Noah Webster's 1852 *An American Dictionary of the English Language:* "1. To surround; to shut in; to confine on all sides; as to inclose a field with a fence; to inclose a fort or an army with troops; to inclose a town with walls. 2. To separate from common grounds by a fence; as to inclose lands." I read *The NC Memorial* as a type of conversion narrative or, more accurately, as the poet's confession of faith in the figure of Mary and in her own poetic project.

82. This final question in section 2 of *The NC Memorial* resonates for me of Jesus' appeal to God on the cross: "And about the ninth hour Jesus cried with a loud voice, saying Eli, Eli lama sabachtani? That is to say, My God, my God, why hast thou forsaken me?" (Mark 27:46, also Matt. 15:34). Like Jesus' words, the speaker's "Oh when when" is as much an entreaty (to be delivered from suffering, perhaps) and a prayer as it is a question.

83. I will quote again at this point from Jefferson Humphries's evocative description of literature that is "like love, . . . a performance of desire, and so of failure to know, to possess. They are both, then, performances of loss" (1986: ix). These words are relevant to our understanding of *The NC Memorial,* a poem in which literature and love are intricately interwoven, both circling an unnamed loss (an empty tomb) that by definition can never be filled.

84. In the recognition scene as described in John and quoted by Howe at the opening of *The NC Memorial,* Mary twice "turned herself" (20:14, 16). Regarding the word *turning,* Blanchot notes that "the verb 'to find' [in French] does not first of all mean 'to find,' in the sense of a practical or scientific result. To find is *to turn,* to take a turn about, to go around . . . No idea here of a goal, still less of stopping" (1993: 25; my italics). *The NC Memorial* is, in many ways, a quest-poem (Mary's search for Jesus, the poet's search for Mary) that incorporates this understanding of finding (i.e., "turning") into its poetics. In a similar vein, biblical scholar Mark Stibbe notes that of the thirty-four times the verb *to seek* (*zetein*) is utilized in John, "only on three occasions does a character who seeks Jesus actually find him" (1994: 15). It is the *not finding* that

transforms the narrative into a tale of the act of seeking rather than into a tale of that which is sought after.

85. It is interesting to note that many of the structural elements of the seventeenth-century American conversion narrative as delineated by Caldwell (1983) are in evidence in this definition of testimony, particularly the open-endedness of the telling that transform the conversion narrative into what Felman here names "language in process" and the "performative" aspect of relating one's conversion experience to an entire congregation.

Epilogue

1. I am echoing here Creeley's words that in writing "[t]hings have happened as they have happened nowhere else." The continuation of the passage states, in words that one could easily apply to Howe's work and that I imagine she would apply to the writing process, that "[i]n writing it has seemed to me . . . that, at last, the world 'came true'" (1973: 273).

Bibliography

Books by Susan Howe

Hinge Picture. New York: Telephone Books, 1974.
The Western Borders. Willits, CA: Tuumba Press, 1976.
Secret History of the Dividing Line. New York: Telephone Books, 1978.
Cabbage Gardens. Chicago: Fathom Press, 1979.
The Liberties. Guilford, CT: Loon Books, 1980.
Pythagorean Silence. New York: Montemora Supplement, 1982.
Defenestration of Prague. New York: Kulchur Foundation, 1983.
My Emily Dickinson. Berkeley, CA: North Atlantic Books, 1985.
Articulation of Sound Forms in Time. Windsor, VT: Awede Press, 1987.
Federalist 10. Abacus 30. Elmwood, CT: Potes and Poets Press, 1987.
A Bibliography of the King's Book or, Eikon Basilike. Providence, RI: Paradigm Press, 1989.
The Captive Morphology. Santa Fe, NM: Weasel Sleeves Press, 1990.
The Europe of Trusts: Selected Poems. Los Angeles: Sun & Moon Press, 1990.
Singularities. Hanover & London: Wesleyan University Press, 1990.
The Nonconformist's Memorial. New York: Grenfell Press, 1992.
The Birth-mark: Unsettling the Wilderness in American Literary History. Hanover and London: Wesleyan University Press, 1993.
The Nonconformist's Memorial: Poems. New York: A New Directions Book, 1993.
Frame Structures: Early Poems 1974–1979. New York: A New Directions Book, 1996.
Pierce-Arrow. New York: A New Directions Book, 1999.

Essays by Susan Howe

"Ether Either." In *Close Listening: Poetry and the Performed Word.* Ed. Charles Bernstein. New York and Oxford: Oxford University Press, 1998. 111–127.
"The Flames and Generosities of the Heart: Emily Dickinson and the Illogic of Sumptuary Values." In *Artifice and Indeterminacy: An Anthology of New Poetics.* Ed.

Christopher Beach. Tuscaloosa: University of Alabama Press, 1998. 319–341.
"Renunciation Is a P(ei)rcing Virtue." *Profession* (1998): 51–61.
"Sorting Facts: Or, Nineteen Ways of Looking at Marker." In *Beyond Document: Essays on Nonfiction Film.* Ed. and intro. Charles Warren. Foreword Stanley Cavell. Hanover, NH: Wesleyan University Press, 1996. 295–343.

Interviews with Susan Howe

Beckett, Tom. "*The Difficulties* Interview." *The Difficulties* 3:2 (1989): 17–27.
Falon, Janet Ruth. "Speaking with Susan Howe." *The Difficulties* 3:2 (1989): 28–42.
Foster, Edward. "An Interview with Susan Howe." In *The Talisman Interviews.* Hoboken, NJ: Talisman House Publishers, 1994. 48–68. First published in *Talisman: Journal of Contemporary Poetry and Poetics* 4 (1990): 14–38. Rpt. in Howe, *Birth-mark,* 155–181.
Keller, Lynn. "An Interview with Susan Howe." *Contemporary Literature* 36:1 (Spring 1995): 1–34.

Criticism on Susan Howe—Works Cited

Adamson, Gregory Dale. "Serres Translates Howe." *Substance: A Review of Theory and Literary Criticism* 83 (1997): 110–124.
Beckett, Tom, ed. *Susan Howe Issue. The Difficulties.* 3:2 (1989).
Bernstein, Charles. "Passed by Examination: Paragraphs for Susan Howe." *The Difficulties* 3:2 (1989): 84–88.
Butterick, George F. "The Mysterious Vision of Susan Howe." *North Dakota Quarterly* 55 (Fall 1987): 312–321.
Daly, Lew. *Swallowing the Scroll: Late in a Prophetic Tradition with the Poetry of Susan Howe and John Taggart.* Buffalo, NY: M Press, 1994.
DuPlessis, Rachel Blau. *The Pink Guitar: Writing as Feminist Practice.* New York and London: Routledge, 1990.
Dworkin, Craig Douglas. "'Waging Political Babble': Susan Howe's Visual Prosody and the Politics of Noise." *Word and Image* 12:4 (Oct.–Dec. 1996): 389–405.
Hogue, Cynthia. "Towards a Poetics of Performative Transformation." In *Women Poets of the Americas: Toward a Pan-American Gathering.* Ed. Jacqueline Vaught Brogan and Cordelia Chavez Candelaria. Notre Dame, IN: University of Notre Dame Press, 1999. 51–67.
Keller, Lynn. *Forms of Expansion: Recent Long Poems by Women.* Chicago and London: University of Chicago Press, 1997.
Kuszai, Joel. "Prayer in a Time of Captivity." Unpublished.
Lazer, Hank. *Opposing Poetries: Volume 2—Readings.* Evanston, IL: Northwestern University Press, 1996.

Ma, Ming-Qian. "Articulating the Inarticulate: Singularities and the Counter-method in Susan Howe." *Contemporary Literature* 36:1 (Spring 1995): 466–489.

Marsh, Nicky. 'Out of My Texts I Am Not What I Play': Poetry and Self in the Poetry of Susan Howe." *College Literature* 24:3 (1997): 124–137.

Martin, Stephen-Paul. *Open Form and the Feminine Imagination (The Politics of Reading in Twentieth Century Innovative Writing)*. Washington, D.C.: Maisonneuve Press, 1988.

McCorkle, James. "Prophecy and the Figure of the Reader in Susan Howe's *Articulation of Sound Forms in Time." Postmodern Culture: An Electronic Journal of Interdisciplinary Criticism* 9:3 (May 1999): 25 para.

McGann, Jerome. *Black Riders: The Visible Language of Modernism*. Princeton: Princeton University Press, 1993.

Middleton, Peter. "On Ice: Julia Kristeva, Susan Howe and Avant Garde Poetics." In *Contemporary Poetry Meets Modern Theory*. Ed. Anthony Easthope and John O. Thompson. Toronto: University of Toronto Press. 81–95.

Naylor, Paul. *Poetic Investigations: Singing the Holes in History*. Evanston, IL: Northwestern University Press, 1999.

Nicholls, Peter. "Unsettling the Wilderness: Susan Howe and American History." *Contemporary Literature* 37:4 (Winter 1996): 586–601.

Perelman, Bob. *The Marginalization of Poetry: Language Writing and Literary History*. Princeton, NJ: Princeton University Press, 1996.

Perloff, Marjorie. *Poetic License: Essays on Modernist and Postmodernist Lyric*. Evanston, IL: Northwestern University Press, 1990.

————. "Language Poetry and the Lyric Subject: Ron Silliman's Albany, Susan Howe's Buffalo." *Critical Inquiry* 25:3 (Spring 1999): 405–434.

Quartermain, Peter. *Disjunctive Poetics: From Gertrude Stein and Louis Zukofsky to Susan Howe*. Cambridge Studies in American Literature and Culture Series. New York: Cambridge University Press, 1992.

Reinfeld, Linda. "On Henry David (Susan Howe's) 'Thorow.'" *The Difficulties* 3:2 (1989): 97–104.

————. *Language Poetry: Writing as Rescue*. Baton Rouge and London: Louisiana State University Press, 1992.

Taggart, John. *Songs of Degree: Essays on Contemporary Poetry and Poetics*. Tuscaloosa and London: University of Alabama Press, 1994.

Talisman: A Journal of Contemporary Poetry and Poetics. Susan Howe Issue 4 (1990).

Williams, Megan. "Howe Not to Erase(her): A Poetics of Posterity in Susan Howe's 'Melville's Marginalia.'" *Contemporary Literature* 38:1 (Spring 1997): 106–132.

General

Achinstein, Sharon. *Milton and the Revolutionary Reader*. Princeton, NJ: Princeton University Press, 1994.

Alien, Donald, and Warren Tallman, eds. *The Poetics of the New American Poetry*. New York: Grove Press, 1973.

Almack, Edward. *A Bibliography of the King's Book; or, Eikon Basilike.* London: Blades, East & Blades, 1896.

Andrews, William L., ed. *Classic American Autobiographies.* New York: Penguin, 1992.

Ashton, John. *Understanding the Fourth Gospel.* Oxford: Clarendon Press, 1991.

Battis, Emery. *Saints and Sectaries: Anne Hutchinson and the Antinomian Controversy in the Massachusetts Bay Colony.* Chapel Hill: University of North Carolina Press, 1962.

Bayley, John. *Shakespeare and Tragedy.* London and Boston: Routledge & Kegan Paul, 1981.

Baym, Nina et. al., eds. *The Norton Anthology of American Literature.* Vols. 1 and 2. New York: W. W. Norton & Co., 1994.

Beach, Christopher, ed. *Artifice and Indeterminacy: An Anthology of New Poetics.* Tuscaloosa and London: University of Alabama Press, 1998.

Beasley-Murray, George R. *World Biblical Commentary.* Vol. 36. Waco, TX: Word Books Publisher, 1987.

Beckett, Samuel. *Waiting for Godot.* New York: Grove Press, 1954.

Benjamin, Walter. "Theses on the Philosophy of History." In *Illuminations.* Ed. and intro. Hannah Arendt. Trans. Harry Zohn. New York: Schoken Books, 1968. Original title of the essay is "On the Concept of History."

––––––. "The Task of the Translator." In *Illuminations.* Ed. and intro. Hannah Arendt. Trans. Harry Zohn. New York: Schoken Books, 1968. 69–82.

––––––. *One Way Street and Other Writings.* Trans. Edmund Jephcott and Kingsley Shorter. London: Verso, 1979.

Bercovitch, Sacvan. *The Puritan Origins of the American Self.* New Haven and London: Yale University Press, 1975.

Bernstein, Charles. *Content's Dream: Essays, 1975–1984.* Los Angeles: Sun and Moon Press, 1986.

––––––. *A Poetics.* Cambridge, MA: Harvard University Press, 1992.

––––––, ed. *Close Listening: Poetry and the Performed Word.* New York and Oxford: Oxford University Press, 1998.

Bernstein, Michael Andre. *The Tale of the Tribe: Ezra Pound and the Modern Verse Epic.* Princeton, NJ: Princeton University Press, 1980.

Blanchot, Maurice. "The Indestructible" (1962). In *The Blanchot Reader.* Ed. Michael Holland. Oxford: Blackwell Publishers, 1995.

––––––. *The Writing of the Disaster.* Trans. Ann Smock. Lincoln and London: University of Nebraska Press, 1986.

––––––. *The Sirens' Song: Selected Essays.* Ed. Gabriel Josipovici. Trans. Sacha Rabinovitch. Bloomington: Indiana University Press, 1982.

––––––. *The Infinite Conversation.* Trans. Susan Hanson. Minneapolis and London: University of Minnesota Press, 1993.

Blau, Herbert. "Notes from the Underground: *Waiting for Godot* and *Endgame.*" In *On Beckett: Essays and Criticism.* Ed. and intro. S. E. Gontarski. New York: Grover Press, 1986. 255–279.

Bloom, Harold. *The Anxiety of Influence: A Theory of Poetry.* Oxford: Oxford University Press, 1973.

Blyth, Caroline. "Touch Wood: Coming to Terms with Bibliography." *Word and Image* 9:1 (Jan.–Mar. 1993): 66–79.

Bohn, Willard. *The Aesthetics of Visual Poet.* Cambridge: Cambridge University Press, 1986.

Bonnefoy, Yves, ed. *Mythologies.* Trans. Gerald Honigsblum, et al. Chicago: University of Chicago Press, 1981.

Bowie, Malcolm. *Lacan.* Cambridge, MA: Harvard University Press, 1991.

Bowlby, John. *Attachment and Loss.* Vol. 2. London: Hogarth Press and Institute of Psycho-Analysis, 1973.

Bozeman, Theodore Dwight. *To Live Ancient Lives: The Primitivist Dimension in Puritanism.* Chapel Hill: University of North Carolina Press, 1988.

Brent, Joseph. *Charles Peirce Sanders: A Life.* Bloomington and Indianapolis: Indiana University Press, 1993.

Brodie, Thomas L. *The Quest for the Origins of John's Gospel: A Source-Oriented Approach.* New York and Oxford: Oxford University Press, 1993.

Bultman, Rudolf. *The Gospel of John: A Commentary.* Trans. G. R. Beasley-Murray. Philadelphia: Westminster Press, 1971.

Byrne, Brenda. "The Faith of the Beloved Disciple and the Community in John 20." In *The Johannine Writings.* Ed. Stanley E. Potter and Craig A. Evans. Sheffield: Sheffield Academic Press, 1995. 31–45.

Cable, Lana. "Milton's Iconoclastic Truth." In *Politics, Poetics and Hermeneutics in Milton's Prose.* Ed. David Loewenstein and James Grantham Turner. Cambridge: Cambridge University Press, 1990. 135–151.

Caldwell, Patricia. *The Puritan Conversion Narrative.* Cambridge: Cambridge University Press, 1983.

———. "The Antinomian Controversy." *Harvard Theological Review* 69:3–4 (July–Oct. 1976): 345–367.

Cardinal, Roger. "Enigma." *20th Century Studies: The Limits of Comprehension* 12 (Dec. 1974): 42–62.

Carroll, Peter N. *Puritanism and the Wildness: The Intellectual Significance of the New England Frontier, 1629–1700.* New York and London: Columbia University Press, 1969.

Castiglia, Christopher. *Bound and Determined: Captivity, Culture-Crossing and White Womanhood from Mary Rowlandson to Patty Hearst.* Chicago: University of Chicago Press, 1996.

Cixous, Helene. "From the Scene of the Unconscious to the Scene of History." In *The Future of Literary Theory.* Ed. Ralph Cohen. New York and London: Routledge, 1989. 1–18.

Cixous, Helene, and Catherine Clement. *The Newly Born Woman.* Trans. Betsy Wing. Minneapolis and London: University of Minnesota Press, 1986.

Cohen, Charles Lloyd. *God's Caress: The Psychology of Puritan Religious Experience.* New York: Oxford University Press, 1986.

Conte, Joseph M. *Unending Design: The Forms of Postmodern Poetry.* Ithaca and London: Cornell University Press, 1991.

Corkery, Daniel. *The Fortunes of the Irish Language.* Cork: Mercier Press, 1954.

Cosgrave, E. MacDowel, and Leonard R. Strangways. *The Dictionary of Dublin: Being a Comprehensive Guide to the City and Its Neighbourhood.* London: Simpkin, Marshall, Hamilton, Kent & Co., 1895.

Crane, Hart. "Hart Crane to Harriet Monroe." In *The Poetics of the New American Poetry.* Ed. Donald Allen and Warren Tallman. New York: Grove Press, 1973. 80–84.

Crawford, Patricia. *Women and Religion in England, 1500–1720.* London and New York: Routledge, 1993.

Creeley, Robert. "I'm Given to Write Poems." In *The Poetics of the New American Poetry.* Ed. Donald Allen and Warren Tallman. New York: Grove Press, 1973. 263–273.

Culler, Jonathan. *Structuralist Poetics: Structuralism, Linguistics and the Study of Literature.* Ithaca, NY: Cornell University Press, 1975.

Damon, Maria. *the dark end of the street: Margins in American Vanguard Poetry.* Minneapolis and London: University of Minnesota Press, 1993.

D'Arbois de Jubainville, H. *The Irish Mythological Cycle and Celtic Mythology.* Trans. Richard Irvine Best. Dublin: Hodges, Fiogiss & Co., 1903.

Davidson, H. R. Ellis. *Gods and Myths of Northern Europe.* Middlesex: Penguin Books, 1969.

Deleuze, Gilles, and Felix Guttari. *Nomadology: The War Machine.* Trans. Brian Massumi. New York: Semiotext, 1986.

Doolittle, Hilda (H. D.). *Trilogy.* New York: A New Directions Book, 1973.

Drucker, Johanna. *The Visible Word: Experimental Typography and Modern Art, 1909–1923.* Chicago and London: University of Chicago Press, 1994.

Duncan, Robert. "Towards an Open Universe." In *The Poetics of the New American Poetry.* Ed. Donald Allen and Warren Tallman. New York: Grove Press, 1973. 212–225.

Eagleton, Terry. "Language and Value in *King Lear.*" In *King Lear: Contemporary Critical Essays.* Ed. and intro. Kiernan Ryan. Hampshire: Macmillan, 1993. 84–91.

Eco, Umberto. *The Open Work.* Trans. Anna Cancogni. Cambridge, MA: Harvard University Press, 1989.

Eisenstein, Elizabeth. *The Printing Press as an Agent of Change: Communications and Cultural Transformations in Early-Modern Europe.* Cambridge: Cambridge University Press, 1979.

Eisler, Robert. *The Enigma of the Fourth Gospel: Its Author and Its Writer.* London: Methuen & Co., 1938.

Ellis, Joseph J. *Founding Brothers: The Revolutionary Generation.* New York: Knopf, 2000.

Ellis, Peter Berresford. *A Dictionary of Irish Mythology.* Santa Barbara, CA: ABC-CLIO, 1987.

Ellmann, Maud. "Introduction." In *Psychoanalytic Literary Criticism.* Ed. Maud Ellmann. London and New York: Longman, 1994. 1–35.

Erikson, Kai T. *Wayward Puritans: A Study in the Sociology of Deviance.* New York: Joyn Wiley & Sons, 1966.

Evans, Dylan. *An Introductory Dictionary of Lacanian Psychoanalysis.* London and New York: Routledge, 1996.

Fabricant, Carole. *Swift's Landscape*. Baltimore and London: Johns Hopkins University Press, 1982.

Felman, Shoshana. *Jacques Lacan and the Adventures of Insight: Psychoanalysis in Contemporary Culture*. Cambridge, MA: Harvard University Press, 1987.

Felman, Shoshana, and Dori Laub , M.D. *Testimony: Crises of Witnessing in Literature, Psychoanalysis, and History*. New York and London: Routledge, 1992.

Fideler, David R., ed. *The Pythagorean Sourcebook and Library*. Trans. Kenneth Sylvan Guthrie. Grand Rapids, MI: Phanes Press, 1987.

Finlayson, Michael G. *Historians, Puritanism, and the English Revolution: The Religious Factor in English Politics before and after the Interregnum*. Toronto: Toronto University Press, 1983.

Fiori, Gabriella. *Simone Weil: An Intellectual Biography*. Trans. Joseph R. Berrigan. Athens: University of Georgia Press, 1989.

Fischer, John Irwin. *On Swift's Poetry*. Gainesville: University Presses of Florida, 1973.

Foster, R. F. *Modern Ireland: 1600–1972*. London: Allen Lane Penguin Press, 1988.

Foucalt, Michel. "Nietzsche, Genealogy, History." In *Language, Counter-Memory, Practice: Selected Essays and Interviews*. Ed. Donald F. Bouchard. Ithaca, NY: Cornell University Press, 1977. 139–164.

Fritze, Ronald H., and William B. Robinson, eds. *Historical Dictionary of Stuart England, 1603–1689*. London: Greenwood Press, 1996.

Frye, Northrop. *On Shakespeare*. Ed. Robert Sandler. New Haven and London: Yale University Press, 1986.

Gallop, Jane. *Reading Lacan*. Ithaca: Cornell University Press, 1985.

———. *The Daughter's Seduction: Feminism and Psychoanalysis*. Ithaca: Cornell University Press, 1982.

Gauden, John / Charles I. *Eikon Basilike: The Portraiture of His Sacred Majesty in His Solitudes and Sufferings in the Works of King Charles*. London: James Flesher Printer, 1662.

Genette, Gerard. *Paratexts: Thresholds of Interpretation*. Trans. Jane E. Lewin. Cambridge: Cambridge University Press, 1997.

Golding, Alan. *From Outlaw to Classics: Canons in American Poetry*. Madison: University of Wisconsin Press, 1995.

Golding, John. *Marcel Duchamp: The Bride Stripped Bare by her Bachelors, Even*. London: Penguin Press, 1973.

Gorman, Peter. *Pythagoras: A Life*. London: Routledge & Kegan Paul, 1979.

Graver, Lawrence. *Beckett: Waiting for Godot*. Cambridge and New York: Cambridge University Press, 1989.

Greenacre, Phyllis. *Swift and Carroll: A Psychoanalytic Study of Two Lives*. New York: International Universities Press, 1955.

Greenblatt, Stephen. *Renaissance Self-Fashioning: From More to Shakespeare*. Chicago: University of Chicago Press, 1980.

Grimm, Jacob and Wilhelm. *Grimm's Fairy Tales*. Ed. and intro. Eleanor Ordman. Middlesex: Penguin Books, 1948.

———. *The Complete Grimm's Fairy Tales*. Intro. Padraic Colum. Commentary Joseph Campbell. New York: Pantheon Books, 1944.

Grosz, Elizabeth. *Jacques Lacan: A Feminist Introduction*. London: Routledge, 1990.

——. *Sexual Subversions: Three French Feminists*. Sydney: Allen & Unwin, 1989.

Gurevitch, Zali. "The Double Site of Israel." In *Grasping Land: Space and Place in Contemporary Israeli Discourse and Experience*. Ed. Eyal Ben-Ari and Yoram Bilu. Albany: State University of New York Press, 1997. 203–216.

Hamilton, Edith. *Mythology*. New York: Signet, 1940.

Hanks, Patrick, and Flavia Hodges. *A Dictionary of First Names*. Oxford: Oxford University Press, 1990.

Hartley, George. *Textual Politics and the Language Poets*. Bloomington and Indianapolis: Indiana University Press, 1989.

Hartman, Geoffrey H. *Criticism in the Wilderness: The Study of Literature Today*. New Haven and London: Yale University Press, 1980.

Helgerson, Richard. "Milton Reads the King's Book: Print, Performance, and the Making of a Bourgeois Idol." *Criticism* 29:1 (Winter 1987): 1–25.

Heninger, S. K., Jr. *Touches of Sweet Harmony: Pythagorean Cosmology and Renaissance Poetics*. California: Huntington Library, 1974.

Holmes, Oliver Wendell. *Speeches*. Boston: Little, Brown & Co., 1934.

Howe, Mark DeWolfe, ed. *Touched with Fire: Civil War Letters and Diary of Oliver Wendell Holmes, Jr., 1861–1864*. Cambridge, MA: Harvard University Press, 1947.

Humphries, Jefferson. *Losing the Text: Readings in Literary Desire*. Athens and London: University of Georgia Press, 1986.

Hutchinson, Thomas. *The History of the Province of Massachusetts Bay*. London: J. Smith, 1768.

Jefferson, Ann, and David Robey, eds. *Modern Literary Theory: A Comparative Introduction*. 2d ed. London: B. T. Batsford, 1986.

Joyce, James. *A Portrait of the Artist as a Young Man*. New York: Penguin Books, 1978.

Kahn, Coppelia. "The Absent Mother in *King Lear*." In *King Lear: Contemporary Critical Essays*. Ed. and intro. Kiernan Ryan. Hampshire: Macmillan, 1993. 92–113.

Kenner, Hugh. *A Reader's Guide to Samuel Beckett*. Syracuse: Syracuse University Press, 1996.

Kenney, Herbert A. *Literary Dublin: A History*. Dublin: Gill & Macmillan, 1974.

Kermode, Frank, and Robert Alter, eds. *The Literary Guide to the Bible*. Cambridge, MA: Belknap Press of Harvard University Press, 1987.

Ketner, Kenneth Laine. *His Glassy Essence: An Autobiography of Charles Sanders Peirce*. Nashville: Vanderbilt University Press, 1998.

Kibbey, Ann. *The Interpretation of Material Shapes in Puritanism: A Study of Rhetoric, Prejudice, and Violence*. Cambridge: Cambridge University Press, 1986.

Klee, Paul. *Notebooks: Volume 1—The Thinking Eye*. Trans. Ralph Manheim. Ed. Jung Spiller. New York: George Wittenborn, 1961.

——. *The Diaries of Paul Klee, 1898–1918*. Ed. and trans. Felix Klee. Berkeley and London: University of California Press, 1968.

Kostelanetz, Richard, ed. *The Avant-Garde Tradition in Literature*. Buffalo, NY: Prometheus Books, 1982.

Kott, Jan. *Shakespeare Our Contemporary.* Trans. Boleslaw Taborski. New York: W. W. Norton & Co., 1974.

Lacan, Jacques. *Ecrits: A Selection.* Trans. Alan Sheridan. New York: Norton, 1977.

Lang, Amy Schrager. *Prophetic Woman: Anne Hutchinson and the Problem of Dissent in the Literature of New England.* Berkeley: University of California Press, 1987.

Lawrence, D. H. *Studies in Classic American Literature.* New York: Viking, 1961.

Levinas, Emmanuel. *Proper Names.* Trans. Michael B. Smith. London: Athlone Press, 1996.

Livingstone, E. A., ed. *The Oxford Dictionary of the Christian Church.* 3d ed. Oxford: Oxford University Press, 1997.

Loewenstein, David. "The Script in the Marketplace." In *Representing the English Renaissance.* Ed. Stephen Greenblatt. Berkeley: University of California Press, 1988. 265–278.

———. *Milton and the Drama of History: Historical Vision, Iconoclasm and the Literary Imagination.* Cambridge: Cambridge University Press, 1990.

Lowney, John. *The American Avant-Garde Tradition: William Carlos Williams, Postmodern Poetry, and the Politics of Cultural Memory.* London: Associated University Presses, 1997.

Macherey, Pierre. *A Theory of Literary Production.* Trans. Geoffrey Wall. London: Routledge & Kegan Paul, 1978.

Madan, Francis F. *A New Bibliography of the Eikon Basilike.* Oxford: Oxford University Press, 1950.

Mahoney, Robert. *Jonathan Swift: The Irish Identity.* New Haven and London: Yale University Press, 1995.

Mather, Cotton. *Magnalia Christi Americana, or the Ecclesiastical History of New England.* Hartford, CT: Silas Andrus, 1853.

McGann, Jerome. *The Textual Condition.* Princeton: Princeton University Press, 1991.

McKnight, Laura Blair. "Crucifixion or Apocalypse? Refiguring the *Eikon Basilike.*" In *Religion, Literature, and Politics in Post-Reformation England, 1540–1688.* Ed. Donna B. Hamilton and Richard Strier. Cambridge: Cambridge University Press, 1996.

Middlebrook, Diane Wood, and Marilyn Yalom, eds. *Coming to Light: American Women Poets in the Twentieth Century.* Ann Arbor: University of Michigan Press, 1996.

Middlekauf, Robert. *The Mathers: Three Generations of Puritan Intellectuals, 1592–1728.* New York: Oxford University Press, 1971.

Miller, Kerby A. *Emigrants and Exiles: Ireland and the Irish Exodus to North America.* New York: Oxford University Press, 1985.

Miller, Nancy K. *Subject to Change: Reading Feminist Writing.* New York: Columbia University Press, 1988.

Miller, Perry. *Errand into the Wilderness.* New York: Harper & Row, 1956.

Miller, Perry, and Thomas H. Johnson, eds. *The Puritans: A Sourcebook of Their Writing.* New York: Harper & Row, 1938.

Milton, John. *Eikonoklastes.* In *The Complete Prose Works of John Milton.* Vol. 3, *1648–1649.* New Haven and London: Yale University Press, 1962. 337–601.

Mitchell, W. J. T. "Holy Landscape: Israel, Palestine and the American Wilderness." *Critical Inquiry* 26:2 (Winter 2000): 193–223.

Morgan, Edmund S. *Visible Saints: The History of a Puritan Idea.* Ithaca, NY: Cornell University Press, 1963.

Muller, John P., and William J. Richardson. *The Purloined Poe, Lacan, Derrida Psychoanalytic Reading.* Baltimore: Johns Hopkins University Press, 1988

Nokes, David. *Jonathan Swift: A Hypocrite Reversed.* Oxford: Oxford University Press, 1985.

Olson, Charles. *Call Me Ishmael.* London: Jonathan Cape, 1967.

———. "Projective Verse." In *The Poetics of the New American Poetry.* Ed. Donald Allen and Warren Tallman. New York: Grove Press, 1973. 147–158.

Ong, Walter. *The Presence of the Word: Some Prolegomena for Cultural and Religious History.* New Haven and London: Yale University Press, 1967.

———. *Orality and Literacy: The Technologizing of the Word.* London and New York: Routledge, 1988.

Ovid. *Heroides.* Trans. Grant Showerman. Cambridge and London: Harvard University Press, 1971.

———. *Metamorphoses.* Trans. Frank Justus Miller. Cambridge, MA: Cambridge University Press, 1946.

———. *Metamorphoses.* Trans. A. D. Melville. Oxford: Oxford University Press, 1986.

Patterson, Annabel. *Censorship and Interpretation: The Conditions of Writing and Reading in Early Modern England.* Madison: University of Wisconsin Press, 1984.

Paz, Octavio. *Children of Mire: Modern Poetry from Romanticism to the Avant-Garde.* Trans. Rachel Phillips. Cambridge, MA: Harvard University Press, 1974.

Pazicky, Diana Loercher. *Cultural Orphans in America.* Jackson: University Press of Mississippi, 1998.

Perloff, Marjorie. "Contemporary/Postmodern: The 'New' Poetry." *Bucknell Review* 26 (Winter 1980): 171–180.

———. *The Poetics of Indeterminacy: Rimbaud to Cage.* Princeton, NJ: Princeton University Press, 1981.

———. *The Dance of the Intellect: Studies in the Poetry of the Pound Tradition.* Cambridge: Cambridge University Press, 1985.

———. *The Futurist Moment: Avant-Garde, Avant Guerre, and the Language of Rupture.* Chicago: University of Chicago Press, 1986.

Phillips, John. *The Reformation of Images: Destruction of Art in England, 1535–1660.* Berkeley: University of California Press, 1973.

Piette, Adam. *Remembering and the Sound of Words: Mallarme, Proust, Joyce, Beckett.* Oxford: Clarendon Press, 1996.

Potter, Lois. *Secret Rites and Secret Writing: Royalist Literature, 1641–1660.* Cambridge: Cambridge University Press, 1989.

Price, William H. *The Civil War Centennial Handbook.* Virginia: Prince Lithograph Co., 1961.

Pye, Christopher. "The Sovereign, the Theater, and the Kingdome of Darknesse:

Hobbes and the Spectacle of Power." In *Representing the English Renaissance*. Ed. Stephen Greenblatt. Berkeley: University of California Press, 1988. 270–301.

Rasula, Jed, and Steve McCaffery, eds. *Imagining Language: An Anthology*. Cambridge MA: MIT Press, 1998.

Rees, Joan. *Sir Philip Sidney and Arcadia*. London and Toronto: Associated University Presses, 1991.

Rhys, John. *Celtic Folklore: Welsh and Manx*. North Stratford, N.H.: Ayer Company Publishers, 1990.

Rose, Mark. *Authors and Owners: The Invention of Copyright*. Cambridge, MA: Harvard University Press, 1993.

Rosenthal, Mark. *Anselm Kiefer*. Chicago and Philadelphia: Philadelphia Museum of Art, 1987.

Royston, R., ed. *The Works of King Charles the Martyr*. London: James Flesher Printer, 1662.

Said, Edward. "The Mind of Winter: Reflections on Life in Exile." *Harper's Magazine* (Sept. 1984): 49–54.

Sayre, Henry M. *The Visual Text of William Carlos Williams*. Urbana: University of Illinois Press, 1983.

Shakespeare, William. *King Lear*. Ed. Russell Fraser. New York: Signet Classics, 1963.

———. *Hamlet*. Ed. Edward Hubler. New York: Signet Classics, 1963.

———. *Richard II*. Ed. Kenneth Muir. New York: Signet Classics, 1963.

Sharpe, J. A. "'Last Dying Speeches': Religion, Ideology and Public Execution in Seventeenth-Century England." *Past and Present* 107 (May 1985): 144–168.

Sidney, Sir Philip Sidney. *The Countess of Pembroke's Arcadia (The New Arcadia)*. Ed. and intro. Victor Skretkowicz. Oxford: Clarendon Press, 1987.

Slotkin, Richard. *Regeneration through Violence. The Mythology of the American Frontier, 1600–1860*. Middletown, CT: Wesleyan University Press, 1973.

Smith, Eldson C. *New Dictionary of American Family Names*. Harper & Row, 1973.

Smith, Gary. "Thinking through Benjamin: An Introductory Essay." In *Benjamin: Philosophy, Aesthetics, History*. Ed. Gary Smith. Chicago: University of Chicago Press, 1989. vii–xlii.

Smith, Robert Jerome. "Irish Mythology." In *Irish History and Culture: Aspects of a People's Heritage*. Kansas: Wolfhound Press, 1979. 1–29.

Staley, Jeffrey Lloyd. *The Print's First Kiss: A Rhetorical Investigation of the Implied Reader of the Fourth Gospel*. Atlanta, GA: Scholars Press, 1988.

Stevens, Williams. *The Palm at the End of the Mind: Selected Poems and a Play*. Ed. Holly Stevens. New York: Vintage Books, 1972.

Stibbe, Mark W. G. *John's Gospel*. London and New York: Routledge, 1994.

Stoppard, Tom. *Rosencrantz and Guildenstern Are Dead*. New York: Grove Press, 1967.

Strauss, Leo. *Persecution and the Art of Writing*. Glencoe, IL: Free Press, 1952.

Swift, Jonathan. *Journal to Stella, Vol. I and II*. Ed. Harold Williams. Oxford: Clarendon Press, 1948.

———. *The Works of Dr. Jonathan Swift*. Edinburgh: A. Donaldson, 1768.

Tiedemann, Rolf. "Historical Materialism or Political Messianism? An Interpretation of the Theses 'On the Concept of History.' In *Benjamin: Philosophy, Aesthetics, History*. Ed. Gary Smith. Chicago: University of Chicago Press, 1989. 175–209.

Tindall, George Brown, and David E. Shi. *America: A Narrative History*. New York and London: W. W. Norton & Co., 1993.

Todorov, Tzvetan. *Introduction to Poetics*. Trans. Richard Howard. Minneapolis: University of Minnesota Press, 1981.

———. *Symbolism and Interpretation*. Trans. Catherine Porter. Ithaca, NY: Cornell University Press, 1982.

———. *The Conquest of America: The Question of the Other*. Trans. Richard Howard. New York: HarperPerennial, 1984.

Wedgwood, C. V. *The Trial of Charles I*. London: Collins, 1964.

Weil, Simone. *Waiting for God*. Trans. Emma Crawford. London and Glasgow: Fontana Books, 1959.

Welch, Robert, ed. *The Oxford Companion to Irish Literature*. Oxford: Clarendon Press, 1996.

Weston, St. John Joyce. *The Neighbourhood of Dublin*. 1912. Dublin: Gill & Macmillan, 1977.

White, John J. *Literary Futurism: Aspects of the First Avant-Garde*. Oxford: Clarendon Press, 1990.

Williams, William Carlos. *In the American Grain*. Ed. Horace Gregory. New York: A New Directions Book, 1956.

———. *Selected Poems*. New York: New Directions, 1949.

Wimsatt, W. K. *The Verbal Icon: Studies in the Meaning of Poetry*. London: Methuen & Co., 1954.

Woolf, Virginia. *A Room of One's Own*. New York: Harvest/HBJ Book, 1957.

———. *The Voyage Out*. London: Grafton Books, 1978.

Woudhuysen, H. R. *Sir Philip Sidney and the Circulation of Manuscripts, 1558–1640*. Oxford: Clarendon Press, 1996.

Wright, Elizabeth. *Psychoanalytic Criticism: Theory in Practice*. London: Routledge, 1989.

Wright, Louis B., and Marions Tinling, eds. *William Bryd of Virginia: The London Diary (1717–1721) and Other Writings*. New York: Oxford University Press, 1958.

Yeats, W. B. *The Collected Plays of W. B. Yeats*. London: Macmillan, 1953.

Zakai, Avihu. *Exile and Kingdom: History and Apocalypse in the Puritan Migration to America*. Cambridge: Cambridge University Press, 1992.

Index

Italic page numbers refer to figures.